Structural Equation Modeling of Writing Proficiency Using Can-Do Questionnaires

WAKAKO KOBAYASHI

BUNSHINDO

I received an academic publishing grant from
College of Humanities and Sciences, Nihon University.

ABSTRACT

The purposes of this study were to validate the writing section of the Eiken Can-Do Questionnaires used in this study and the second purpose was to determine the effects of ten affective orientations (i.e., Desire to Write English, Attitude Toward Learning to Write English, Motivational Intensity, Instrumental Orientation for Writing in English, L2 Writing Anxiety, L2 Writing Self-Confidence, Willingness to Communicate in L2 Writing, Self-Esteem, Cognitive Competence, and General Self-Worth), on the participants' responses to the Eiken Can-Do Questionnaires. This purpose is valuable because little is known about the relationship between Can-Do Questionnaire and affective variables investigated in this study. The final purpose of this study was to develop Can-Do Questionnaires as an internal measure for a university writing class.

The participants of this study were 204 university students studying in two private universities in Tokyo, Japan. The first instrument was the writing section of the Eiken Can-Do Questionnaire; this questionnaire served as the outside measure in this study. The second, six out of nine essays written by the students were assessed as a measure of their writing ability in English. The Affective Orientation Questionnaire was administered to measure ten Affective Orientations. The questionnaire and essay data were analyzed using the Rasch rating scale. All of the participants completed the Background Questionnaire and Affective Orientation Questionnaire in April 2010 and 2011 and completed the writing section of the Eiken Can-do Questionnaire in April, July, and December 2010 and 2011. six writing assignments were produced by 179 out of the 204 participants wrote during the 2010 and 2011 academic year, and the relationships among the variables were analyzed using Structural Equation Modeling.

The results indicated that the use of the Eiken Can-Do Questionnaires as the proficiency level measure was appropriate for this group of university students. The Eiken Can-Do Questionnaires were predictors of Motivation and L2 Self-Confidence. Motivation was a predictor of WTC in L2 Writing. Therefore, it should be noted that the Eiken Can-Do Questionnaires had an indirect effect with WTC in L2 Writing. The result implies that through having Eiken Can-Do questionnaires and Classroom Can-do Questionnaires to achieve their future goals, their English classes and their future learning objectives were connected.

It is necessary to provide students with adequate practice and guidance in using the Eiken Can-Do Questionnaires in order to promote a deeper understanding of their purposes and uses.

ACKNOWLEDGMENTS

I wish to express my sincerest gratitude to my advisors, Dr. David Beglar and Dr. James Elwood, for their kind, energetic, warm, and conscientious supports throughout the long years of challenges in writing this dissertation. Dr. David Beglar patiently read my drafts many times, gave me helpful comments, and guided me to improve my writing throughout the dissertation writing process. Without his kind help and encouragement, I could not have finished writing this dissertation. Thanks to Dr. Beglar's professional and long guidance and instruction, I had a positive experience, especially in terms of statistical research; this experience enabled me to see the beauty of statistical analyses.

Dr. James Elwood took a great deal of time on Saturday mornings and afternoons to help me conduct the structural equation modeling and to make detailed checks of my dissertation. Without his warm support and instruction, I would not have been able to complete this study.

I would also like to thank my dissertation committee members, Dr. Robert Nelson and Dr. Matthew Apple, from the bottom of my heart. Their comments helped me to polish my writing and address numerous shortcomings and limitations.

I would also like to thank my friends, colleagues, and students who assisted in this research. I would especially like to thank my former colleagues at Kunitachi College of Music. I also thank the Vice Deans, Professor Kensuke Kono, and Professor Masahiko Suzuki, and the Director at Foreign Language Education Center, Professor Masahiro Shiina, at the College of Humanities and Sciences, Nihon University. Their warm encouragement led me to continue working on this study for the past several years.

I would also like to extend my gratitude to all individual members in the seventh Tokyo doctoral cohort. We studied, discussed, and shared ideas on Fridays and Saturdays for the two years it took us to complete our doctoral course work. I learned from their sincere attitude toward conducting research.

iv   ACKNOWLEDGMENTS

Last but not least, I would like to express my deepest gratitude to my parents, Tomoko and Koji Nagano, for their unconditional love, humor, and encouragement throughout my life. Without their understanding and full support, I could not have finished this long writing process.

Wakako Kobayashi
Yokohama, Japan
January, 2017

TABLE OF CONTENTS

Page

ABSTRACT ⋯⋯⋯⋯⋯⋯⋯⋯⋯⋯⋯⋯⋯⋯⋯⋯⋯⋯⋯⋯⋯⋯⋯⋯⋯⋯⋯⋯⋯ *i*

ACNOWLEDGEMENTS ⋯⋯⋯⋯⋯⋯⋯⋯⋯⋯⋯⋯⋯⋯⋯⋯⋯⋯⋯⋯⋯⋯ *iii*

TABLE OF CONTENTS ⋯⋯⋯⋯⋯⋯⋯⋯⋯⋯⋯⋯⋯⋯⋯⋯⋯⋯⋯⋯⋯ *v*

LIST OF TABLES ⋯⋯⋯⋯⋯⋯⋯⋯⋯⋯⋯⋯⋯⋯⋯⋯⋯⋯⋯⋯⋯⋯⋯⋯⋯ *x*

LIST OF FIGURES ⋯⋯⋯⋯⋯⋯⋯⋯⋯⋯⋯⋯⋯⋯⋯⋯⋯⋯⋯⋯⋯⋯⋯⋯ *xiii*

CHAPTER

1. INTRODUCTION ⋯⋯⋯⋯⋯⋯⋯⋯⋯⋯⋯⋯⋯⋯⋯⋯⋯⋯⋯⋯⋯⋯⋯ *1*

    The Background of the Issue ⋯⋯⋯⋯⋯⋯⋯⋯⋯⋯⋯⋯⋯⋯⋯⋯ *1*

    Statement of the Problems ⋯⋯⋯⋯⋯⋯⋯⋯⋯⋯⋯⋯⋯⋯⋯⋯⋯ *5*

    Purposes and Significance of the Study ⋯⋯⋯⋯⋯⋯⋯⋯⋯⋯ *6*

    The Audience for the Study ⋯⋯⋯⋯⋯⋯⋯⋯⋯⋯⋯⋯⋯⋯⋯⋯ *7*

    Delimitations ⋯⋯⋯⋯⋯⋯⋯⋯⋯⋯⋯⋯⋯⋯⋯⋯⋯⋯⋯⋯⋯⋯⋯ *7*

    The Organization of the Study ⋯⋯⋯⋯⋯⋯⋯⋯⋯⋯⋯⋯⋯⋯ *8*

2. REVIEW OF THE LITERATURE ⋯⋯⋯⋯⋯⋯⋯⋯⋯⋯⋯⋯⋯⋯ *9*

    Self-Assessment in Second Language Testing ⋯⋯⋯⋯⋯⋯⋯ *9*

    Assessment by Self and Others ⋯⋯⋯⋯⋯⋯⋯⋯⋯⋯⋯⋯⋯⋯ *11*

    The Roles of the Can-Do Questionnaires ⋯⋯⋯⋯⋯⋯⋯⋯⋯ *13*

    The Use of Can-Do Statements in Japanese Universities ⋯⋯ *15*

    The Common European Framework of Reference: Objectives and Limitations ⋯ *16*

    Autonomous Learning and Partial Competence ⋯⋯⋯⋯⋯ *27*

    MEXT Policies Concerning English Education ⋯⋯⋯⋯⋯⋯ *29*

    Gardner's (1985a) Socio-Educational Model ⋯⋯⋯⋯⋯⋯⋯ *30*

    MacIntyre's (1994) Willingness to Communicate Model ⋯⋯ *32*

    Yashima (2002) and EFL Contexts ⋯⋯⋯⋯⋯⋯⋯⋯⋯⋯⋯ *34*

    Affective Orientation Variables ⋯⋯⋯⋯⋯⋯⋯⋯⋯⋯⋯⋯⋯ *35*

Desire to Write English ·· 35

Attitude Toward Learning to Write English ······································ 36

Motivational Intensity to Write English ··· 36

Instrumental Orientation for Writing in English ···························· 37

L2 Writing Anxiety ··· 38

L2 Writing Self-Confidence ··· 39

Willingness to Communicate in L2 Writing ······································ 41

Self-Esteem ·· 42

Cognitive Competence ·· 44

General Self-Worth ··· 44

Gaps in the Previous Literature ··· 45

Purposes of the Study and Research Questions ·· 46

3. METHODS ·· 48

Participants and Setting ·· 48

Classroom Context ··· 51

Instrumentation ·· 52

Background Questionnaire ·· 52

The Writing Section of the Eiken Can-Do Questionnaires ············· 53

The Classroom Can-Do Questionnaires ·· 53

The Eiken Placement Test ··· 54

Writing Grades ··· 55

Essay Assignments ·· 55

Affective Orientation Questionnaire ·· 57

A Quantitative Methodology ·· 60

Analyses ·· 61

The Rasch Model ·· 61

Path Analysis, Structural Equation Modeling and Hierarchical Multiple
Regression ··· 62

Item Parceling in SEM ··· 63

Mediation, Direct Effects and Indirect Effects ·································· 64

A Hypothesized Structural Equation Model Including Can-Do
Questionnaires·· 65
Procedures and Schedule for Gathering Data ······································· 71

4. PRELIMINARY ANALYSES ·· 74
Desire to Write English ··· 74
Attitude Toward Learning to Write English······························· 76
Motivational Intensity to Write English··································· 79
Instrumental Orientation for Writing in English ····················· 82
L2 Writing Anxiety ·· 85
L2 Writing Self-Confidence ··· 89
Willingness to Communicate in L2 Writing ···························· 92
Self-Esteem ··· 95
Cognitive Competence·· 98
General Self-Worth ··· 101
EIKEN Can-Do Questionnaires ··· 104

5. RESULTS··· 109
Research Question 1: Writing Performance and Affective Orientation
Variables··· 109
Research Question 2: The Relationship Between Each Variable in Structural
Equation Models ··· 111
The Measurement Models ·· 112
Measurement Model A: Motivation ································· 112
Measurement Model A': Motivation with Item Parceling··········· 113
Measurement Model B: Self Variables ····························· 117
Measurement Model B': Self Variables with Item Parceling ······· 118
Measurement Model C': Affective Orientations with Item Parceling ········ 120
The Structural Models ··· 121
Complete Structural Model C' With Writing Outcome··········· 121
Complete Structural Model D Without Anxiety and Writing
Outcome ·· 124

Research Question 3: The Transition of Perceived Writing Performance and
Students' Writing Ability ⋯⋯ *127*

6. DISCUSSION ⋯⋯ *131*

Unidimensionality and Item Difficulty in the Rasch Analysis of the Eiken
Can-Do Questionnaires ⋯⋯ *131*

The Relationship Among the Eiken Can-Do Questionnaires, Affective
Orientation Variables, and Writing Outcomes ⋯⋯ *132*

The Transition in the Students' Self-Perceived Writing Ability and Writing
Ability over One Academic Year ⋯⋯ *137*

Theoretical Implications ⋯⋯ *139*

Pedagogical Implications ⋯⋯ *140*

7. CONCLUSION ⋯⋯ *142*

Summary of the Findings ⋯⋯ *142*

Limitations ⋯⋯ *144*

Suggestions for Future Research ⋯⋯ *145*

Final Conclusions ⋯⋯ *147*

REFERENCES ⋯⋯ *149*

APPENDICES

A. STUDENTS' PROFICIENCY LEVEL BY CEFR ⋯⋯ *170*

B. CLASS SYLABUSES IN THE 2010 AND 2011 ACADEMIC YEARS ⋯⋯ *171*

C. BACKGROUND QUESTIONNAIRE (ENGLISH VERSION) ⋯⋯ *179*

D. BACKGROUND QUESTIONNAIRE (JAPANESE VERSION) ⋯⋯ *180*

E. THE WRITING SECTION OF THE EIKEN CAN-DO QUESTIONNAIRE ⋯ *181*

F. THE ORIGINAL JAPANESE VERSION OF THE CLASSROOM CAN-DO
QUESTIONNAIRE ⋯⋯ *182*

G. CLASSROOM CAN-DO QUESTIONNAIRES AND DEGREE
OF ATTAINMENT (ENGLISH VERSION) ⋯⋯ *183*

H. CLASSROOM CAN-DO QUESTIONNAIRES AND DEGREE
OF ATTAINMENT IN THE 2010 AND 2011 ACADEMIC YEAR ⋯⋯ *184*

I. THE CLASSROOM CAN-DO QUESTIONNAIRE (ENGLISH VERSION) ···· *196*

J. THE CLASSROOM CAN-DO QUESTIONNAIRE (JAPANESE VERSION) ··· *199*

K. SAMPLE QUESTIONS OF THE EIKEN PLACEMENT TEST B ···················· *202*

L. THE PROMPTS OF EACH WRITING ASSIGNMENT AND WRITING
SAMPLES ··· *208*

M. RATING CRITERIA FOR STUDENT ESSAYS ··· *215*

N. AFFECTIVE ORIENTATION QUESTIONNAIRE (ENGLISH VERSION) ····· *216*

O. AFFECTIVE ORIENTATION QUESTIONNAIRE (JAPANESE VERSION) ···· *219*

P. WILLINGNESS TO COMMUNICATE (WTC) IN WRITING (ENGLISH
VERSION) ··· *222*

Q. WILLINGNESS TO COMMUNICATE (WTC) IN WRITING (JAPANESE
VERSION) ··· *223*

R. SELF-ESTEEM (ENGLISH VERSION) ·· *224*

S. SELF-ESTEEM (JAPANESE VERSION) ··· *225*

T. COGNITIVE COMPETENCE (ENGLISH VERSION) ································· *226*

U. COGNITIVE COMPETENCE (JAPANESE VERSION) ······························· *227*

V. GENERAL SELF-WORTH (ENGLISH VERSION) ······························ *228*

W. GENERAL SELF-WORTH (JAPANESE VERSION) ································· *229*

X. CONFIGURATION OF THE VARIABLES AFTER PARCELING ···················· *230*

LIST OF TABLES

Table		Page
1.	Common Reference Levels: Global Scale	18
2.	The Relationship Among CEFR's Six Indexes, TOEFL iBT, TOEIC, and EIKEN (STEP) Tests	20
3.	Overall Written Production Criteria	20
4.	Criteria for Assessing Creative Writing	21
5.	Criteria for Assessing Reports and Essays	22
6.	Equation Table for the EIKEN, TOEFL iBT, and TOEIC Test Scores	49
7.	The Participants' Major, Proficiency Levels and Overseas Experiences	50
8.	The Writing Section of the Eiken Can-Do Questionnaires and Classroom Can-Do Questionnaires	54
9.	English Writing Topics (Spring Semester, 2010 and 2011)	56
10.	English Writing Topics (Fall Semester, 2010 and 2011)	57
11.	Overview of the Study	73
12.	Category Structure Statistics for Desire to Write English	74
13.	Rasch Descriptive Statistics for the Desire to Write English Items	75
14.	Rasch Standardized Residual Variance Results for Desire to Write English	75
15.	Category Structure Statistics for Attitude Toward Learning to Write English	78
16.	Rasch Descriptive Statistics for the Attitude Toward Learning to Write English Items	78
17.	Rasch Standardized Residual Variance Results for Attitude Toward Learning to Write English	79
18.	Category Structure Statistics for Motivational Intensity	81
19.	Rasch Descriptive Statistics for the Motivational Intensity Items	81
20.	Rasch Standardized Residual Variance Results for Motivational Intensity	82
21.	Category Structure Statistics for Instrumental Orientation	84
22.	Rasch Descriptive Statistics for the Instrumental Orientation Items	84

LIST OF TABLES   *xi*

23. Rasch Standardized Residual Variance for instrumental Orientation ························· *85*

24. Category Structure Statistics for L2 Writing Anxiety ································· *87*

25. Rasch Descriptive Statistics for the L2 Writing Anxiety Items ······························· *87*

26. Rasch Standardized Residual Variance Results for L2 Writing Anxiety ····················· *88*

27. Category Structure Statistics for L2 Writing Self-Confidence ···························· *90*

28. Rasch Descriptive Statistics for the L2 Writing Self -Confidence Items ··············· *90*

29. Rasch Standardized Residual Variance Results for L2 Writing Self-Confidence ······· *91*

30. Category Structure Statistics for Willingness to Communicate in Writing ············· *93*

31. Rasch Descriptive Statistics for the Willingness to Communicate in Writing Items
    ··· *93*

32. Rasch Standardized Residual Variance Results for Willingness to Communicate
    in Writing ··· *93*

33. Category Structure Statistics for Self-Esteem ·· *95*

34. Rasch Descriptive Statistics for Self-Esteem Items ······································· *96*

35. Rasch Standardized Residual Variance Results for Self-Esteem ·························· *96*

36. Category Structure Statistics for Cognitive Competence ································· *98*

37. Rasch Descriptive Statistics for Cognitive Competence Items ··························· *99*

38. Rasch Standardized Residual Variance Results for Cognitive Competence ············· *99*

39. Category Structure Statistics for General Self-Worth ···································· *101*

40. Rasch Descriptive Statistics for the General Self-Worth Items ························· *102*

41. Rasch Standardized Residual Variance Results for General Self-Worth ················· *102*

42. Category Structure Statistics for the EIKEN Can-Do Questionnaires ··················· *104*

43. Rasch Descriptive Statistics for the EIKEN Can-Do Questionnaires ···················· *105*

44. Rasch Standardized Residual Variance Results for the EIKEN Can-Do
    Questionnaires ·· *107*

45. Winsteps Output for Residual Loadings for Each EIKEN Item ························ *108*

46. Measurement Models Tested ··· *110*

47. Pearson Correlations Among Affective Orientation Variables, Eiken Can-Do and
    Writing Outcome ··· *111*

48. Inter-Item Correlations for Motivation Subscales ······································ *116*

LIST OF TABLES

49. Summary of Fit Indices for Model A and Model A' ⋯⋯⋯⋯⋯⋯⋯⋯⋯⋯ *117*

50. Summary of Fit Indices for Model B and Model B' ⋯⋯⋯⋯⋯⋯⋯⋯⋯⋯ *120*

51. Summary of Fit Indices for Model C' ⋯⋯⋯⋯⋯⋯⋯⋯⋯⋯⋯⋯⋯⋯⋯⋯ *122*

52. The FACETS Output Table for Essays Assignments ⋯⋯⋯⋯⋯⋯⋯⋯⋯⋯ *129*

53. The FACETS Output Table for Rating Criteria ⋯⋯⋯⋯⋯⋯⋯⋯⋯⋯⋯ *129*

54. The FACETS Output Table for Raters of Writing Assignments ⋯⋯⋯⋯⋯ *129*

55. Eiken Can-Do Results' Transition over One Academic Year (April, July, and December) ⋯⋯⋯⋯⋯⋯⋯⋯⋯⋯⋯⋯⋯⋯⋯⋯⋯⋯⋯⋯⋯⋯⋯⋯⋯⋯⋯ *129*

LIST OF FIGURES

Figure   Page

1. Portion of MacIntyre's (1994) Willingness to Communicate Model 33

2. Yashima's (2002) Willingness to Communicate Model 34

3. The Hypothesized Motivation Model: Measurement Model A and Measurement Model B 72

4. Wright map for Desire to Write English 77

5. Wright map for Attitude Toward Learning to Write English 80

6. Wright map for Motivational Intensity to Write English 83

7. Wright map for Instrumental Orientation for Writing in English 86

8. Wright map for L2 Writing Anxiety 89

9. Wright map for L2 Writing Self-Confidence 92

10. Wright map for Willingness to Communicate in L2 Writing 94

11. Wright map for Self-Esteem 97

12. Wright map for Cognitive Competence 100

13. Wright map for General Self-Worth 103

14. Wright map for the EIKEN Can-Do Questionnaires 106

15. Measurement Model A: Motivation 113

16. Factor loadings for Items in Measurement Model A' 115

17. Revised Measurement Model A': Motivation with Item Parceling 116

18. Measurement Model B: Self Variables 118

19. Measurement Model B' Self Variables with Item Parceling 119

20. Measurement Model C': Affective Orientation with Item Parceling 121

21. The Complete Structural Model C' with Writing Outcome 123

22. Results for re-specified revised model of the Complete Structural Model D without Anxiety and Writing Outcome 125

23. Results of the FACETS analysis for writing assignments 128

24. Model of direct effects and indirect effects 135

1

CHAPTER 1
INTRODUCTION

The Background of the Issue

Can-Do Questionnaires, which consists of sentences describing what individuals believe they can accomplish in a foreign language, are now used by major high-stakes English test organizations used in Japan to aid in the interpretation of test scores for tests such as the TOEFL[1], TOEIC[2], GTEC for STUDENTS,[3] and the EIKEN (STEP)[4] as more qualitative indicators of the current English abilities of test-takers. Other sources of Can-Do Questionnaires are the Common European Framework of Reference for Language Learning, Teaching and Assessment (CEFR), which was announced by the Council of Europe in 1996, and frameworks prepared by governmental organizations in England, Canada, Australia, or the United States as goals for learners to pursue and standards for level of achievement (Naganuma, 2008). Individuals who take the TOEFL iBT test also complete competency descriptors in the form of Can-Do statements. As part of their test results, they receive feedback in the form of the percentile of activities they can do according to the score band. For instance, in the writing skills section, an essay assessed at score level 5

---

1 TOEFL is an abbreviation of Test of English as a Foreign Language, and is a standardized test to measure the English language ability of non-native speakers wishing to enroll in English-speaking universities.

2 TOEIC is an abbreviation of Test of English for International Communication, and is an English language test designed specifically to measure the everyday English skills of people working in an international environment.

3 GTEC (Global Test of English Communication) for Students is an English test that is made for fostering the English proficiency not only for entrance examinations but also for business situations. There are three levels: Core, Basic, and Advanced.

4 The EIKEN (STEP) is an abbreviation of Jitsuyo Eigo Gino Kentei (Test in Practical English Proficiency), Japan's most widely used English testing program. There are seven tests within the Eiken framework, each representing a different ability level, from 5th Level to 1st Level.

2   CHAPTER 1 INTRODUCTION

largely accomplishes all of the following: (a) effectively addresses the topic and task, (b) is well organized and well developed, using clearly appropriate explanations, exemplifications, and/or details, (c) displays unity, progression, and coherence, (d) displays consistent facility in the use of language, demonstrating syntactic variety, appropriate word choice, and idiomaticity, though it might have minor lexical or grammatical errors.

A Can-Do guide was published for a previous version of the TOEIC when the test was redesigned under the concept of Evidence Centered Design (ETS, 2008). The developers adopted a new Can-Do instrument and included score descriptors on the test-takers' score sheet. The TOEIC Can-Do Guide allows users of TOEIC test results to link TOEIC scores to the activities that examinees might be able to carry out successfully in English. For example, in English listening on the TOEIC, two Can-do statements are (a) "I can understand simple questions in social situations such as *How are you? Where do you live?, How do you feel?*, and (b) *I can understand a salesperson when she or he tells me prices of various items.*

Benesse Corporation and Masashi Negishi from the Tokyo University of Foreign Languages jointly developed a Can-Do Questionnaire for the GTEC for STUDENTS and investigated the validity of the questionnaire by analyzing the test-takers' performance (Negishi, 2006). The developers of the GTEC for STUDENTS provided Can-do statements in order to provide feedback to test-takers' regarding their ability to perform everyday tasks. Examples in the writing category include, *You can generally write a schedule in English, You can write a letter, email, or diary in English without the help of dictionary*, and *You can take notes in English in a class in an English-speaking country.* The primary advantage of this form of assessment is that the statements allow test-takers to refer to what they can do in each Level as well as to their test score (Naganuma, 2008).

The Eiken Can-Do List (2006), which consists of descriptive statements by which Eiken test-takers indicate what they believe they can accomplish in English in real-life situations, provides Can-Do statements describing the test-takers' self-perceived ability to use English for the four major skills of reading, listening, speaking, and writing for each of the seven Eiken levels. The primary aim of the list is to help test users gain a better understanding of the levels of language proficiency targeted by the Eiken tests (STEP, 2006). For this reason,

The Background of the Issue   *3*

the list is designed to be accessible to a variety of test users and is written in everyday, non-specialist language so that it is accessible to as wide a range of learners as possible. Eiken (STEP) also hopes that the Can-Do list provides information that allows educators and researchers to achieve a better understanding of the proficiency of Japanese learners of English in general.

In the field of Japanese education, the Business Japanese Test (BJT) administered by Japan External Trade Organization (JETRO) also includes Can-Do statements. The BJT test-takers engage in self-assessment using the Can-Do statements, which are divided into five levels. For instance, they self-assess their Japanese writing ability using Can-Do statements such as, *I can write my own address or affiliation in Japanese*, or *I can exchange an e-mail in Japanese* (BJT, 2009). The assessment standard consists of a 5-point Likert scale: 5 = *I can do 80-100%*; 4 = *I can do 60-80%*; 3 = *I can do 40-60%*; 2 = *I can do 20-40%*, and; 1 = *I can do 0-20%*.

In addition, the Japanese Language Proficiency Test (JLPT), which is administered by the Japan Foundation, which is Japan's only institution dedicated to carrying out comprehensive international cultural exchange programs throughout the world, added a Can-Do List in 2010 (Naganuma, Okuma, Wada, Ito, Kumagaya & Noguchi, 2007). Each section on the test (i.e., listening, speaking, reading, and writing) has 20 Can-Do statements, for a total of 80 statements, which are divided into five levels. The Japan Foundation investigated the candidates who passed the test and what they can and cannot do at each level. Sample items for each skill are as follows: *You can roughly understand the contents when you listen to the announcement at school, office or public places* (listening); *You can concretely describe your hopes and past experiences when you are interviewed for jobs* (speaking); *You can understand the contents of the newspaper or journals which are a relevant topic* (reading); *You can write letters or emails which express any gratitude, apology, or emotion* (writing) (JLPT, 2010).

Can-Do statements have also been adopted in some Super English Language High Schools (SELHi schools), where in 2003 the government launched a three-year project and around 50 schools were designated for Super English Language High Schools. Super English Language High Schools, which are Ministry of Education, Culture, Sports, Sci-

4   CHAPTER 1 INTRODUCTION

ence and Technology (MEXT) promoted projects, aim for researching advanced English education in Japan. The teachers in SELHI schools are in an effort to develop better syllabuses and clearer classroom objectives. For example, in Kasumi High School, Naganuma and Nagasue (2006) reported that teachers adopted the tasks listed in the CEFR Can-Do Questionnaires for use in the classroom, developed a more concrete and clearer syllabus and classroom objectives, and identified which levels of CEFR Can-Do Questionnaires correspond to the Kasumi Can-Do Grade through an analysis of the CEFR Can-Do statements. The authors also pointed out which of CEFR's Can-Do statements are usable in Kasumi's classrooms.

In another SELHi, Fukiai High School in Kobe, the teachers developed the Common Fukiai Framework (CFF) in order to develop and present the descriptors, and administered classroom-based Can-Do Questionnaires (Takeshita, 2008). Takeshita stated that in Fukiai High School, the teachers have developed clearer learning objectives using Can-Do statements, and the teachers as well as the students can more effectively consider how to attain those objectives. The teachers in Fukiai High School monitor each student and provide individual instruction using Can-do statements.

As seen from the above brief descriptions, a number of major testing corporations and educational institutions provide not only quantitative, objective ability measures in the form of test scores, but also subjective ability measures in the form of Can-Do statements in which the test-takers indicate what they believe they can do in English. Can-Do statements have been used because a number of stakeholders have not been satisfied with objective, multiple-choice test results. As noted above, one of the benefits of Can-Do statements is that they allow test users and administrators to interpret the test scores subjectively. A further advantage was provided by Blanche and Merino (1989), who summarized the literature on self-assessment on foreign language skills and pointed out that self-assessment accuracy can lead to greater learner autonomy and help teachers become aware of learners' individual needs.

Statement of the Problems

The first problem is that there is little international research on investigation for the relationship between writing performance as measured by six essay writing assignments, the students' self-assessed writing ability using Eiken Can-Do Questionnaires and ten affective orientation variables, such as Desire to Write English, Attitude Toward Learning to Write English, Motivational Intensity, Instrumental Orientation for Writing in English, L2 Writing Anxiety, L2 Writing Self-Confidence, Willingness to Communicate in L2 Writing, Self Esteem, Cognitive Competence, and General Self-Worth. Especially there is little international research on investigation for this relationship using structural equation modeling.

Moreover, research in the Japanese EFL setting is even more limited. As Japanese university students' learning environments and frequency of classes might differ greatly from those of the participants in past studies, research involving Japanese university students is necessary to fill some of the gaps between the current research on Can-Do statements in the Japanese EFL context.

The second problem is that little is known about the value and motivational effects of using Can-Do statements in EFL classrooms. Naganuma (2008a) stated that Can-Do statements can be used as a tool for monitoring students' English learning processes and developing more autonomous learners. Researchers should investigate how Eiken Can-do questionnaires affect students' motivation. Moreover, previous researchers have not investigated self-assessment and its relationship to affective variables. Can-Do Questionnaires can be used as a form of self-assessment, and self-assessment tasks not only can help foster a greater awareness of foreign language but also fulfill a subjective role for the learners' self-learning process.

The third problem is that little is known about the degree to which self-assessment changes over time, and if it changes, why it changes. The relationship between Perceived Writing Performance as measured by the Eiken Can-Do Questionnaires and the students' writing proficiency, as measured by essay writing performance over one year is not known at all. The quality of the self-assessment depends on the persons who are doing the self-as-

6   CHAPTER 1 INTRODUCTION

sessment. Nakanishi, Hayashi, Kobayashi and Sakuma (2010a) pointed out that teachers and students need explanations before doing the self-assessment because students can underestimate or overestimate their actual ability when completing the self-assessments. More specifically, it might be more accurate to say that students need experience using Can-Do statements once or twice to become accustomed to that form of assessment.

Purposes and Significance of the Study

The first purpose of this study is to investigate the relationship between the writing performance as measured by six writing assignments, the students' self-assessed writing ability using the Eiken Can-Do Questionnaires, and ten affective orientation variables used in this study. This purpose is important because little is known about the relationship among these variables using structural equation modeling. Also, it will enable researchers to have a clearer understanding of the effect of distributing Eiken Can-Do Questionnaire over an extended period of time.

The second purpose is to determine the effects of ten affective variables on the participants' use of the Eiken Can-Do Questionnaire. This purpose is valuable because little or nothing is known about the relationship between Can-Do Questionnaires and affective variables investigated in this study. It will allow researchers to have a clearer understanding of the students by illuminating the relationship between the Eiken Can-Do Questionnaires and ten affective orientations.

The third purpose of this study is to investigate the transition of perceived writing performance, as measured by the Eiken Can-Do Questionnaires and students' writing proficiency as measured by essay writing performance over one year. This purpose is valuable because little is known about the relationship between them. It will allow researchers to have a better understanding of the transition of perceived writing performance and students' writing proficiency.

The Audience for the Study

This study will benefit researchers in the field of foreign language assessment because it provides them with an additional perspective on Can-Do statement research. As noted above, research on Can-Do Questionnaires is limited; therefore, this investigation of writing for communication meets the increasing need for empirical support for Can-Do Questionnaires. Researchers will also gain a better understanding of what types of items work most effectively, at least in this context. Finally, researchers will gain a better understanding of the relationship between ten affective variables and students' performances on the Eiken Can-Do Questionnaires.

The results of this study can potentially benefit students enrolled in English writing classes by providing them with a way to more accurately assess their writing proficiency and to specify what they can and cannot do in terms of writing English. When students complete Can-Do statements as an external measure, they can potentially arrive at a clearer understanding of their own general proficiency level, become more aware of their strengths and weaknesses, increase their motivation by becoming more aware of which tasks they are able to do successfully, and form appropriate learning objectives by focusing on tasks they cannot yet perform successfully.

The third audience for this study is university teachers and administrators. The results of the study can show them the degree to which Can-Do statements can be used to estimate students' classroom performance, provide attainable learning objectives, and help students know what they can accomplish at each development stage. Teachers will see concrete examples of validated questionnaires, and these examples will prove useful should they decide to develop Can-Do Questionnaires in their own institution.

Delimitations

The results can be generalized to Japanese university students whose proficiency levels are similar to those of the participants in this study and generalized with caution to uni-

8 CHAPTER 1 INTRODUCTION

versity students with other L1s, whose English proficiency levels are similar to the participants in this study. It should, however, be recognized that students from other cultures might interpret both the Can-Do items and the affective questionnaire items differently from the participants in this study.

Several delimitations restrict the generalizability of the study. The participants in this study are Japanese university students, whose ages range from 20 to 21. Their first language and cultural backgrounds are Japanese and they are non-English majors. The results of this study cannot be generalized with confidence to young children, junior and high school students, or adult learners.

The Organization of the Study

This study consists of seven chapters. Chapter 2 is a review of the literature and is divided into 13 main sections: Self-assessment in Second Language Testing, Assessment by Self and Others, The Roles of Can-Do Questionnaires, The Use of Can-Do statements in Japanese Universities, The Common European Framework of Reference: Objectives and Limitations, Autonomous Learning and Partial Competence, MEXT Policies Concerning English Education, Gardner's (1985a) Socio-educational Model, MacIntyre's (1994) Willingness to Communicate Model, Yashima (2002) and EFL context, Affective Orientation Variables, Gaps in the Previous Literature, and Purposes of the Study and Research Questions. The methodology of the study is described in Chapter 3. This chapter is divided into six sections: Participants and Setting, Classroom Context, Instrumentation, A Quantitative Methodology, Analyses, and Procedures and Schedule for Gathering Data. In Chapter 4, Preliminary Analysis, the instruments used in this study are validated primarily using the Rasch rating scale model and the multifaceted Rasch model. In Chapter 5, Results, the findings for each research question are presented through the quantitative approach, EQS, Structural Equation Modeling. Those results are interpreted in Chapter 6, Discussion, and a summary of the findings, the limitations of the study, suggestions for future research, and final conclusions are presented in Chapter 7, Conclusion.

CHAPTER 2
REVIEW OF THE LITERATURE

In this chapter, I review the literature concerning Self-Assessment in Second Language Testing, Assessment by Self and Others, The Roles of Can-Do Questionnaires, The Use of Can-Do Statements in Japanese Universities, The Common European Framework of Reference: Objectives and Limitations, Autonomous Learning and Partial Competence, MEXT Policies Concerning English Education, Gardner's (1985a) Socio-educational Model, MacIntyre's (1994) Willingness to Communicate Model, Yashima (2002) and EFL contexts, and Affective Orientation Variables. At the end of this chapter, I describe the gaps in the previous literature, and present the purposes of this study and the research questions investigated in this study.

Self-Assessment in Second Language Testing

While researchers investigating self-assessment have considered various aspects of measurement theory, such as reliability and construct validity, there has been relatively little discussion of the value of self-assessment as an alternative to more expensive and logistically problematic approaches to proficiency and achievement assessment, particularly in the area of second and foreign language testing (Ross, 1998). Moral reasons, such as the sharing of power between teacher and learner, as well as motivational ones, such as the excitement of self-discovery, are often used to justify self-assessment practices against the accusation of lack of reliability (Davies et al., 1999). Ross also stated that self-assessment has frequently been viewed as being opposed to the concerns of traditional educational measurement because self-assessment often introduces a large number of unwanted measurement facets. Despite these drawbacks, there are advantages to using self-assessment, including its potential to increase student and teacher motivation.

10 CHAPTER 2 REVIEW OF THE LITERATURE

Ross (1998, p. 16) stated that learners provide more accurate self-assessments if the criterion variable exemplifies the achievement of functional skills. For example, if students in English as a Foreign Language (EFL) environment are provided with the statement, *You can order a meal at a fast food restaurant in English*, many of them cannot respond because they have never ordered a meal at a fast food restaurant in English. When the self-assessment instrument contains abstract items designed to assess general language proficiency, learners can be expected to have had less direct experience in practicing those language skills, and as a result, self-assessment can be relatively inaccurate in these cases. However, if learners are asked to assess skills with which they have had direct and possibly repeated experience, their judgments are relatively accurate. This suggests that the episodic memory of using particular skills in the classroom enhances the accuracy of self-assessment.

Teacher assessment can be considered more generalizable than student assessment, as it is based on the teacher's cumulative experience observing student performance in classroom contexts over long periods of time (Ross, 1998). It is, however, possible to argue that teachers only observe any particular student a fraction of the class time, whereas students constantly observe their own performance; this would presumably put the student in a better position to assess their performance accurately.

Sato (2010) explained the relationship between self-assessment ratings and test scores: two claims have been made regarding self-assessment ratings and test scores. One is that they correlate moderately, and the other is that they correlate poorly. Blanche and Merino (1989) found that Pearson product-moment correlation values higher than $r = .70$ were not unusual. Another meta-analysis of self-assessment (Falchikov & Boud, 1989) showed that the mean value of correlation coefficients between self-assessment and teacher's evaluation was moderate ($r = .39$). Several independent studies also indicated a moderate correlation (Alderson, 2005; Bailey, 1998; Brantmeier & Vanderplank, 2008).

On the other hand, several researchers reported a low correlation and cast doubt on incorporating self-assessment in formal settings. As reported by Matsuno (2009) and Sullivan and Hall (1997), even advanced-proficiency learners occasionally overestimate or underestimate their proficiency to a large extent. Self-assessment statements that are not closely related to the learner's immediate situation or past experiences are assessment are most difficult for learners to assess accurately (Oscarson, 1997; Ross, 1998).

The Eiken Can-Do Questionnaires were produced on the basis of questionnaires responded to by more than 20,000 Eiken test-takers (STEP, 2008). In spite of its research potential, only a few validation studies of the Eiken Can-Do Questionnaires have been carried out (Sato, 2010; Takemura, 2008; Usuta, 2009). Sato (2010) examined the validity of 16 Can-Do items taken from the four Eiken Can-Do Questionnaires, Level 5, Level 4, Level 3, and Level pre-2 respectively. The coded data were analyzed using the Rasch-based computer software WINSTEPS (Linacre, 2004). The results showed that the 16 Can-Do Questionnaire items were highly reliable and unidimensional.

Takemura (2008) investigated the validity of the writing Can-Do Questionnaires for Eiken level 3 and Level pre-2. He found that the learners who assessed themselves highly tended to perform the writing tasks more successfully than their peers who gave themselves lower ratings. Similarly, Usuta (2009) examined the validity of the speaking Can-Do Questionnaires for Eiken Pre-2 Level examination. Usuta concluded that the items were moderately correlated with task performance.

Having shown evidences that self-assessment in the second language testing is useful, I address a similar topic, peer- and self-assessment in the next section.

Assessment by Self and Others

The Council of Europe (2001, p. 191) stated that two kinds of assessments are related to Can-Do instruments. The first concerns assessment by a teacher or examiner, which involves the measurement of person ability or the quality or success of instruction. The other is self-assessment in which the student makes a judgment about his or her own proficiency. Learners can be involved in all of the assessment techniques outlined above. Frequently used approaches in the area of self-assessment have been the use of rating scales, checklists, and questionnaires. These three techniques have been used as a means of allowing learners to rate their perceived general language proficiency or ability to carry out specific tasks in the L2. The second example of self-assessment concerns the use of learner diaries and dialogue journals, which have been proposed as a way of systematizing student self-assessment

12 CHAPTER 2 REVIEW OF THE LITERATURE

(Dickinson, 1987; Oscarsson 1989). Learners should be encouraged to write about what they learned, their perceived level of mastery over the course content, and what they plan to do with their acquired skills. The third example is that students can be videotaped or they can videotape each other and then assess their language skills. An obvious advantage to use of video in self-assessment is that students can assess not only their communicative language skills, but also their paralinguistic skills, such as their use of body language (Coombe & Canning, 2010).

Research suggests that except for high-stakes testing, self-assessment can be an effective complement to classroom tests, placement tests, and teacher assessments (Oscarsson, 1989). Accuracy in self-assessment is increased when the assessment is related to clear descriptions defining standards of proficiency and/or when the assessment is related to specific experiences, including taking tests. Self-assessment is also more accurate when learners receive an explanation about the purposes and usages of the Eiken Can-Do Questionnaires (Nakanishi, Hayashi, Kobayashi & Sakuma, 2010b). Self-assessment can achieve high correlations with teachers' assessments and objective tests. These correlations can equal those commonly reported between teachers themselves, between two tests of the same skill, and between teacher assessment and tests (The Council of Europe, 2001, p. 191).

The main potential for self-assessment, however, is in its use as a tool for motivation and awareness-raising (The Council of Europe, 2001). According to Dörnyei and Ottó's (1998) definition of L2 motivation, motivation is "the dynamically changing cumulative arousal in a person that initiates, directs, coordinates, amplifies, terminates, and evaluates the cognitive and motor processes whereby initial wishes and desires are selected, prioritized, operationalized and (successfully or unsuccessfully) acted out" (p. 65). In addition, learners' awareness of their strengths, weaknesses, and their orientations toward learning can be increased through the use of self-assessment.

As one form of self-assessment, I consider the roles that Can-Do Questionnaires can play in educational curricula in the next section.

The Roles of the Can-Do Questionnaires

Can-Do Questionnaires have two major roles in the field of educational assessment. Nakanishi et al. (2010b) stated that the first role is to help test administrators and teachers interpret test scores. The results of certified English examinations, such as TOEFL, TOEIC, GTEC for STUDENTS, and the EIKEN (STEP) are expressed using numerical scores, together with descriptive sentences from Can-do questionnaires, which concretely indicate what test-takers believe they can do with the foreign language in specific situations. For instance, one Eiken pre-2nd Level writing descriptor (Eiken, 2006) states that the student *can write a simple notice (e.g., the date, time and place of a party, the program for a school festival)* or *can write short letters and e-mails (e.g. a simple letter to a friend or pen pal).*

These descriptive Can-Do statements provide learners with an opportunity to assess their current English proficiency level in specific ways, which is the second role of Can-do statements. This role of Can-Do statements serves as an external measure of the learners' developmental stage. In this context, external measure means that the Can-Do results are used by the general public to refer to levels of English proficiency. When used in conjunction with large-scale proficiency tests, the purpose of a Can-Do questionnaire is to provide an alternative indication of students' current developmental stage for a number of stakeholders, including teachers, parents, and the students themselves. The information provided is also useful for teachers when they formulate learning objectives for their students (Naganuma, 2008).

However, Can-Do statements that are used to interpret the test scores of certified examinations sometimes do not fit the activities used in a particular classroom because they are written for the general public rather than a specific group of students. Therefore, when developing Can-Do statements as an internal measure in a single educational institution, test developers must initially write concrete learning objectives for that particular course; the Can-Do statements are then derived from the class objectives.

For instance, Koike (2008) assessed the Japanese version of CEFR, CEFRjapan's (Oka, Kawanari, Takada, Tominaga & Nakamura, 2008) attainable objectives, based on the

14 CHAPTER 2 REVIEW OF THE LITERATURE

CEFR version written in Finland and the Young Learner English Test (2010) published by English for Speakers of Other Language (ESOL) in Cambridge University. Koike stated that the importance of improving English communicative ability is evident given that the governments of many countries have officially recognized that English is a necessary tool for achieving international competitiveness. However, in terms of English communicative ability, Japanese lag far behind people in other Asian countries such as Korea, China, and Taiwan, and behind many Europeans. Koike (2008) concluded that a new paradigm of TEFL policy standardization based on the CEFR should be implemented so that Japanese can improve their communicative ability in English.

The Koike Kaken[5] (2004-2007), which is a Leading Research to Coordinate Primary, Secondary and Tertiary level English Education based on Second Language Research, proposed a new, comprehensive, and consistent English language curriculum that extends from elementary school to university. Those curricula are designed to enhance Japan's competitive English ability. After investigating 7,354 international business people's English communicative ability, need for English, and communication strategies, they concluded that Japanese must have attainable English objectives, and it is important to set up a common framework of reference for English communicative ability and a national standard for English education (Koike et al., 2010).

Furthermore, Kyushu Industrial University (2009) analyzed the relationship between scores on the TOEIC Bridge test and English Communication Proficiency and developed Can-Do Questionnaires based on the results. The participants were 2,671 first-year students who were enrolled the English education program in Kyushu Industrial University. The teachers made Can-Do items based on the students' self-assessment and teachers' assessments. The researchers concluded that the Can-Do items were effective because they allowed teachers to share a common understanding of the students' proficiency, grasp more appropriate educational goals and objectives, and make better decisions regarding textbooks for the students. They also concluded that completing the Can-Do statements helped students set attainable goals and objectives, and become more motivated to study

---

5 Kaken is Grant in Aid for Scientific Research, which is supported by MEXT in Japan

English (ETS, 2006).

Regarding developing more concrete versions of CEFR's or Eiken Can-Do Questionnaires, Green (2011) advocated a process for working with the CEFR to generate locally appropriate educational tools. He stated that when applied to a classroom, CEFR should consist of three layers: abstract, which is made up of can-do objectives, elaboration, which refers to reference level descriptions, and concrete, which concerns classroom and real-life tasks undertaken by language learners. He also emphasized the necessity of linking the interpretation of Can-Do Questionnaires to specific learning contexts.

Having looked at Can-Do Questionnaires in this section, I describe how Can-Do statements have been used in Japanese universities in the next section.

The Use of Can-Do Statements in Japanese Universities

Under the influence of MEXT's announcements, Seisen University and Ehime University made the statements on their Can-Do Questionnaires into curricular objectives (Hiromori, 2009; Naganuma & Miyajima, 2006; Yamanishi & Hiromori, 2008). The purpose of the Seisen Academic Can-Do Scale is to measure the academic English abilities of learners in the classroom, rather than daily communicative English abilities outside of class. As such, the scale performs an important role in defining course objectives. The scale is made up of 20 Can-Do statements divided into four skill areas, each of which describes a level of performance (at least four levels) in accomplishing learning tasks.

As a result of CEFR's publication, some Japanese junior high schools, high schools, and universities are using Can-Do statements as one part of their foreign language curricula (Naganuma, 2008; Naganuma & Nagasue, 2008; Tadaki, 2007; Tanaka, 2008). For instance, in Ibaraki University, which has been a pioneer in the use of Can-do statements, teachers referred to CEFR and defined comprehensive English reference levels in Can-Do statements for all students in 2005 (Fukuda, 2007). Two examples of Can-Do statements used for assessing writing skills at Ibaraki University are *I can describe dreams, hopes and ambitions* and *I can describe the plot of a book or film and describe my reactions* (Fukuda, 2007).

16   CHAPTER 2 REVIEW OF THE LITERATURE

In Seisen University, Naganuma and Miyajima (2006) developed the Seisen Can-Do statements and introduced them into the classrooms as a part of a reformulation of the compulsory English Curriculum. The Seisen Can-Do statements, which are designed to be comprehensive by covering the four skills as well as past English experiences and students' needs, were developed as an external measure. Two examples of Can-Do statements used for assessing writing skills at Seisen University are *I can correct my grammatical mistakes when I read my essay in English*, and *I can write emails to my friends, teachers and acquaintances after I read the email letters from them* (Naganuma & Miyajima, 2006).

In Meijo University as well, a framework based on CEFR was introduced into the English language curriculum in 2007 (Tadaki, 2007). Tadaki stated that whether the teachers could guide the students to the objective levels depended on higher consciousness or awareness regarding language learning and education among the teachers and students. Through these trials, Can-Do statements are gradually coming to be viewed as an effective educational tool in Japan.

Having gained a concrete image about how Can-Do statements are used in Japanese universities, I next address the objectives the Common European Framework has targeted with Can-Do Questionnaires and how some researchers have pointed out limitations of Can-Do Questionnaires.

The Common European Framework of Reference:
Objectives and Limitations

The Council of Europe announced the Common European Framework of Reference for Languages: Learning, Teaching, Assessment (CEFR) in 1996. The Council of Europe (2001) described CEFR as a document indicating what language learners have to learn to do in order to use a foreign language for communicative purposes and what knowledge and skills they have to develop to communicate effectively. CEFR also defined six proficiency levels that allow learners' progress to be measured at each stage of learning on a lifelong basis (The Council of Europe, 2001, p. 1).

The Common European Framework is intended to overcome the barriers to communi-

The Common European Framework of Reference: Objectives and Limitations   *17*

cation among professionals working in the field of modern language arising from the different educational systems in Europe. As such, the aims and objectives of the Council's language policy are to (a) ensure that all segments of their populations have access to effective means of acquiring knowledge of the languages of other member states as well as the skills that will enable them to satisfy their communicative needs, (b) promote, encourage, and support the efforts of teachers and learners at all levels to apply in their own situation the principles of the construction of language-learning systems, and (c) promote research and development programs leading to the introduction, at all educational levels, of methods and materials best suited to enabling different classes and types of students to acquire a level of communicative proficiency appropriate to their specific needs.

The Council of Europe (2001, p. 4) also stated that the concept of plurilingualism has grown in importance in the Council of Europe's approach to language learning, and that plurilingualism differs from multilingualism, which is the knowledge of a number of languages or the co-existence of different languages in a given society. The plurilingual approach emphasizes the notion that as an individuals' experience of a language and its cultural context expands, from the language of the home to that of society at large and then to the languages of other peoples, they develop a communicative competence to which all knowledge and experience of language contributes and in which languages interrelate and interact.

According to the Council of Europe (2001, p. 9), a comprehensive, transparent, and coherent frame of reference for language learning, teaching, and assessment must be related to a general view of language use and learning. The approach adopted here is action-oriented as users and learners of a foreign language primarily are seen as "social agents" who have particular tasks to accomplish in a specific environment and within a particular field of action. In accordance with the action-oriented approach, it is assumed that language learners are in the process of becoming language users, so the same set of categories applies. Learners do not simply acquire two unrelated ways of acting and communicating; they become plurilingual and develop interculturality (Council of Europe, 2001, p. 43).

To carry out communicative tasks, users have to engage in communicative language activities and use communication strategies (Council of Europe, 2001, p. 57). Productive ac-

18　CHAPTER 2 REVIEW OF THE LITERATURE

tivities and strategies include both speaking and writing activities; however, as the focus of this study is on writing, I have omitted a discussion of speaking skills.

When engaged in writing activities, language users produce a written text that is re-

Table 1. *Common Reference Levels: Global Scale* (Adopted from the Council of Europe, 2001, p. 24)

Proficient User	C2	Can understand with ease virtually everything heard or read. Can summarize information from different spoken and written sources, reconstructing arguments and accounts in a coherent presentation. Can express him/herself spontaneously, very fluently and precisely, differentiating finer shades of meaning even in more complex situations.
	C1	Can understand a wide range of demanding, longer texts and recognize implicit meaning. Can express him/herself fluently and spontaneously without much obvious searching for expressions. Can use language flexibly and effectively for social, academic and professional purposes. Can produce clear, well-structured, detailed text on complex subjects, showing controlled use of organizational patterns, connectors and cohesive devices.
Independent User	B2	Can understand the main ideas of complex text on both concrete and abstract topics, including technical discussions in his/her field of specialization. Can interact with a degree of fluency and spontaneously that makes regular interaction with native speakers quite possible without strain and explain a viewpoint on a topical issue giving the advantages and disadvantages of various options.
	B1	Can understand the main points of clear standard input on familiar matters regularly encountered in work, school, leisure, etc. Can deal with most situations likely to arise whilst travelling in an area where the language is spoken. Can produce simple connected text on topics which are familiar or of personal interest. Can describe experiences and even dreams, hopes and ambitions and briefly give reasons and explanations for opinions and plans.
Basic User	A2	Can understand sentences and frequently used expressions related to areas of most immediate relevance (e.g. very basic personal and family information, shopping, local geography, employment). Can communicate in simple and routine tasks requiring a simple and direct exchange of information on familiar and routine matters. Can describe in simple terms aspects of his/her background, immediate environment and matters in areas of immediate need.
	A1	Can understand and use familiar everyday expressions and very basic phrases aimed at the satisfaction of needs of a concrete type. Can introduce him/herself and others and can ask and answer questions about personal details such as where he/she lives, people he/she knows and things he/she has. Can interact in a simple way provided the other person talks slowly and clearly and is prepared to help.

ceived by a readership of one or more readers. Examples of writing activities include (a) completing forms and questionnaires, (b) writing articles for magazines newspapers, or newsletters, (c) producing posters for display, (d) writing reports or memoranda, (e) making notes for future reference, (f) taking messages, (g) creative and imaginative writing, and (h) writing personal or business letters (Council of Europe, 2001, p. 61).

The Council of Europe has provided a framework divided into six broad levels labeled A1 (Breakthrough), A2 (Waystage), B1 (Threshold), B2 (Vantage), C1 (Effective), and C2 (Mastery). A1 and A2 are categorized as Basic User, B1 and B2 as Independent User, and C1 and C2 as Proficient User. This framework provides coverage of the learning space relevant to European language learners for the above purposes.

Koike (2010) showed how CEFR's six indexes align with the TOEFL iBT, TOEIC, and STEP total scores. Table 1 summarizes the proposed Common Reference Levels, and shows that CEFR's six indices are divided into three categories, Basic User, Independent User, and Proficient User.

Table 2 shows the relationship between CEFR levels and those tests, and shows that CEFR's six indexes have more detailed categories than the TOEFL, TOEIC, and EIKEN (STEP) tests. For example, TOEFL does not provide a score for CEFR A1 and A2, which are the lower proficiency levels, and CEFR C2, which is the highest level. TOEFL speaking, though it is aligned with CEFR A1 and A2, does not extend to the CEFR C2 level. TOEIC Listening and Reading, and the EIKEN (STEP) test also do not extend to the CEFR C2 level.

Table 3 shows the scale provided for Overall Written Production. The descriptors on this scale and on the two sub-scales that follow (Creative Writing; Reports and Essays) have not been empirically calibrated with a measurement model; thus, the validity of the sub-scales is unknown. The descriptors for these three scales have been created by recombining elements of descriptors from other scales (The Council of Europe, 2001, p. 61).

The development of learners' linguistic competences is a central aspect of language learning. The development of writing skills can be facilitated in a number of ways including: (a) simple transfer from the L1, (b) exposure to authentic written L2 texts, (c) memorization of target language orthography and its associated phonetic values, together with

20   CHAPTER 2 REVIEW OF THE LITERATURE

diacritics and punctuation marks, (d) practicing cursive writing and noting the characteristic national handwriting conventions, (e) memorizing word forms and punctuation conventions, and (f) the practicing dictation (Council of Europe, 2001, p. 153).

The Association of Language Testers in Europe (ALTE) Can-do statements, described in the Common European Framework of Reference for Languages: Learning, Teaching, Assessment by the Council of Europe (2001, p. 244), constitute a central part of a long-term

Table 2. *The Relationship Among CEFR's Six Indexes and the TOEFL iBT, TOEIC, and EIKEN (STEP) Tests* **(Adopted from British Council, 2015)**

Test	CEFR Index					
	A1	A2	B1	B2	C1	C2
TOEFL Total			57-86	87-109	110-120	
TOEFL Reading			8	22	26	29
TOEFL Listening			13	21	26	
TOEFL Speaking	8	13	19	23	28	
TOEFL Writing		11	17	21	28	
TOEIC Total		400	520	740	900	
TOEIC Listening	60	110	275	400	490	
TOEIC Reading	60	115	275	385	455	
EIKEN Level	Levels 3, 4, & 5	Level Pre-2	Level 2	Level Pre 1	Level 1	

Table 3. *Overall Written Production Criteria* **(Adopted from Council of Europe, 2001, p. 61)**

Level	Criterion descriptions
C2	Can write clear, smoothly flowing, complex texts in an appropriate and effective style and a logical structure which helps the reader to find significant points.
C1	Can write clear, well-structured texts of complex subjects, underlining the relevant salient issues, expanding and supporting points of views at some length with subsidiary points, reasons and relevant examples, and rounding off with an appropriate conclusion.
B2	Can write clear, detailed texts on a variety of subjects related to his/her field of interests, synthesizing and evaluating information and arguments from a number of sources.
B1	Can write straightforward connected texts on a range of familiar subjects within his field of interest, by linking a series of shorter discrete elements into a linear sequence.
A2	Can write a series of simple phrases and sentences linked with simple connectors like "and", "but" and "because".
A1	Can write simple isolated phrases and sentences.

research program set by the ALTE, the aim of which is to establish a framework of key levels of language performance, within which examinations can be described objectively. The aims of the Can-do statements are two-fold. First, they provide a useful tool for foreign language teachers and assessment professionals in that they can be used as a checklist of what language individuals can use and they provide a definition of their current stage of development. Second, they provide a basis for developing diagnostic test tasks, activity-based curricula, and teaching materials. Third, they can serve as a means of carrying out an activity-based linguistic audit with people concerned with language training and recruitment in companies. Finally, they provide a means of comparing the course objectives and materials in different languages that exist in the same context.

Table 4 shows that criteria for assessing creative writing, made by Council of Europe (2001, p. 62). The descriptors on this scale provide information about the written produc-

Table 4. *Criteria for Assessing Creative Writing*

Level	Criterion descriptions
C2	Can write clear, smoothly flowing, and fully engrossing stories and descriptions of experience in a style appropriate to the genre adopted.
C1	Can write clear, detailed, well-structured and developed descriptions and imaginative texts in an assured, personal, natural style appropriate to the reader in mind.
B2	Can write clear, detailed descriptions of real or imaginary events and experiences, making the relationship between ideas in clear connected text, and following established conventions of the genre concerned. Can write clear, detailed descriptions on a variety of subjects related to his/her field of interest. Can write a review of a film, book or play.
B1	Can write a straightforward, detailed description on a range of familiar subjects within his/her field of interest. Can write accounts of experiences, describing feelings and reactions in simple connected text. Can write a description of an event, a recent trip–real or imagined. Can narrate a story.
A2	Can write about everyday aspects of his/her environment, e.g., people, places, a job or study experience in linked sentences. Can write very short, basic descriptions of events, past activities and personal experiences.
	Can write a series of simple phrases and sentences about their family, living conditions, educational background, present or most recent job. Can write short, simple imaginary biographies and simple poems about people.
A1	Can write simple phrases and sentences about themselves and imaginary people, where they live and what they do.

22 CHAPTER 2 REVIEW OF THE LITERATURE

tion activities and language uses as the writer produces a creative written text received by a readership of one or more readers. The descriptors on these scales (Creative Writing in Table 4 and Reports and Essays in Table 5) have not been empirically calibrated with the measurement model. The descriptors for these scales have therefore been created by recombining elements of descriptors from other scales (Council of Europe, 2001).

Table 5 shows that the criteria for assessing reports and essays produced by the Council of Europe (2001, p. 62). The descriptors on this scale provide information about when teachers and researchers assess students' reports and essays from A1 to C2.

An important aspect of the Can-Do statements is that they have been translated into 12 of the languages represented in the ALTE: Catalan, Danish, Dutch, English, Finish, French, German, Italian, Norwegian, Portuguese, Spanish, and Swedish. Furthermore, the

Table 5. *Criteria for Assessing Reports and Essays*

Level	Criterion descriptions
C2	Can produce clear, smoothly flowing, complex reports, articles or essays which present a case, or give critical appreciation of proposals or literary works.
	Can provide an appropriate and effective logical structure which helps the reader to find significant points.
C1	Can write clear, well-structured expositions of complex subjects, underlining the relevant salient issues.
	Can expand and support points of view at some length with subsidiary points, reasons and relevant examples.
B2	Can write an essay or report which develops an argument systematically with appropriate highlighting of significant points and relevant supporting detail.
	Can evaluate different ideas or solutions to a problem.
	Can write an essay or report which develops an argument, giving reasons in support of or against a particular point of view and explaining the advantages and disadvantages of various options.
	Can synthesize information and arguments from a number of sources.
B1	Can write short, simple essays on topics of interest.
	Can summarize report and give his/her opinion about accumulated factual information on familiar routine and non-routine matters within his/her field with some confidence.
	Can write very brief reports to a standard conventionalized format, which pass on routine factual information and state reasons for actions.
A2	No descriptor available
A1	No descriptor available

The Common European Framework of Reference: Objectives and Limitations   23

Can-Do scale currently consists of about 400 statements, organized into three general areas: Social and Tourist, Work, and Study. Each general area includes a number of more specific areas. For instance, the Social and Tourist area has sections on Shopping, Eating out, and Accommodation. Each of these includes up to three scales for the four skills of listening, speaking, reading, and writing.

Validating a Can-Do instrument involves transforming the Can-Do statements from a subjective set of level descriptions into a calibrated measuring instrument. The Council of Europe (2001, p. 246) stated that early efforts at data collection have been based primarily on self-reports. However, researchers have started empirical investigations of the statements by investigating the internal coherence of the Can-Do scale, the aims being to check the functioning of individual statements in each Can-Do scale, equate different Can-Do scales, and investigate the neutrality of the Can-Do scales with respect to different languages.

The European Language Portfolio, which is also in the form of Can-Do statements, was developed and piloted by the Language Policy Division of the Council of Europe, Strasbourg, from 1998 until 2000 (Council of Europe, 2010). This document allows those who are learning or have learned a language at school or outside school to record their language learning and cultural experiences. The portfolio has three parts. The first part contains a language passport that its owner regularly updates. A grid is provided where the person's language competences can be described according to common criteria accepted throughout Europe. The second part of the document contains a detailed language biography describing the owner's experiences in each language; the purpose is to guide the learner in planning and assessing progress. Finally, there is a dossier where examples of personal work can be kept to illustrate an individual's language competence.

The European Language Portfolio has two main aims: (a) to motivate learners by acknowledging their efforts to extend and diversify their language skills and (b) to provide a record of the linguistic and cultural skills they have acquired. This record can be useful when they are moving to a higher learning level or seeking employment at home or abroad. These two aims coincide with the two basic functions of the European Language Portfolio: the pedagogical function and the reporting function. For example, the portfolio

24 CHAPTER 2 REVIEW OF THE LITERATURE

reflects the learner's objectives, ways of learning, success in language learning, plans for further learning, and ability to learn autonomously. The European Language Portfolio has a bank of descriptors for self-assessment.

Therefore, both CEFR and the European Language Portfolio currently provide learners a good opportunity to experience self-assessment in the form of Can-Do statements. The main feature in CEFR is to present a Can-Do Questionnaire describing the skills and knowledge required by language learners at each proficiency level in order to use the foreign language as a communication tool (CEFR; Council of Europe, 2001). In order to fulfill its functions, the Common European Framework must be comprehensive, transparent and coherent. Comprehensive means that the Common European Framework should specify as full a range of language knowledge, skills, and use as possible and that all users should be able to describe their learning objectives. Transparent means that information must be clearly formulated, explicit, easily available, and readily comprehensible to users. Coherent means that the description of information is free from internal contradictions. With regard to educational systems, coherence requires that there is a harmonious relation among their components. The construction of a comprehensive, transparent, and coherent framework for language learning and teaching does not imply the imposition of a single uniform system. On the contrary, the framework should be open and flexible so that it can be applied with such adaptations as prove necessary to particular situations (Council of Europe, 2001, p. 7; Koike, 2009, p. 16). The Common European Framework should be multi-purpose, flexible, open, dynamic, user-friendly, and non-dogmatic. Multi-purpose means that it is usable for the full variety of purposes involved in the planning and provision of educational facilities for language learning. Flexible means that it can be adapted for use in different circumstances. Open means that the framework can be further extended and refined. Dynamic means that the framework is continuously evolving in response to experience in its use, and user-friendly means that it is presented in a form readily understandable and usable by those to whom it is addressed. Non-dogmatic means that the framework is not irrevocably and exclusively attached to any one of a number of competing linguistic or educational theories or practices.

Weir (2005) pointed out several limitations of CEFR regarding reading, listening, writing, and speaking skills. First, he observed that CEFR does not specify the purposes for which individuals use language at different levels of proficiency and lacks a specification of the sub-skills of comprehension, such as comprehending main ideas, important details, making inferences, drawing conclusions, and recognizing connections between parts of the text (Alderson, Figueras, Kuijper, Nold, Takala, & Tardieu, 2004).

Second, Alderson et al. (2004) noted that CEFR does not address the issue of response format (e.g., a cloze test, open-ended test, or a summary writing test), even though CEFR is supposed to be a reference point for assessment. For example, Weir (2005) stated that in a writing assessment, the choice of format determines whether knowledge telling or knowledge transformation occurs during task completion; these are two very different processing experiences; knowledge telling involves language users in just describing the knowledge they have while knowledge transformation requires users to change the form and nature of the knowledge substantially.

Third, Alderson (2000) noted that speed in reading or writing should not be measured without reference to comprehension, but at present comprehension is all too often measured without reference to speed. For example, when testing writing, it is important to consider the time constraints on brainstorming activity and responding to the items associated with a given topic, because students can plan more effectively when they are provided with a specific time constraint, such as *Write a movie review in 40 minutes* (Weir, 2005).

Fourth, Alderson (2000) pointed out that CEFR (2001) provides little information as to the content of any given level of proficiency, other than what is contained in the numerous scales. As a result, it is not easy to determine what sort of written and spoken text is appropriate for each level. Huhta et al. (2002) also found that CEFR provides little information concerning what discourse types are suitable across different levels of the four skills.

Fifth, Alderson et al. (2004) pointed out that text length is not defined clearly by CEFR, which relies on vaguely defined terms such as *short* or *long*. The problem with these terms is that it is not possible to determine precisely what they mean. For instance, if students are told to write a long essay, they do not have a clear idea what long means. Specifying length in terms of a word count (e.g., 1,000-1,500 words) would be clearer.

26 CHAPTER 2 REVIEW OF THE LITERATURE

Sixth, CEFR provides no guidance as to what topics are suitable for any particular proficiency level. Weir (2005) stated that the relationship between the content of a text and the candidate's background knowledge (general knowledge that might or might not be relevant to the content of a particular text), and subject matter knowledge (specific knowledge directly relevant to topic and content of a text) must be considered.

Seventh, CEFR provides little assistance in identifying the breadth and depth of productive or receptive lexis that might be needed at various proficiency levels. Weir (2005) stated that the argument that CEFR is intended to be applicable to a wide range of different languages is used as an explanation for the fact that CEFR does not provide information concerning the breadth and depth of productive or receptive lexis, but this offers little assistance to test writers who must select texts or activities for use at a particular CEFR level.

Eighth, Weir (2005) stated that CEFR provides little help in determining what level or range of syntax might define a particular proficiency level despite the finding that texts with less complex grammar are generally easier to comprehend than texts with more complex grammar. In relation to teaching, Keddle (2004) noted that there are challenges in using the CEFR framework in schools, as it does not measure grammatical proficiency and this lack creates a barrier between the aims of descriptors (Can-do statements) and the students' achievement. The integration of CEFR standards with pre-existing courses has also been difficult because of this mismatch between the Can-Do statements and the grammatical syllabus used in the classroom. Some course designers have stated that they could work more effectively if there were more guidance concerning grammar.

Alderson et al. (2004) showed how many formulations in the Can-Do statements are inconsistent. They provided a number of examples showing that similar descriptions occur at different levels; some operations, such as *recognize* are only mentioned in three out of the six levels (A1, B1, and C1), some verbs (e.g., *infer*) do not appear in all reading and listening levels, and some conditions appear in some levels and not in others (e.g., *with a large degree of independence* is only mentioned in level B2).

Weir (2005) concluded that CEFR is expected to be useful in helping define objectives for pedagogy and assessment (Council of Europe, 2001), but deficiencies still remain. Language test constructors not only need to know what learners can do at each of the six

CEFR scale levels, but also under what performance conditions these activities are normally carried out and what quality the performance is expected to meet in terms of specified criteria. CEFR must also address the demands of theory-based validity, which is a function of the processing involved in carrying out the Can-Do statements, context-based validity, which is to comprehensively define the construct to be tested and scoring validity, which is both reliable in terms of rater agreement and valid in terms of descriptor interpretation in a rating process.

Although a number of commentators have pointed out that some CEFR Can-Do statements are vague, a possible advantage of this is that it provides teachers with more choices and greater autonomy when selecting and conducting classroom tasks. If CEFR's Can-Do statements are more clearly specified, teachers will have less freedom to develop classroom-based Can-do statements.

In the next section, I discuss autonomous learning and partial competence, which are the two of the main rationales for using the CEFR.

Autonomous Learning and Partial Competence

One aspect of the underlying rationale of the CEFR is learner autonomy. It is important to promote methods of modern language teaching that strengthen independence of thought, judgment and action, combined with social skills and responsibility (The Council of Europe, 2001, pp. 3-4). Having different ideas and tradition concerning social responsibilities and roles of individuals, some Japanese researchers have tried to apply CEFR in the Japanese contexts (Touno, 2013).

As Collett and Sullivan (2010) explained, autonomy is widely considered to be one of the central characteristics of successful language learners. Autonomy is frequently defined in terms of control, in particular "the capacity to take control over one's learning" (Benson, 2001, p. 2). As Benson and others argue, autonomy is not a strategy or skill but "an attribute of the learner's approach to the learning process" (p. 2). Although there is some argument over whether the development of autonomy should be left to individual learners themselves, the prevailing belief is that autonomy can be developed and that training is

28   CHAPTER 2 REVIEW OF THE LITERATURE

necessary to promote its successful development (Benson, 2001, 2006; Ushioda, 2007).

CEFR's Can-Do statements have already been identified as a possible tool for facilitating self-regulated or reflective learning process (Collet & Sullivan, 2010). For example, Little (2005) explained the function of self-assessment based on Can-Do statements within the European Language Portfolio (ELP) as facilitating a reflective learning cycle of "planning, monitoring and evaluating learning" (p. 326).

As for life-long or autonomous learning, three aspects can be identified as contributing to life-long or autonomous learning; the ability to reflect on one's language and one's learning and draw relevant conclusions, the development of learning to learn strategies, and the ability to take responsibility for one's own learning (The Council of Europe, 2001, p. 144). It can be seen from these three aspects that the notion of life-long learning entails, by its very definition, an adherence to an autonomous view of learning. As CEFR stated, "once teaching stops, further learning has to be autonomous. Autonomous learning can be promoted if learning to learn is regarded as an integral part of language learning, so that learners become increasingly aware of the way they learn, the options open to them and the options that best suit them (The Council of Europe, 2001, p. 141).

According to the CEFR, partial competence is defined as at the same time a functional competence with respect to a specific limited objective. Can-Do Questionnaires, which promote the partial competence, can enhance learner motivation (Naganuma, 2008). Learners can work independently with self-study materials including self- assessment such as Can-Do Questionnaires. Even for lower proficiency leaners, it is important to set an attainable goal and confirm what they can partially achieve the goal to produce a sense of self-efficacy. Using the form *I can*, Can-Do Questionnaires adopt a positive, added-value approach. As learners use the Can-Do Questionnaires as a positive self-assessment check list, they can participate more actively in the learning process in co-operation with the teacher and other students, reach an agreement on course objectives and methods, accept compromises, engage in peer teaching and peer assessment, and progress steadily towards autonomy (The Council of Europe, 2001, p. 144).

The term *partial competence* in a given language can concern receptive language activities, for example with the emphasis on oral or written comprehension. It can concern a particular domain and specific tasks; for example, the functional competence that allows a post office clerk to give information on the most useful post office operations to foreign clients speaking a particular language. However, it can also involve general competences, such as non-linguistic knowledge about the characteristics of other languages and cultures and their communities, so long as there is a functional role to this complementary development of a dimension of the specified competence. In other words, in the framework of reference proposed in CEFR, the notion of partial competence is to be viewed in relation to the different components of the model (Tables 1, 3, 4, and 5) and variation in objectives (The Council of Europe, 2001, p. 135).

In the following section, I look at policies enacted by the Ministry of Education, Culture, Sport, Science and Technology.

MEXT Policies Concerning English Education

In Japan, the Ministry of Education, Culture, Sports, Science and Technology (hereinafter MEXT) (2003) announced plans to develop Japanese who can use English effectively by the time they graduate from a university. MEXT has stated that each university should set attainable objectives, seek to develop persons who can use English communicatively in business situations, and improve course syllabi so that university administrators and instructors can help students increase their English proficiency.

MEXT (2003) announced that they had administered a survey designed to investigate the current conditions of university English education in Japan. In the same document, MEXT (2003) published a standard of attainable objectives for each university for English education, urging university administrators to exert more efforts to improve English education. In a 2008 survey conducted by MEXT, 99 universities reported that they had identified attainable English-language objectives, such as the ability to write an essay or thesis in English, make an oral presentation at an international conference, or pass a particular standard on a certified examination such as the TOEFL, TOEIC, or Eiken (STEP).

In the next three sections, I explore the literature concerning the motivational models that are a part of this study. First, I address Gardner's socio-educational model, which sug-

30   CHAPTER 2 REVIEW OF THE LITERATURE

gests that the learning context and attitudes toward that context is a crucial aspect of learners' motivation.

Gardner's (1985a) Socio-Educational Model

It is no accident that L2 motivation research was initiated in Canada and that it was dominated by a social psychological emphasis there. The understanding of the unique Canadian situation with the coexistence of the Anglophone and Francophone communities speaking two of the world's most vital languages has presented an ongoing challenge for researchers in the social sciences, and the Canadian government has always actively promoted (and sponsored) research in this vein (Dörnyei, 2001).

A key issue in Gardner's (1985a) Socio-educational Model is the relationship between motivation and orientation. One of the most elaborate and researched aspects of Gardner's Socio-educational Model has been the concept of motivation in learning, which is defined as a "motivation to learn second language because of positive feelings toward the community that speaks that language (Gardner, 1985, pp. 82-83). Gardner started developing the socio-educational model in the 1960's and there are two main factors that influence L2 performance: aptitude and motivation in learning. The model, however, has undergone numerous revisions to capture the sub-process underlying each individual factor. Gardner (1985b) introduced three sub-measures, motivational intensity, the desire to learn, and attitude towards learning, to explain motivation. Gardner modified his model at least twice after 1985 (Gardner, 2010). The Attitude and Motivation Test Battery (AMTB) (Gardner, 1985b) measures several construct including (a) integrativeness, which consists of integrative orientation, Attitude toward English speaking people, and Interest in foreign languages, (b) Attitudes toward the learning situation, which consists of English teacher evaluation and English course evaluation, (c) Motivation, which consists of Motivational intensity, Desire to learn English, and Attitudes toward learning English, and (d) Language Anxiety, which consists of English class anxiety and English use anxiety.

As noted above, Canada is an officially bilingual country, and its immigrant population is typically in an English or French L2 situation (or conceivably both). In that situation, as

Elwood (2011) discussed, the notion of integrativeness involves actual or metaphorical integration into a community. That notion is appropriate for that context, in which there is a clear need for non-English speaking immigrants to repeatedly use at least one L2 in order to function in daily life.

On the other hand, many Japanese learners of English, who are in EFL contexts, are not seeking to integrate into an L2 community, as one of their primary goals is simply to communicate with the target language group or to achieve instrumental goals such as passing an English proficiency examination such as the Eiken, TOEFL, or TOEIC.

Gardner and MacIntyre (1993) are concerned with the role of various individual difference characteristics of L2 learners in the socio educational model, which was originally conceptualized by Gardner and Lambert (1972). Its main importance lies in its clear separation of four distinct aspects of the second language acquisition process: (a) antecedent factors, which can be biological or experiential such as gender, age or learning history; (b) individual difference (learner variables); (c) language acquisition contexts, and; (d) learning outcomes. Dörnyei (2001) noted that the main learner variables covered by the model are intelligence, language aptitude, language learning strategies, language attitudes, motivation, and language anxiety. These variables, in turn, affect L2 attainment in formal and informal learning contexts, resulting in both linguistic and non-linguistic outcomes.

As Gardner, Tremblay, and Masgoret (1997) stated, many researchers have focused on the relationship among individual difference measures such as language attitudes, motivation, anxiety, self-confidence, language aptitude, learning strategies, field independence, and measures of achievement in language use. They reported substantial links among the affective measures, such as language attitude, language aptitude, field independence, motivation, language strategies, self-confidence, and language achievement.

The original socio-educational model proposed that Language Attitudes influence Motivation, and that Motivation influences both Self-Confidence and the use of Language Learning Strategies. It further proposed that Motivation, Language Aptitude, and Learning Strategies influence Language Achievement.

In Gardner, Tremblay, and Masgoret (1997)'s model, Self-Confidence and the four Can-Do scales, which consists of listening, speaking, reading and writing, were summed to

32   CHAPTER 2 REVIEW OF THE LITERATURE

form one measure of Self-Rated Proficiency (ß = .81). Language Aptitudes is seen to cause Motivation, Motivation causes both Self-Confidence (ß = .31) and Language Learning Strategies (ß = .48) and Motivation (ß = .48), and Language Aptitude (ß = .47) and Language Learning Strategies (ß = -.29) cause Language Achievement. Moreover, Field Independence relates significantly with Language Aptitude (ß = .38).

Orientations do not necessarily reflect motivation. Noels and Clément (1989), for example, demonstrated that some orientations are associated with motivation and some are not. That is, one might profess an integrative orientation in language study but still might not be motivated to learn the language. Similarly, one might profess an instrumental orientation and either be motivated or nor to learn the language. In the socio-educational model of second language acquisition, the factor most directly linked to achievement is motivation. Thus, it is conceivable that an individual who is instrumentally oriented can be more motivated than one who is integrative oriented and because of the differences in motivation can experience more success at learning the language (Masgoret & Gardner, 2002).

In the next section I describe MacIntyre's (1994) willingness to communicate model, which is closely related to motivation to speak the foreign language.

MacIntyre's (1994) Willingness to Communicate Model

MacIntyre (1994) proposed an L2 Willingness to Communicate Model, which was designed to predict the amount of oral output produced by foreign language learners. MacIntyre was Gardner's student, and his interest in Willingness to Communicate was informed by Gardner's work on motivation and anxiety, leading them to co-publish several studies that eventually led to the L2 willingness to communicate model (MacIntyre & Gardner, 1991; Gardner & MacIntyre, 1993).

The concept of Willingness to Communicate (WTC) was developed by McCroskey and associates as an expansion of Burgoon's (1976) work on unwillingness to communicate (McCroskey & Richmond, 1987). WTC was developed in an L1 educational context in the United States as McCroskey had little to no interest in L2 learners and his field was communication studies (McCroskey, 1977; McCroskey & Baer, 1985; McCroskey & Richmond, 1987; McCroskey & Richmond, 1990; McCroskey & Richmond, 1991).

As shown in Figure 1, MacIntyre hypothesized Introversion to be a predictor of both Perceived Competence and Communication Anxiety, while Self-Esteem predicted Communication Anxiety. Anxiety influenced Perceived Competence, and both Perceived Competence and Communication Anxiety significantly predicted L2 WTC. The original MacIntyre model (MacIntyre et al., 1999, p. 223) uses the factor Communication Apprehension, not Communication Anxiety, which they used with regard to state level of apprehension, as they try to make a distinction between trait and state level.

The results offered empirical support for the predictive roles of Communication Anxiety and Perceived Competence. Furthermore, MacIntyre (1994) suggested that Communication Anxiety has its roots in broader personality variables, such as Introversion and Self-Esteem (p. 139). MacIntyre, Babin, and Clément (1999) also argued that Communication Anxiety and Perceived Competence strongly predict L2 WTC.

In this study, I use the term *Willingness to Communicate in Writing* because the focus of this study is on writing, and WTC can exist in written form. However, as MacIntyre's model was developed and tested in an ESL context, some researchers questioned its appropriateness in EFL contexts. Yashima's (2002) work, which extends MacIntyre's basic model to the Japanese EFL context is discussed in the following section.

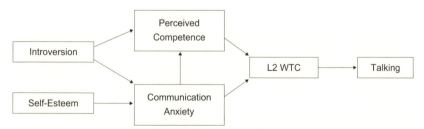

Figure 1. Portion of MacIntyre's (1994) Willingness to Communicate Model. From P. D. MacIntyre & C. Charos (1996), "Conceptualizing willingness to communicate in a L2: A situated model of confidence and affiliation." *Journal of Language and Social Psychology, 15*(1), p. 8. Copyright 1996 by the Journal of Language and Social Psychology. Reprinted by permission.

Yashima (2002) and EFL Contexts

Yashima and her colleagues (Yashima, 2002; Yashima & Zenuk-Nishide, 2008; Yashima et al., 2004) advanced the notion of international posture, which appears to satisfactorily supplant the concepts of motivation in learning. Yashima (2002) noted that some learners are interested in or have favorable attitudes toward what English symbolizes. This orientation can thus include interest in foreign or international affairs, willingness to go overseas

FIGURE 5
1.2 Communication Model in the Japanese EFL Context with Stndardived Estimanes

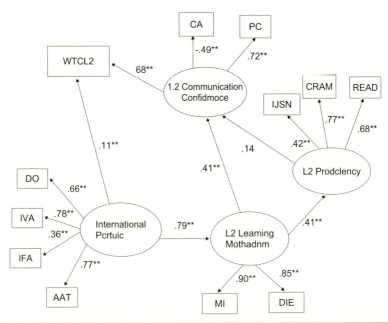

Note. **p< .01; $x^2(49)$=62.63. n.s.; GFI=0.97: AGFI=0.95: GFI=0.99: RMSEA=0.051; WTC 1.2: Willingness to Communicate in 1.2; GA: Communication Anxiety in 1.2; PC: Perceived Communication Competence in 1.2; LISN: Listening Comprehension; GRAN: Grammar $ Vocabulary; READ: Reading Comprehension; IFO: International Friendship Orientation in Leaming English; IVA: Interesi in International Vocation/Activities; IFA: Interesi in Foreign Affairs; AAT: Intergroup Approcth Avoidance Tendency; MI: Motivational Intensity; DLE: Desite to Learn English.

Figure 2. Yashima's (2002) Willingness to Communicate model.

to stay or work, readiness to interact with intercultural partners and one hopes, openness or a non-ethnocentric attitude toward different cultures among others. Furthermore, Yashima and colleagues (e.g., Yashima, 2002; Zenuk-Nishide, 2008) have demonstrated that international posture plays an important role in models of SLA.

Figure 2 shows the importance of international posture in L2 communication as measured in Yashima's (2002) model. International Posture directly influenced Frequency of L2 Communication, Willingness to Communicate in the L2, and L2 Learning Motivation. L2 Learning Motivation in turn influenced L2 Communication Confidence with L2 Proficiency playing an indeterminate mediating role. On the other hand, L2 Communicative Confidence directly influenced L2 WTC, which together with Motivation determined the Frequency of L2 Communication.

In the following section, I describe the ten affective variables included in this study, state who created the variable, indicate how the variable has been used in other fields, and discuss its relationship with other variables.

Affective Orientation Variables

In this study, ten affective orientation variables are measured: Desire to Write English, Attitude toward Learning to Write English, Motivational Intensity, Instrumental Orientation, L2 Writing Anxiety, L2 Writing Self-Confidence, Willingness to Communicate in Writing, Self- Esteem, Cognitive Competence, General Self-Worth.

Desire to Write English

Desire to Write English, which is defined as the strength of a learner's desire to write in English, is modified from Beglar (2009b) based on Gardner (1985a) (see Appendix C for the English version and Appendix D for the Japanese version). In his book, *Social psychology and second language learning*, Gardner (1985b) developed the Attitudes/Motivation Test Battery (AMTB) and Desire to Learn French was included on the battery. Ten multiple-choice items were included on this scale with a high score expressing a strong desire to learn French. In this study, in which the focus is on writing in an EFL context, I modified

36 CHAPTER 2 REVIEW OF THE LITERATURE

the original items to create the Desire to Write English scale, which is made up of six items measured on a 6-point Likert scale. An example item is *I plan to write as much as possible during the class.*

Attitude Toward Learning to Write English

Attitude Toward Learning to Write English, which is defined as a positive attitude that writers of different languages have toward each other's languages in writing English, is based on Gardner's (1985a) notion that attitudes toward learning a second language and attitudes toward the second language community play an important role in successful second language acquisition (see Appendix C for the English version and Appendix D for the Japanese version). Gardner stated that attitudes can be classified along a dimension of specificity/generality. Thus, Gardner's original variable, attitudes toward learning French, is relatively specific in that the object of the attitude (i.e., learning French) is fairly clearly circumscribed and definite.

In this study, Gardner's (1985a), Attitude toward Learning to Speak English was modified into a construct designed to measure Attitude toward Learning to Write English. This scale is made up of six items measured on a 6-point Likert scale. The items were modified from Beglar (2009b) based on Gardner (1985a). An example item is, *Writing English is really enjoyable.* Strong endorsement of these items indicates that the participant has a positive attitude toward writing English.

Motivational Intensity to Write English

Motivational Intensity to Write English is defined as the desire to learn to write English to communicate with people from other cultures that speak that language and the desire to identify closely with the target language group (see Appendix C for the English version and Appendix D for the Japanese version). This variable, which was adopted from Gardner (1985a), originally consisted of ten multiple-choice items designed to measure the intensity of students' motivation to learn French in terms of classroom assignments, future plans to use the language, and future plans to study the language. A high score represented a student's self-report of a high degree of effort being spent in acquiring the language.

Although motivational intensity can be influenced by both the want and the attitude components, it is possible that other situational variables (e.g., a demanding teacher) or personality characteristics (i.e., need achievement, compulsiveness) can also influence motivational intensity.

According to Masgoret and Gardner (2002), motivation refers to goal-directed behavior (Hackhausen, 1991) and when attempting to measure motivation, attention can be directed toward a number of features of the individual. The motivated individual expends effort, is persistent and attentive to the task at hand, has goals, desires, and aspirations, enjoys the activity, experiences reinforcement from success and disappointment from failure, is aroused, and makes use of strategies to aid in achieving goals. That is, the motivated individual exhibits many behaviors, feelings, and cognitions that the unmotivated individual does not.

The items measuring this variable are from Gardner's (1985a), Motivational Intensity items. This scale is made up of six items measured on a 6-point Likert scale. The items were modified from Beglar (2009b) based on Gardner (1985a) so that a writing version could be collected. An example item is, *I plan to study hard in writing class.* Strong endorsement of these items indicates that the participant has a strong motivation to write English.

Instrumental Orientation for Writing in English

This variable, which was defined as the desire to learn a language in writing English because it would fulfill certain utilitarian goals, such as getting a job or passing an examination, was adopted from Gardner (1985a) (see Appendix C for the English version and Appendix D for the Japanese version). Students were presented with four items measuring the utilitarian value of learning French. A high score indicated that the student had instrumental reasons for learning French, without implying any interest in getting closer socially to the language community (Masgoret & Gardner, 2002).

Because this study is focused on writing, the Instrumental Orientation scale based on Gardner (1985a) was converted into a writing version named Instrumental Orientation for Writing in English. This scale is made up of six items measured on a 6-point Likert scale that were modified from Beglar (2009b) based on Gardner (1985a) so that the items

38 CHAPTER 2 REVIEW OF THE LITERATURE

for a writing version could be collected. An example item is, *Improving my English writing ability is important because it will help me get higher test scores (e.g., on the Eiken)*. Strong endorsement of these items indicates that the participant has a utilitarian reason for learning English and the participant is studying English in order to further a career or achieve academic success.

L2 Writing Anxiety

L2 Writing Anxiety, which was defined as the anxiety that language learners experience in second language writing, was based on Gardner (1985a), who created a five-item scale, called French Class Anxiety, with a high score reflecting the participants' degree of discomfort while participating in the French class (Gardner, 2002) (see Appendix C for the English version and Appendix D for the Japanese version). In the Attitude / Motivation Test Battery (AMTB), language anxiety is an affective variable, which corresponds to what individuals feel when performing the L2. In the AMTB, it is measured by determining how anxious the learner feels when in the classroom or when using the language in general.

Language anxiety has long been included as a variable in Gardner's socio-educational model, but within the model it has not received the attention assigned motivation nor has it been assigned a consistent place (MacIntyre & Gardner, 1991). In some formulations, anxiety is an antecedent of motivation (Tremblay & Gardner, 1995) and in others a predictor of proficiency (Gardner, Tremblay, & Masgoret, 1997). Gardner and MacIntyre (1993) suggested that anxiety and motivation have a reciprocal relationship. Clément (1980, 1986) proposed a model in which anxiety combines with self-perceptions of language proficiency to create self-confidence, which is viewed as a second motivational process (MacIntyre et al., 2001). The relationship between anxiety and L2 proficiency is a larger issue and raises an important question about the causal direction of the variables (MacIntyre, 2002): Is lower anxiety a predictor of higher proficiency, higher proficiency a predictor of lower anxiety, or is the relationship reciprocal?

Park and Lee (2005) stated that anxiety is one of the most influential affective variables, as it can prevent learners from successfully learning a foreign language. One factor that is negatively correlated with anxiety is self-confidence, which involves judgments and evaluation about one's own value and worth. Self- confidence can be negatively influenced when the language learner thinks of oneself as deficient and limited in the target language. On the other hand, high self-confidence can be positively correlated with oral performance (Heyde, 1979).

Park and Lee (2005) noted that anxiety is a complex affective concept associated with feelings of uneasiness, frustration, self-doubt, apprehension, or worry. Resent research on anxiety and language learning distinguishes foreign language anxiety from trait anxiety, which is one's general and global disposition, focusing specifically on the situational nature of language learning. Horwitz, Horwitz, and Cope (1986) defined foreign language anxiety as "a distinct complex of self-perception, beliefs, feelings and behaviors related to classroom language learning arising from the uniqueness of the language learning process" (p. 128). Three components of foreign language anxiety have been identified and examined: communication apprehension, test anxiety, and fear of negative evaluation. The focus of this study is on a form of L2 communication apprehension, which is a person's level of fear or anxiety associated with either real or anticipated communication with another person or persons.

Phillips (1992) showed that there is relationship between language anxiety and oral performance, reporting that the more anxious the students were, the lower performance they displayed on oral tests. Furthermore, the anxious students expressed negative attitudes toward oral tests. The results of the study suggested that language anxiety can affect learners' oral performance and their attitudes toward language learning (Cheng, Horwitz, & Schallert, 1999).

In this study, the focus being on writing, I modified Gardner's (1985a) L2 Speaking Anxiety scale and created a L2 Writing Anxiety scale. This scale is made up of six items measured on a 6-point Likert scale. The items were modified from Beglar (2009b) based on Gardner (1985a). An example item is *I feel nervous when I write English.* Strong endorsement of these items indicates that the participant feels anxious when writing English.

L2 Writing Self-Confidence

This measure, which is defined as the idea that language learners have enough self-confi-

40 CHAPTER 2 REVIEW OF THE LITERATURE

dence in second language writing, combines six items from the three self-confidence scales presented in Gardner et al. (1997) from AMTB (see Appendix C for the English version and Appendix D for the Japanese version). The first scale contains 10 positively worded items. For example, *I am sure I could speak French well in almost any circumstances.* The second scale is called *ability controlled* and is made up of six positively worded items that distinguish self-confidence from achievement. For example, *Regardless of how much French I know, I feel confident about using it.* The third scale is called *given ability* and is made up of three positively and three negatively worded items that account for differences in self-confidence as well as differences in ability. For example, *I am as confident using French as other people who know as much French as I do.*

In MacIntyre, Clément, Dörnyei, and Noels' (1998) conceptualization of L2 WTC, self-confidence is used as one of the motivational propensities variables. L2 Self-Confidence concerns the relationship between the individual and the L2. This corresponds to the overall belief in being able to communicate in the L2 in an adaptive and efficient manner. There are two components to L2 confidence: The first component is cognitive and corresponds to the self-evaluation of L2 skills, a judgment made by the speaker (writer) about the degree of mastery achievement in the L2. The second component is affective and corresponds to language anxiety, specifically, the discomfort experienced when using L2 (p. 551). Therefore, this variable was used as one of the affective orientation variables in this study.

In the model tested by Clément and Kruidenier (1985), self-confidence was a significant predictor of achievement. Yashima (2002) found that higher proficiency positively affected confidence in communication, and Gardner, Tremblay, and Masgoret (1997) reported that the path in this direction was significant in their research. Clément and his associates found that indices of self-confidence correlate significantly and appreciably with measures of proficiency in the L2 (Clément, Dörnyei, & Noels, 1994; Clément, Gardner, & Smythe, 1980; Clément & Kruidenier, 1985).

Every human being possess some self-confidence, self-esteem, and belief in one's own abilities in carrying out tasks, though the degree differs from one individual to the next (Park & Lee, 2005). People develop a concept of their capabilities based on experiences with themselves and others and the external world. MacIntyre, Dörnyei, Clément, and Noels (1998) suggested that self-confidence significantly contributes to the learner's willingness to communicate in a foreign language. According to them, affective factors such as motivation, personality, intergroup climate, and self-esteem underlie willingness to communicate, and the factor of self-esteem including overall self-esteem in L2 and situational self-confidence in communication play and important role in determining the learner's willingness to communicate.

In this study, the focus being on writing, I modified Gardner's (1985a) scale, L2 Speaking Self-Confidence, into L2 Writing Self-Confidence. This scale is made up of eight items measured on a 6-point Likert scale. The items were modified from Beglar (2009) based on Gardner (1985a) so that I could have the items for a writing version. An example item is *I can write about common topics (e.g., hobbies and vacation) in English*. Strong endorsement of these items indicates that the participant has self-confidence in writing English.

Willingness to Communicate in L2 Writing

Willingness to Communicate in L2 Writing is defined as the readiness to enter into discourse at a particular time with a specific person or persons, using a L2 (see Appendix P for the English version and Appendix Q for the Japanese version). McCroskey and Baer (1985) conceptualized the construct as the probability of initiating conversation when given the choice to do so. MacIntyre et al. (1998) adapted WTC to the L2 situation in a model that is intended to explain individual and contextual influences in the choice to initiate L2 communication. MacIntyre et al. (1998)'s model is more extensive than Ajzen (1988)'s model of theory of planned behavior, however, they share the conviction that behavior is strongly predicted by intention or willingness to act. The taxonomical model proposed by Ajzen (1988) traces L2 usage through a number of layers of influence ranging from WTC (Layer 2) as the most immediate behavioral intention preceding usage (MacIntyre, Babin, & Clément, 1999) to the social and individual context (Layer 6) as the most remote influence. Intermediate layers include situated antecedents such as communicative confidence (Layer 3), motivational propensities tied to the group and to the interlocutor (Layer 4), and the affective-cognitive context (Layer 5), which includes intergroup

42   CHAPTER 2 REVIEW OF THE LITERATURE

attitudes, communicative competence, and aspects of the social situation.

Past research has shown that the strongest predictors of WTC are two individual charac-teristics, communication anxiety and perceived communication competence (Baker & MacIntyre, 2000; MacIntyre, Clément, Baker, & Conrad, 2001; McCroskey & Rich-mond, 1991). Communication anxiety corresponds to the level of fear associated with ac-tual or anticipated communication (McCroskey, 1977). Perceived communication compe-tence is the belief that one can communicate effectively in a given situation (McCroskey & Richmond, 1990). Although actual competence might influence communication, it is the perception of competence that ultimately determines the choice of whether to communi-cate. In the WTC model, these two variables are combined into the single construct of L2 confidence (Layer 3), borrowed from Clément (1980).

In this study, I modified Weaver's (2010) Willingness to Communicate scale into L2 Willingness to Communicate in Writing, since Weaver (2010)'s study is originally related to willingness to communicate in Speaking. This scale is made up of eight items measured on a 6-point Likert scale. An example item is, *I would be willing to write about a recent va-cation on a post card in English.* Strong endorsement of these items indicates that the par-ticipant has a willingness to engage in written communication in English.

Self-Esteem

Self-Esteem, which is defined as a positive or negative orientation toward oneself and an overall evaluation of one's worth or value, is based on Rosenberg (1965) (see Appendix R for the English version and Appendix S for the Japanese version). The Rosenberg Self-Es-teem Scale is perhaps the most widely used measure of self-esteem in social science re-search (Owens, 2001). People are motivated to have high self-esteem, and having it indi-cates positive self-regard, not egoism. However, self-esteem is only one component of the self-concept, which Rosenberg (1965) defined as the totality of the individual's thoughts and feelings with reference to himself as an object. Besides self-esteem, self-efficacy or mas-tery, and self-identities are important parts of the self-concept (Owens, 2001).

Much of Rosenberg's work examined how social structural positions like racial or ethnic statuses and institutional contexts like schools or families relate to self-esteem. Here, patterned social forces provide a characteristic set of experiences that are actively interpreted by individuals as the self-concept is shaped. At least four key theoretical principles, reflected appraisals, social comparisons, self-attributions, and psychological centrality, underlie the process of self-concept formation (Owens, 2001).

In addition to examining self-esteem as an outcome of social forces, self-esteem is often analyzed as an independent or intervening variable that is conceptualized as a generally a stable characteristic of adults. Balscovich and Tomoka (1993) indicated that experimentally manipulated success or failure is unlikely to have any measurable impact when assessed against a lifetime of self-evaluative experiences. It is also unrealistic to think that self-esteem can be taught; rather it is developed through an individual's like experiences.

Self-esteem is considered to be the overall value that one places on oneself as a person (Harter, 1989), whereas self-concept is viewed as the body of self-knowledge that individuals possess about themselves (Rosenberg, 1986). Also, it is considered as a person's overall emotional evaluation of their own worth. It is a judgment of oneself as well as an attitude toward self.

A favorable attitude towards oneself has been considered to be important by several personality theorists as well as psychologists (Coopersmith, 1981; Rogers & Dymond, 1954). They found that people who frequently seek psychological help often report suffering from feelings of inadequacy and see themselves as helpless and inferior, as incapable of improving their situations, and as lacking the inner resources to tolerate or to reduce the anxiety readily aroused by everyday events and stress (Liu, 2011). People whose performance does not match their personal aspirations evaluate themselves as inferior no matter how great their achievements. People with high self-esteem are more creative, and more likely to assume an active role in social groups and to express their views frequently and effectively. Students with greater self-esteem are more likely to be successful academically in school (Dalgas-Pelish, 2006, Ja, Huai, & Guo, 2007; Pepi, Faria, & Alesi, 2006; Rayle, Arredondo, & Kurpius, 2005; Stringer & Heath, 2008), happier (Zhang, 2005), less anxious (Situ & Li, 2007; Wray & Stone 2005) and to adopt higher quality learning strategies (Watkins, 2000).

The Rosenberg Self-Esteem Scale is used to measure overall feelings of self-worth or self-

44 CHAPTER 2 REVIEW OF THE LITERATURE

acceptance, and has been widely used in numerous studies on self-esteem (Daglas-Pelish, 2006; Pepi et al., 2006; Rayle et al., 2005; String & Heath, 2008). It includes two dimensions, positive self- esteem and negative self-esteem, with five items measuring each aspect (Liu, 2011).

In this study, all ten items from the Rosenberg Self-Esteem Scale were used. An example item is *I believe that I have a number of good qualities.* I modified the original 4-point Likert scale to a 6-point scale ranging from 1 (*Strongly disagree*) to 6 (*Strongly agree*).

Cognitive Competence

Cognitive Competence, which is defined as the brain-based skills people need to carry out both simple and complex tasks (see Appendix T for the English version and Appendix U for the Japanese version). This variable has more to do with the mechanisms of how people learn, remember, problem-solve, and direct attention rather than with any actual knowledge, is based on Harter (1982). Harter emphasized the importance of assessing children's sense of competence across different domains, instead of viewing self-perceived competence as a unitary construct. She identified three domains of competence: (a) cognitive, (b) social, and (c) physical. This is originally designed for children over age 8 and has also been adapted specifically for adolescents. Cognitive competence concerns academic performance and involves self-perceptions of doing well at schoolwork, being smart, and feeling good about one's classroom performance.

In this study, all seven items of Harter's (1982) items were used. An example item is *I am good at school work.* The original 4-point scale was modified into a 6-point scale ranging from 1 (*Strongly disagree*) to 6 (*Strongly agree*).

General Self-Worth

General Self-Worth is based on work by Harter (1982), who defined general self-worth as being sure of oneself, being happy with the way one is, feeling good about the way one acts, and thinking that one is a good person (see Appendix V for the English version and Appendix W for the Japanese version). Harter hypothesized that children age 8 and older not only make discrete judgments about their competence in different domains, but that by they also construct a view of their general self-worth as a person over and above competence judgments. Harter saw self-esteem or self-worth as a superordinate construct and competence judgments as a lower order evaluative dimension (Epstein, 1973; Rosenberg, 1979). According to this model, judgments concerning one's overall self-worth are assessed by items that directly measure how much individuals like themselves as a person. Items measuring self-worth refer to being sure of oneself, being happy with the way one is, feeling good about the way one acts, and thinking that one is a good person. An example item is *I am sure of myself*. In this study, all seven items are from Harter (1985). The original 4-point scale was modified into a 6-point scale ranging from 1 (*Strongly disagree*) to 6 (*Strongly agree*).

Gaps in the Previous Literature

Three gaps can be identified in the Can-Do literature. First, previous researchers have not investigated the relationship between writing performance as measured by six essay writing assignments, the students' self-assessed writing ability using Eiken Can-Do Questionnaires and ten affective orientation variables, such as Desire to Write English, Attitude Toward Learning to Write English, Motivational Intensity , Instrumental Orientation for Writing in English, L2 Writing Anxiety, L2 Writing Self-Confidence, Willingness to Communicate in L2 Writing, Self Esteem, Cognitive Competence and General Self-Worth. Especially there is little international research on investigation for this relationship using structural equation modeling. Moreover, the previous researchers have not investigated the writing section of Eiken Can-Do Questionnaires thoroughly.

Second, previous researchers have not investigated self-assessment and its relationship to affective variables such as confidence, motivation, and anxiety. Therefore, such a study is necessary to fill some of the gaps between the current research on Can-Do statements in Japanese EFL classrooms. As stated above, Can-Do Questionnaires can be used as a form of self-assessment, and self-assessment tasks can not only help foster a greater awareness of the foreign language, but also play a subjective role in the learners' self-learning process (Nunan, 1988).

46 CHAPTER 2 REVIEW OF THE LITERATURE

Third, it is unclear to what degree self-assessment changes over time, and if it changes, why it changes. Can-Do statements as a form of self-assessment are potentially important in promoting learners' success in language learning (Oxford, 1990). Self-assessment embodies three processes that self-regulating students use to observe and interpret their behavior (Schunk, 1996). First, students produce self-observations by deliberating focusing on specific aspects of their performance related to their subjective standards of success. Second, students make self-judgments in which they determine how well their general and specific goals were met. The third process of self-assessment is self-reactions, interpretations, or reflections of the degree of satisfaction students feel with the results of their actions. Training in self-assessment increases the likelihood that students will interpret their performance as a mastery experience, the most powerful source of self-efficacy information (Bandura, 1997). However, previous researchers have not investigated to what degree the self-assessment changes over one academic year.

Purposes of the Study and Research Questions

The first purpose of this study is to investigate the relationship between the writing performance as measured by six writing assignments, the students' self-assessed writing ability using the Eiken Can-Do Questionnaires and, and ten affective orientation variables used in this study. This purpose is important because little or nothing is known about the relationship among these variables using structural equation modeling. Also, it will enable researchers to have a better and clearer understanding of the effect of distributing Eiken Can-Do Questionnaire on the participants in this study.

The second purpose of this study concerns how Can-Do Questionnaires relate with ten affective orientation variables and present a new model using Structural Equation Modeling. The second purpose is to determine the effects of ten affective variables on the use of the Eiken Can-Do Questionnaires used in this study. This purpose is valuable because nothing is known about the relationship between Can-Do Questionnaires and the affective variables investigated in this study. The results for this research question will allow researchers to gain a clearer understanding of the relationship between the Eiken Can-Do

Questionnaires and the affective orientations investigated in this study. Also, the results of this research question will show that how Can-Do Questionnaires behave well in the ten affective orientation variables' model.

The third purpose of this study is to conduct a longitudinal study from 2010 April to 2012 March, to determine how the participants' self-assessed writing ability changes over one academic year in two universities in Tokyo. By doing this, I could obtain how a longitudinal study provides the different results from the other short term studies and acquire a different knowledge about that. As Brown (2001) noted, it is important to recognize that quantitative analysis can be appropriate to examine the relationship among variables. These variables can be measured so that numbered data can be analyzed using statistical procedures.

The following three research questions are the focus of this study.

1. What is the relationship between Writing performance and the Affective Orientation Variables?

2. What is the relationship between teacher ratings of the students' writing performances, the three Eiken Can-do questionnaires (April, July, and December) and the following affective orientation variables: Desire to Write English, Attitude Toward Learning to Write English, Motivational Intensity, Instrumental Orientation for Writing in English, L2 Writing Anxiety, L2 Writing Self-Confidence, Willingness to Communicate in L2 Writing, Self Esteem, Cognitive Competence, General Self-Worth?

3. To what degree does the students' self-perceived writing ability, as measured by the Eiken Can-Do Questionnaires, change across one academic year?

CHAPTER 3
METHODS

Participants and Setting

Students enrolled in the English classes at two four-year private universities, a music college and a prestigious private university (hereafter Sakura University, a pseudonym) in Tokyo, Japan in 2010 and 2011 participated in this study. The main participants were 204 native speakers of Japanese (157 female [76.9%] and 47 male [23.1%] students) from 20 to 21 years old. Out of 204 participants, I taught 179 participants in 2010 and 2011 in the music college and Sakura University. I asked one colleague to collect the data from her classes in order to complete this study in the music college. In the music college, 112 of the participants were music performance majors, 10 were music culture design majors, 41 were music education majors, and eight students did not respond to the question. In Sakura University, 21 students were business majors and 12 students were marketing majors. All of the participants had studied English in the Japanese educational system for six years in junior high school and high school. The general English proficiency levels of the music college participants varied from elementary to intermediate according to the placement test given in April. In terms of CEFR's criteria, their proficiency levels range from A1 to B1. According to the Eiken Placement Test in Practical English Proficiency, the participants' English proficiency levels varied from Level 5 to Level 2. They were enrolled in classes focused on English for communicative purpose at the time of the study.

Table 6 shows information regarding how Eiken level, TOEFL iBT, and TOEIC align with one other. This table indicates that the Eiken 4th and 5th levels do not have a TOEFL iBT and TOEIC counterpart.

In their first year in the music college, the 171 second-year participants took two

Table 6. *Equation Table for the EIKEN, TOEFL iBT, and TOEIC Test Scores*

Eiken level	TOEFL iBT	TOEIC
1st	97-110	840-960
Pre-1st	68-97	640-840
2nd	56-68	540-640
Pre-2nd	46-56	400-540
3rd	32-46	200-400
4th	—	—
5th	—	—

Note. English Quest Group (2011). http:/eq-g.com/article/exam-hikaku/

90-minute English communication classes that were held once a week. In all, 232 second-year students in the music college took two English communication classes per semester, a reading/writing class, and a listening/speaking class. Each class was held once a week for 90 minutes and ran for 14 weeks. Thus, over the academic year, the students took 28 reading and writing classes, and 28 listening and speaking classes. The students in the music college were classified into four levels: S (the highest), A (the second highest), B (the second lowest), and C (the lowest) based on the results of the Eiken placement test taken in April. I taught two A classes and two B classes in 2010 and two B classes and two C classes in 2011. Each class had 17 to 22 students (Appendix B). The students were divided into four levels based on the Eiken Placement test results: S (Eiken 2nd Level), A (Eiken pre-2nd and 2nd Level), B (Eiken 3rd Level), and C (Eiken 5th to 3rd Level).

In Sakura University, 33 third-year participants attended an Advanced English class. Each class was held once a week for 90 minutes and ran for 14 weeks per semester. Thus, over the academic year, the students took 28 reading and writing classes.

Of the 171 participants attending the music college, nine had lived overseas, three for two to three years, six for less than six months. Eight of those nine students had lived in a country where English is the dominant language (e.g., the United States or England) while one lived in a country where English is not widely spoken (e.g., Thailand). Only three of the participants from Sakura University reported living overseas, two of them for less than six months and one for over three years. All three reported living in a country where English was the dominant language. They also participated in this study.

50   CHAPTER 3 METHODS

When asked what rank the music college had when they were seeking a university to attend, 146 participants stated that the music college was their first choice, 13 persons said it was their second choice, and nine students did not respond to the question. Of the 33 participants at Sakura University, 14 reported that the university was their first choice, five stated that it was second choice, nine reported that it was their third choice, and five students reported that it was their fourth choice or lower (Table 7).

Table 7 shows the information on participants' background data, and it tells that (a) the major parts of the participants are female, music college students, and (b) their proficiency

Table 7. *The Participants' Majors, Proficiency Levels, and Oversea Experience*

Major	Music performance	112	Music College
	Music culture design	10	
	Music education	41	
	Did not answer	8	
	Business	21	Sakura University
	Marketing	12	
Levels	S: Highest		Music College
	A: Second highest		
	B: Second lowest		
	C: Lowest		
	One level		Sakura University
Lived	Two to three years	3	Music College
overseas	Less than six months	6	
	Over three years	1	Sakura University
	Less than six months	2	
Rank	First choice	146	Music College
	Second choice	13	
	Did not answer	9	
	First choice	14	Sakura University
	Second choice	5	
	Third choice	9	
	Fourth choice or lower	5	

levels are not so high, (c) the most of the participants entered the university with their first or second choice. There were 47 male students (23.1%) and 157 female students (76.9%).

Classroom Context

On Mondays, I taught a first-period class (Class MC1) with 17 female students, majoring in piano. These students were generally serious, they liked repetitive practice, and they enjoyed participating in pair and group work tasks. In the second period, I taught a class (Class MC2) of 20 students (5 male and 15 female students) who were majoring in various musical instruments (e.g., woodwinds, strings, and percussion), composition, and music education. They tended to be loud and outgoing, but they preferred individual work to pair work.

On Wednesdays, I taught a first-period class (Class MC3), which consisted of 22 students (3 male and 19 female students) majoring in music education. Some students in this class were serious about learning English, so they asked good questions during the reading and writing activities. In the second period, I taught a class with 3 male and 20 female students (Class MC4). Most of the students in this class were majoring in piano, while others were majoring in composition or string instruments. Two students were very serious about studying English, and they took the Eiken second Level examination after I encouraged them to do so.

Six out of 80 students were removed from the study because they were unable to fulfill the attendance requirements for the course during the 2010 academic year.

In 2011, I taught a first-period class (Class MC5) on Mondays with 16 students (2 male and 14 female students) majoring in piano, music education, and composition. This class was classified as C, so their English proficiency and motivation toward learning English were relatively low compared with the other classes in the music college. In the second period, I taught a class (Class MC6) of 16 students (3 male and 13 female students). This class was also classified as C class, so in general, their English proficiency and motivation were low, although some of the students were friendly and eager to study English writing.

In 2011, on Wednesdays I taught a first-period class (Class MC7) consisting of 18 stu-

52 CHAPTER 3 METHODS

dents (3 male and 15 female students) majoring in piano, music education, composition, and various musical instruments (e.g., woodwinds, strings, and percussion). In the second period, I taught a class (Class MC8), of 16 female students majoring in various musical instruments. Students in both of the Wednesday classes were serious and they enjoyed pair work activities more than individual work. Their English proficiency levels were higher than that of the Monday classes.

In 2011, I taught an Advanced English class fourth period on Tuesdays with 26 male and 7 female students majoring in business and marketing in Sakura University. These students were generally serious, eager to learn English, and eager to obtain high levels. Three male students had lived in the United States or England. In general, their English proficiency levels were the highest of all the classes in this study.

The A level classes in the music college (MC3 and MC4) and a class in Sakura University used *Skills for Better Writing* (Ishitani & Andrews, 2008), and the B and C classes (MC1, MC2, MC5, MC6, MC7, and MC8) used *Writing Within from Intro* (Kelly & Gargagliano, 2004).

Instrumentation

The following instruments were used in this study: (a) Background Questionnaire, (b) The writing section of the Eiken Can-Do Questionnaires, (c) The Classroom Can-Do Questionnaires, (d) The Eiken Placement Test, (e) Writing Grades, (f) Essay Assignments, (g) Affective Orientation Questionnaire.

Background Questionnaire

The purpose of the Background Questionnaire (See Appendix C for the English version and Appendix D for the Japanese version) was to obtain background information about the participants concerning their gender, university major, nationality, and whether they have lived in a foreign country. In April 2010 and 2011, 204 students completed the Background Questionnaire.

The Writing Section of the Eiken Can-Do Questionnaires

The Eiken Can-Do Questionnaires were designed to contribute to a better understanding of typical Japanese language learners and to create a comprehensive snapshot of what Eiken test-takers believe they can accomplish in English in real-life situations (STEP, 2006). One purpose of using the Eiken Can-Do Questionnaires was to help the participants gain a better understanding of the levels of language ability targeted by the Eiken tests. The questionnaire was designed to elicit information from test-takers about what they believe they can do in English outside the testing situation. Therefore, being able to perform language activities included on the Can-Do questionnaires for a particular Eiken level does not guarantee that a person can pass that level of the Eiken test.

The participants completed the 24-item writing section of the Eiken Can-Do Questionnaires, in April, July, and December in 2010 and 2011 (Appendix E). The writing section of Eiken Can-Do Questionnaires was administered in Japanese. The items were taken from the 4th Level, 3rd Level, pre-2nd Level, and 2nd Level of the Eiken Can-Do Questionnaires. The original Eiken Can-Do Questionnaires in the writing section has not been changed. Sample items from each level are as follows: *Can write at some length about topics from everyday life* (2nd Level); *Can write simple texts about things that he/she is interested in* (Pre-2nd Level); *Can write simple texts about himself/herself* (3rd Level); *Can write simply constructed sentences and messages* (4th Level). The students answered using a 4-point Likert scale (1 = *I cannot do this at all*; 2 = *I can do this a little*; 3 = *I can do this fairly well*; 4 = *I can do this very well*).

The Classroom Can-Do Questionnaires

I developed the Classroom Can-Do questionnaires based on the writing activities used in the university writing courses (see Appendix F for The Original Japanese Version of the Classroom Can-Do Questionnaire, Appendix G for Classroom Can-Do Questionnaires and Degree of Attainment (English Version), Appendix H for Classroom Can-Do Questionnaires and Degree of Attainment: In the Year 2010 and 2011 Academic Year, Appendix I for The Classroom Can-Do Questionnaire (English Version), and Appendix J for The Classroom Can-Do Questionnaire (Japanese Version). The purpose of these questionnaires

54 CHAPTER 3 METHODS

Table 8. *The Writing Section of the Eiken Can-Do Questionnaires and Classroom Can-Do Questionnaires*

Writing section of the Eiken Can-Do Questionnaire: External measure	Classroom Can-Do Questionnaires: Internal measure
Can write a simple notice (e.g. the date, time, and place of a party, the program for a school festival) (from Level pre-2)	Can write prepositional phrases to refer to places, such as *at school, on a bench, in the park*. (May 17th, 2010, 5th class)
Can write a simple self-introduction (from Level 3)	Can write an email letter of self- introduction in paragraph style in 45 minutes in more than 100 words. (April 26th, 2010, 3rd class)
Can write about his/her hobbies or interests (from Level 3). Can describe the details of memorable experiences (e.g., school events, trips) (from Level 2).	Can write an essay on "Special Place and me" in 45 minutes using more than 100 words. (May 10th, 2010, 4th class)

was to adapt the Eiken Can-Do statements into everyday classroom objectives and to better understand the students' achievement in the writing course. The students' degrees of attainment were calculated by informal examinations and observations.

Table 8 shows the information of the difference between Eiken Can-Do Questionnaires and Classroom Can-Do Questionnaires. It tells that Eiken Can-Do Questionnaires are more general, widespread and common than Classroom Can-Do Questionnaires, which are more concrete and informative.

The Eiken Placement Test

At the beginning of spring semester 2010, the Eiken Placement Test B was administered to 232 second-year students in the music college to obtain estimates of the students' reading, listening, and writing proficiency levels. The Eiken Placement Test B (from 2nd to 3rd level) is made up of vocabulary, structure, and reading and listening sections, and took 60 minutes to administer (Appendix K). The students were divided into four levels based on the test results: S (Eiken 2nd Level), A (Eiken pre-2nd and 2nd Level), B (Eiken 3rd Level), and C (Eiken 5th to 3rd Level). MC3 and MC4 were made up of students in Eiken pre-2nd and 2nd Level, and MC1 and MC2 were made up of students in Eiken 3rd Level in 2010. MC7 and MC8 were made up of students in Eiken 3rd Level and MC5 and

MC6 were from Eiken 3rd Level to 5th Level in 2011.

Writing Grades

A concern with Can-Do statements is that they are subjective, so it is important to gather objective test scores and scores from people other than the students. The writing grades, which are based on the teacher's assessment of the students' writing performance, are one way to verify the accuracy of the Eiken Can-Do Questionnaires and Classroom Can-Do Questionnaires. The Can-Do Questionnaires are hypothesized to correlate positively with writing grades and essay quality.

The writing grades are based on four or five writing assignments in one semester. In total, the students were required to write nine essays in one academic year. For example, in the A classes in the music college and the class in Sakura University, the assignments were (a) Should English be taught in primary school?, (b) Why have personal computers spread so quickly?, (c) Experimental report: Hypothesis: Women can do more things at the same time than men, and (d) What are the merits and demerits of e-learning? In the B classes and C classes in the music college, the assignments were (a) Email letter of self-introduction, (b) Special place, (c) Ideal partner, and (d) Favorite photo (Appendix L). Attendance, homework, vocabulary quizzes, reading ability, class attitude, pair work participation, and final examinations were not included in the calculation of the writing grades.

Essay Assignments

The participants were required to write four or five essays in one semester. In total, they were required to write nine essays in one academic year. In the A classes in the music college and the class in Sakura University, the students were required to write about the following topics: (a) Should English be taught in primary school?, (b) Why have personal computers spread so quickly?, (c) Women can do more things at the same time than men, and (d) What are the merits and demerits of e-learning? In the B classes and C classes in the music college, the students wrote about the following topics: (a) An email letter of self-introduction, (b) A special place and what happened there, (c) My ideal partner, the character of my ideal partner, and three reasons why I chose those characteristics, and (d) My

56   CHAPTER 3 METHODS

favorite photo and the reasons why the photo is important to me. Topics that were familiar to the students were chosen because that increases the students' motivation for writing. These textbooks were published by ETS based on TOEFL writing topics, which suggests that the difficulty level should be equivalent even though the students chose different topics. The students were required to write more than 100 words in English on each topic. In the A classes, the students chose one topic from the topics shown in Tables 9 and 10. I rated the written products with a modified version of the EFL Composition Profile (Jacobs et

Table 9. *English Writing Topics (Spring Semester, 2010 and 2011)*

Class	Topic number	Topic
A in the music college and class in Sakura University	1	Should English be taught in primary school? Should mothers stay at home until their children go to school? Should the marriage system be abolished? Should children leave home after they reached the age of 20? Should university entrance examinations be abolished?
A	2	Hot springs are now popular again. Chinese noodles are booming. Why have personal computers spread so quickly? Why have mobile phones spread so quickly? Why are karaoke boxes so popular?
A	3	Experimental report: Hypothesis: Women can do more things at the same time than men. Other free topics
A	4	What are the merits and demerits of the Japanese school system? What are the merits and demerits of e-learning? What are the merits and demerits of living alone? What are the merits and demerits of living in an apartment rather than in a house?
B and C in the music college	1	Write an email letter of self-introduction.
B	2	Describe a special place and what happened there.
B	3	Write about your ideal partner, the character of your partner, and three reasons to support the characteristics you chose.
B	4	Describe your favorite photo and give the reasons why the photo is important to you.

Table 10. *English Writing Topics (Fall Semester, 2010 and 2011)*

Class	Topic number	Topic
A in the music college and class in Sakura University	5	Compare Japanese and American family life.
		Compare television news and newspaper news.
		Compare public school education with private school education.
		Compare city life and country life
		Other free topics on comparison.
A	6	Developed, rapidly developing and still underdeveloped countries.
		Countries with hot, temperate, and cold climates.
		Europe, Asia, Africa and America.
		Other free topics on classification.
A	7	How to save paper/water / electricity. (Choose one.)
		How to succeed in an exam.
		How to make friends.
		How to stay fit. (How to stay healthy.)
		Other free topics on giving instructions.
A	8	What effects have computers had on society?
		What is the influence of the spread of mobile phones on society?
		How did the Meiji Restoration affect Japanese history?
		Other free topics on causes and effects.
A	9	Write your thank-you letter.
B and C in the music college	5	Write about your personal seal.
B	6	Write a party invitation.
B	7	Write a thank-you letter.
B	8	Write a movie review.
B	9	Should English be taught in primary school?

al., 1981) (Appendix M), which is made up of five analytical criteria: Content, Organization, Vocabulary, Language Use, and Mechanics.

Affective Orientation Questionnaire

The purpose of the affective orientation questionnaire was to obtain information about the participants concerning ten affective factors, Desire to Write English, Attitude Toward

58 CHAPTER 3 METHODS

Learning to Write English, Motivational Intensity, Instrumental Orientation for Writing in English, L2 Writing Anxiety, L2 Writing Self-Confidence, Willingness to Communicate in L2 Writing, Self-Esteem, Cognitive Competence, General Self-Worth (see Appendix N, P, R, T, and V for the English version and Appendix O, Q, S, U, and W for the Japanese version of the questionnaire).

Desire to write English. The Desire to write English scale, which was based on Gardner (1985b), concerns how strong a desire the participants have to write in English. A sample question is *I plan to write as much as possible during the class.* Six items were designed to measure Desire to write English.

Attitude toward learning to write English. The Attitude toward learning to write English scale, which was based on Gardner (1985b), is designed to measure the degree to which the participants have a positive attitude toward writing English. An example item is *Writing English is really enjoyable.* Six items are hypothesized to measure attitude toward learning to write English.

Motivational intensity to write in English. The Motivational intensity scale, which was based on Gardner (1985b), is designed to measure the intensity of the participants' motivation to write English. An example item is *I plan to study hard in writing class.* Six items are hypothesized to measure motivational intensity.

Instrumental orientation for writing in English. The Instrumental orientation for writing in English scale, which was based on Gardner (1985b), concerns learners' utilitarian reasons for learning English and the degree to which learners are studying English in order to further a career or achieve academic success. An example item is *Improving my English writing ability is important because it will help me get higher test scores (e.g., on the Eiken).* Six items are hypothesized to measure instrumental orientation.

L2 writing anxiety. The L2 writing anxiety scale, which was based on Gardner

(1985b), measures how anxious the participants feel when writing English. An example question is *I feel nervous when I write English*. Six items are hypothesized to measure L2 writing anxiety.

L2 writing self-confidence. The L2 writing self-confidence scale, which was based on Gardner (1985b), is designed to measure the participants' self-confidence in writing English. A sample question is *Compared to other students, I think I can write English well*. Eight items are hypothesized to measure L2 writing self-confidence.

Willingness to communicate in writing. The Willingness to communicate in writing scale, which was adapted from Weaver (2010), was designed to assess the participants' willingness to engage in written communication in English. A sample items is *I would be willing to write a self-introduction in English*. The respondents answered using a 6-point Likert scale (1 = *Very unwilling*; 2 = *Unwilling*; 3 = *Slightly unwilling*; 4 = *Slightly willing*; 5 = *Willing*; 6 = *Very willing*). Eight items are hypothesized to measure willingness to communicate in writing.

Self-esteem. The self-esteem scale, which was originally created by Rosenberg (1965), was designed to assess the participants' self-esteem, which concerns a person's opinion of their own worth. The students answered using a 6-point Likert scale (1 = *Strongly disagree*; 2 = *Disagree*; 3 = *Slightly disagree*; 4 = *Slightly agree*; 5 = *Agree*; 6 = *Strongly agree*). One sample item is *I believe I have a number of good qualities*. Ten items are hypothesized to measure self-esteem.

Cognitive competence. The Cognitive competence scale, which was originally created by Harter (1982), is defined as competence concerning the mental process of understanding. Cognitive competence emphasizes academic performance (doing well at school work, being smart, feeling good about one's classroom performance). A sample item is *I am good at schoolwork*. Seven items are hypothesized to measure cognitive competence.

60 CHAPTER 3 METHODS

General self-worth. The General self-worth scale, which was originally created by Harter (1982), concerns an individual's feeling of confidence that he/she is a good and useful person. Items make reference to being sure of oneself, being happy with the way one is, feeling good about the way one acts and thinking that one is a good person. One sample item is *I am sure of myself.* Seven items are hypothesized to measure general self-worth.

A Quantitative Methodology

In this study, I chose a quantitative method, which means for testing objective theories by examining the relationship among variables (Cresswell 2009). In this design, I collected and analyzed the quantitative data by administering the Eiken Can-Do Questionnaires, the Classroom Can-Do Questionnaires, the Background Questionnaire, and the Affective Orientation Questionnaire.

In this study, as Brown (2001) stated, questionnaires can seem relatively rigid and impersonal to respondents. However, questionnaires are well suited to gathering a large amount of data quickly and efficiently once the issues, research questions, and specific survey questions have been clearly delineated.

After I administered the Eiken Can-do Questionnaires in April, July, and December, 2010 and 2011, and I distributed Classroom Can-Do Questionnaires in November, 2010 and 2011, I then compiled the data to put it into a form that could later be stored, sorted, and analyzed. I entered the data into an Excel 2010 spreadsheet. I also evaluated nine essay assignments written by 179 students through the 2010 and 2011 academic years, using the Jacobs' rating scale, which consists of contents, organization, vocabulary, grammar, and mechanics. I asked three raters, who were my colleagues at a Japanese university in Tokyo, to assess six out of nine essay assignments. The three raters had completed doctoral courses in education and they had more than three years' teaching experience in Japanese universities.

Analyses

The study's three research questions are answered utilizing quantitative analysis of the participants' responses to the Eiken Can-Do Questionnaires, and the Affective Orientation Questionnaire. The first research question asks to what degree each writing section of the Eiken Can-Do item measures a unidimensional construct. Is the difficulty of the Eiken Can-Do items appropriate for the target students? This question will be answered using Rasch analysis.

The second research question asks, what the relationship between teacher ratings of the students' writing performances, as measured by essay measures, the students' self-assessed writing ability using the Eiken Can-Do questionnaires and the following Affective Orientation variables is: Desire to Write English, Attitude Toward Learning to Write English, Motivational Intensity, Instrumental Orientation to write in English, L2 Writing Anxiety, L2 Writing Self-Confidence, Willingness to Communicate in L2 writing, Self-Esteem, Cognitive Competence, and General Self-Worth?" The relationships among the participants' writing performances as measured by essay measures, self-assessed writing ability using the Eiken Can-Do Questionnaires, and the Affective Orientation variables will be modeled using Structural Equation Modeling. I test two models here: in one model, the DV is the Eiken Can-Do Questionnaires results and in the second, the DV is the estimated writing ability of the participants, which is based on their performance on six essays.

The third research question concerning the degree to which the students' self-perceived writing ability (as measured by the Can-Do Questionnaires) changes across one academic year is answered using a multi-faceted Rasch analysis.

The Rasch Model

The Rasch measurement model (Rasch, 1960) is an effective tool for validating a wide variety of instruments, the model allows for investigations of dimensionality and the ordering of items and persons on a common interval scale. The fit of the data to the Rasch measurement model is carried out with item level fit statistics that compare the discrepan-

62   CHAPTER 3 METHODS

cy between the observed and model expected responses. Additionally, the Rasch model re-
duces complex data matrices to a unidimensional variable, as all systematic variation in the
data is explained by one latent variable. The use of Rasch principal component analysis of
item residuals provides an effective way of detecting relevant secondary constructs in the
data.

The Rasch rating scale model (Andrich, 1978) was used to analyze the questionnaire
data and obtain estimates of the degree to which the respondent endorsed the items. Rating scale structure, Rasch descriptive statistics, Principle Component Analysis of the residuals results, Rasch item and person reliability and separation, and Wright maps are presented.

Criteria for the proper scale functioning set by Linacre (1999) are applied in this study.
The criterion is larger than 1.4 and less than 5 logits. The .60 to 1.40 infit MNSQ and
outfit MNSQ criterion set by Wright and Linacre (1994) for rating scale models was used,
as it is slightly more stringent than the .50 to 1.50 criterion suggested by Linacre. The
Rasch PCA of item residual is run to check the degree of unidimensionality of each construct. According to Linacre (1999), in fundamentally unidimensional constructs 50% of
the variance is account for by the Rasch measures and the eigenvalue of the first residual
component is < 3.0, and < 1.5 is considered excellent.

Path Analysis, Structural Equation Modeling and Hierarchical Multiple Regression

Path analysis is a special case of structural equation modeling (SEM) in which only single indicators are employed for each variable in the causal model. Thus, path analysis is
SEM with a structural model, but no measurement model (Tabachnick & Fidell, 2001).
SEM, also referred to as causal modeling, allows researchers to test cause-effect relationships based on correlational data. Thus, it is a powerful analytical tool, as it combines the
versatility of regression analysis and the ability to test hypothesized causal models. Because
SEM is concerned with the adequacy of hypothesized theoretical constructs (i.e., abstract
or latent variables), it is particularly suitable for studying motivational issues (Dörnyei,
2001).

Item Parceling in SEM

Item parceling is a procedure for combining individual items and using these combined items as observed variables. It is typically used in confirmatory factor analysis (CFA) or structural equation modeling. Parcels are an alternative to using the individual items, and the use of item parceling in SEM has become common in recent years (Bandalos, 2002). A parcel can be defined as an aggregate-level indicator comprised of the sum or average of two or more items, responses, or behaviors (Little, Cunningham, Shabar, & Widaman, 2002). Item parceling can help to (a) circumvent problems with so-called difficulty factors, (b) provide a useful approximation to continuous scales, and (c) create indicators with greater reliability and more definite rotational results than individual items (Cattell & Burdsal, 1975; Hagtvet & Nasser 2004; Rushton, Brainerd, & Pressley, 1983).

Item parcels are typically created by taking the sum or mean of a set of items within a factor. For example, if six items (i1, i2, i3, i4, i5, i6) load on factor 1 (f1) and the goal is to create three parcels (p1, p2, p3), then summing pairs of items creates the desired parcels (Anglim, 2014):

p1 = i1 + i2

p2 = i3 + i4

p3 = i5 + i6

There are other ways of creating parcels and debate exists in the literature on the pros and cons of the different approaches (e.g., Hagtvet & Nasser, 2004; Hall et al., 1999; Little et al., 2002). For example, item parceling has been constructed based on random combinations of items, such as split halves or odd-even combinations (Kim & Hagtvet, 2003; Prat, 1990). In this study, I parceled the items by odd-even combinations; so, for example, Self-Esteem Parcel 1 = i1 + i3, Self-Esteem Parcel 2 = i2 + i4, Self-Esteem parcel 3 = i5 + i7, Self-Esteem Parcel 4 = i6 + i8, and Self-Esteem Parcel 5 = i9 + i10.

In large part, the decision to parcel or not depends on one's philosophical stance regarding scientific inquiry (e.g., empiricist vs. pragmatist) and whether the substantive goal of a study is to understand the structure of a set of items or to examine the nature of a set of constructs. I chose the former reason when I conduct the item parceling. Little et al. (2002) strongly recommended that investigators acquire a thorough understanding of the

64   CHAPTER 3 METHODS

nature and dimensionality of the items to be parceled.

Bandalos (2002) pointed out that one advantage of parceling is that parcel solutions typically result in better model fit than solutions produced by the item level. Furthermore, many scales have 50 or 100 items. Modeling this many items with moderate sample sizes (e.g., n = 200) can work poorly (Anglim, 2014). Little et al. (2002) also suggested that parcels are preferred when the sample size is relatively small, which is the case in this study. As I was left with the choice of reducing the number of observed variables (e.g., by parceling) or not conducting structural modeling, which led me to conduct item parceling.

A potential problem with item parceling concerns the need for the unidimensionality of the items being combined (Bandalos & Finney 2001; Kim & Hagtvet, 2003). Bandalos (2002) stated that parceling results in improved fit as well as a less-biased solution in the presence of coarsely categorized items, non-normally distributed items, or both, if the items have a unidimensional structure. In this study, each variable was checked for unidimensionality; therefore, parceling was a viable option. A danger of parceling is that it can result in biased estimates of other model parameters (Hall, Snell, & Foust, 1999).

Mediation, Direct Effects, and Indirect Effects

For the purpose of structural equation modeling, mediation refers to a situation in which there is a causal process between three or more variables. In a mediation relationship, there is a direct effect between an independent variable and dependent variable. Thus, direct effects between the independent variable and the mediator variable and between the mediator variable and the dependent variable comprise an indirect effect (Kenny, 2014). In other words, a direct effect occurs when a construct or variable is directly regressed onto another construct or variable, whereas an indirect effect occurs when a construct or variable is related to a subsequent datum point, but only through an intervening variable or construct. An indirect effect is a measure of association that is the result of the product of two or more direct effects. Each indirect pathway is indexed as the product of each direct pathway that links constructs or variables together.

In the next section I show one hypothesized structural equation model tested in this study.

A Hypothesized Structural Equation Model Including Can-Do Questionnaires

Within the configurations of Gardner (1985a), MacIntyre (1994), and Yashima's (2002) models, the following relationships are hypothesized concerning the ten affective variables, and Writing Ability.

1. Self-Esteem affects current writing ability and writing level both directly and via its effect on motivation and anxiety (Christou et al., 2001; Hein & Hagger, 2006). According to Christou et al. (2001), the proposed model is based on the assumption that self-esteem is both a social force and a social product (Rosenberg, 1965). In Christou et al.'s (2001) study, in the context of mathematics learning and teaching, preservice teachers' self-esteem influenced and was influenced by mathematics achievement. The researchers proposed two variables, motivation and anxiety, as mediators of the causal effect from general self-esteem to mathematics achievement. General self-esteem affects academic achievement both directly and via its effects on motivation and anxiety. Self-esteem theory suggests that individuals with negative self-attitudes tend to exhibit various psychological symptoms of distress because positive self-attitudes constitute ultimate personal goals; failure to obtain positive self-feeling should be highly distressing. Consistent with this reasoning, low self-esteem is associated with various types of psychological and emotional distress, which lead to anxiety and depression (Skaalvik & Hagtvet, 1990). Distress can also have motivational effects, reflected in a negative outlook on life and a lack of interest in related activities. According to Clute (1984), low general self-esteem creates high anxiety, which in turn leads to low achievement. In a similar fashion, low general self-esteem affected preserved teachers' mathematics self-esteem and consequently led to low achievement.

Hein and Hagger (2006) examined a theoretical model of global self-esteem that incorporated constructs from achievement goal and self-determination theories. The researchers hypothesized that self-determined or autonomous motives mediate the influence of achievement goal orientation on global self-esteem. The adapted version of the Behavioral Regulation in Exercise Questionnaire (Mullan et al., 1997), the Perception of Success Questionnaire (Roberts & Balague, 1991) and Rosenberg's (1965) self-esteem scales were administered to 634 high school students aged 11-15 years. A structural equation model supported the hypotheses and demonstrated that autonomous motives mediated the effect of goal orientation on global self-esteem. The results suggest that generalized motivational orientations influence self-esteem by affecting autonomous motivation and are consistent with theory that suggests that experiences relating to intrinsic motivation are the mechanism by which global motivational orientations are translated into adaptive outcomes such as self-esteem.

2. Cognitive Competence directly affects Motivation (Hui et al., 2011; Tanaka et al., 2002). Hui et al. (2011) used self-determination theory (Ryan & Deci, 2000), which provides a lens for understanding psychological accounts of academic motivation (Ballmann & Muellerr, 2008). Self-determination theory assumes competence, autonomy and relatedness as three important factors contributing to human motivational tendencies. Competence represents the need to feel capable of meeting the demands of one's environment.

Furthermore, Tanaka et al. (2002) investigated the interrelations of approach and avoidance achievement motives (Motive to Achieve Success and Motive to Avoid Failure), two types of competence (Cognitive and Social competence), achievement goals (Mastery, Performance-approach, Performance-avoidance, and Work Avoidance goals) of 131 eighth and ninth grade students from a Japanese junior high school. Multiple regression analysis indicated positive relations between Mastery goals and the Motive to Achieve Success and Cognitive Competence, Performance-Approach Goals and both the Motive to Achieve Success and the Motive to Avoid Failure, and Performance Avoidance Goals and both the Motive to Achieve Success and the Motive to Avoid Failure. Negative relations were found between Work Avoidance goals and the Motive to Achieve Success and Cognitive Competence.

3. Cognitive Competence directly influences Current Writing Ability and Writing grade (Hardré et al., 2007). Hardré et al. investigated the predictive relationship among student characteristics that influence motivation for learning and achievement. They tested a hypothesized path model in which the variables included perceptions of classroom climate, perceived ability, perceived instrumentality of instruction, and achievement goals as predictors of engagement and effort in school. The model fit the data reasonably well, with

relatively minor variations in the strength of the paths between subsamples.

Goal theory posits that achievement goals students pursue with regard to academic tasks have an influence on the quality of their effort and engagement regarding those tasks (Ames & Archer, 1988). Moreover, aspects of the classroom climate are proposed to influence the achievement goals that students pursue (Church, Elliot, & Gable, 2001). Finally, the relationship between classroom climate and students' achievement goals is partially mediated by students' perceptions of their ability regarding the academic task (Dweck, 1986; Elliot, 1999) and whether they perceive an instrumental relationship between the academic task and personally valued future goals (Mensch, Miller, & Brickman, 2004). Those relationships are illustrated in the hypothesized model in this study.

Concerning perceived ability, student's self-perception of ability might influence their motivation for a particular subject and class (Dupeyrat & Marine, 2005; Sansone & Morgan, 1992). Perceived ability is the feeling that one is able to learn the content and accomplish classroom tasks (Miller et al., 1996). Ability perceptions are influenced by past and present experiences in school overall and in the specific discipline (Meece et al., 1990), and those perceptions often differ across subject areas for the same individual (Bransford et al., 1999; Stipek & Gralinski, 1996).

4. Motivation has four subcategories, Desire to Write English, Attitude Toward Learning to Write English, Motivational Intensity, and Instrumental Orientation (Gardner, et al., 1997). A study conducted by Gardner and Lambert (1959) found that an individual's orientation to learning French as a L2 was related to his or her motivation to learn French, attitudes toward French Canadians, and proficiency in French. The Attitude/Motivation Test Battery (AMTB; Gardner 1985) was developed to measure these variables. Motivation refers to the individual's attitudes, desires, and effort to learn the L2 and is measured by three scales: (a) Attitudes toward Learning the Language, (b) Desire to Learn the Language, and (c) Motivational Intensity.

5. Motivation directly influences Writing Ability and Writing Grade (Solberg Nes et al., 2009; Unrau & Schlackman, 2006). In Solberg Nes et al.'s (2009) study, in order to un-

68 CHAPTER 3 METHODS

derstand the mechanisms through which optimism might impact outcomes, so they first conducted a series of regression analyses to show that optimism predicted retention, motivation, performance, and adjustment. The authors simultaneously tested the relationship among optimism, previous academic performance, college GPA, motivation, distress, and college retention using structural modeling. Several assumptions were made regarding the structural model. First, because it was hypothesized that optimism would increase levels of motivation but decrease levels of distress, motivation and distress were allowed to cover in the model. Second, based on evidence of the association between motivation and GPA (Aspinwall & Taylor, 1992; Pajares & Urdan, 2002) as well as between distress and GPA (Brunelle-Joiner, 1999; Hishinuma et al., 2001), motivation and distress were each allowed to cover with GPA. Third, HGPA and ACT were allowed to cover because of previous research suggesting a significant association between the two (Stumph & Stanley, 2002).

Unrau and Schlackman (2006) investigated the effects of intrinsic and extrinsic motivation on reading achievement for urban middle school students. The authors initially developed a research based theoretical model representing the interrelationships among students' ethnicity, gender, proficiency level, intrinsic motivation, extrinsic motivation, and reading achievement. Through the perspective of self-determination theory (Deci & Ryan, 1985; Ryan & Deci 2000), the authors explored motivation to read in an urban middle school. A multiple-groups SEM analysis indicated that intrinsic motivation had a stronger positive relationship with reading achievement for Asian students than for Hispanic students.

6. Instrumental Orientation, which is one of the subcategories of Motivation, is hypothesized to directly influence Writing Ability and Writing Level (Hardré et al., 2007). According to Hardré et al. (2007), perception of the instrumentality of instruction can influence striving toward various types of achievement goals. Brickman and Miller (2001) pointed out that an important element of motivation is the student's perception of an instrumental relationship between the current task and a personally valued future outcome (Brickman & Miller, 2001; Menschu, Miller, & Brickman, 2004). If the student does not perceive a

connection between the current task and the eventual valued outcome, perceived instrumentality and its consequent incentive value will be diminished or absent (Reeve, Jang, Hardré, & Omura, 2003). High perceived instrumentality adds incentive value to the learning task beyond that associated with other goals (e.g., performance goals; Miller, DeBacker, & Greene, 1999).

7. Self-Confidence directly influences responses on the Eiken Can-do Questionnaires, with greater self-confidence resulting in more positive responses. Gardner et al. (1997) suggested that the concept of self-confidence is conceptually related to that of language anxiety, except it is a positive rather than a negative component. Clément (1980) proposed that self-confidence is an important determinant of the motivation to learn a L2, and that this form of self-confidence develops in multicultural contexts as a function of the frequency and quality of contact with members of the L2 community. He proposed that self-confidence consisted of perceptions of confidence in the L2 as well as an absence of anxiety about learning or using the language. Clément, Dörnyei, and Noels (1994) stated that self-confidence is made up of anxiety as an affective aspect and the learner's self-evaluation of his or her proficiency as a cognitive component. Clément and his associates have reported that self-confidence correlates significantly and appreciably with measures of L2 proficiency (Clément, Dörnyei, & Noels, 1994; Clément, Gardner, & Smythe, 1977; Clément & Kruidenier, 1985).

Gardner et al.'s (1997) participants rated their French proficiency using a modified version of the Can-do measure developed by Clark (1984). This measure required individuals to rate their French proficiency in terms of Speaking (α = .93; 15 items), Understanding (α = .93; 8 items), Reading (α = .89; 7 items) and Writing (α = .77; 6 items). A sample Speaking item is, *Order a simple meal in a restaurant*. Ratings were made on a 7-point scale ranging from 1 = *Very difficult for me* to 7 = *Very easy for me*.

8. Self-Confidence and Anxiety directly influence responses on the Willingness to Communicate in writing, with greater self-confidence resulting in more positive responses on WTC in writing and with smaller anxiety resulting in more positive responses on WTC in

70   CHAPTER 3 METHODS

writing. Past research has shown that two of the strongest predictors of WTC are individual characteristics—communication anxiety and perceived communication competence (Baker & MacIntyre, 2000; MacIntyre, Clément, Baker, & Conrod, 2001). Communication anxiety corresponds to the level of fear associated with actual or anticipated communication (McCroskey, 1977). Perceived communication competence is belief that one can communicate effectively in a given situation (McCroskey & Richmond, 1990). Furthermore, MacIntyre, Babin, and Clément (1999) stated that people can experience communication apprehension if their perceived competence level is too low for the demands of the current situation. Thus, the consideration of how the combination of perceived competence and apprehension affects one's willingness to communicate is advisable.

9. No empirical research has been conducted on this relationship. However, logically higher scores on Self-Esteem, Cognitive Competence, and General Self-Worth indicate a more positive self-image. If students have higher score on Self-Esteem, Cognitive Competence and General Self-Worth, they will have higher Self-Confidence. On the other hand, if students have lower score on Self-Esteem, Cognitive Competence and General Self-Worth, they will have higher Anxiety.

10. WTC in Writing is hypothesized to directly and positively influence the Eiken Can-Do Questionnaires results. The Eiken Can-Do Questionnaires results positively predict current writing ability measured by the raters. People who are more willing to write will probably write more and/or more often and therefore, can develop their current writing ability more rapidly than those who write less and/or less often. People with higher writing ability will assess themselves more highly on the Can-Do Questionnaires.

11. Self Esteem and General Self Worth are considered to be Antecedent Factors or Fundamental Personality Issues in the Hypothesized Structural Equation model in Level 1. Again, Motivation, Desire to Write English, Attitude Toward Learning to Write English, Motivational Intensity, Instrumental Orientation, Cognitive Competence, Self-Confidence Anxiety and WTC in Writing are referred to as Individual Difference Variables in

Procedures and Schedule for Gathering Data   *71*

Level 2, Eiken Can-Do is the results of Self- Assessment in Level 3 and finally Current Writing ability is considered to be outcome in Level 4. Figure 3 shows two hypothesized models, Measurement Model A and Measurement Model B.

Procedures and Schedule for Gathering Data

Table 11 and the numbered points below show the data that were gathered. The information is organized chronologically.

1. All 232 second-year students in a music college took the Eiken Placement test in April, 2010 and 2011 (Week 1).

2. 204 students completed the Background Questionnaire, and Affective Orientation Questionnaire in the music college and Sakura university in 2010 and 2011 (Weeks 2 and 3).

3. Nine writing topics were completed by 179 students after they had worked through the learning resources materials for each one in 2010 and 2011 (Week 2-Week 28).

4. 204 students completed the Eiken Can-Do Questionnaire (writing part), in April, July, and December in 2010 and 2011. The teacher compared the students' self-assessments and writing course grades.

5. The Classroom Can-do questionnaires for each class were developed so that I could obtain a specific classroom objective for each class (Week 1-Week 28).

6. Four raters rated 179 students' essays after they had completed the 28-week sessions (Weeks 29-30).

Table 11 shows an overview of the study by listing the number of participants, time, and instruments.

72 CHAPTER 3 METHODS

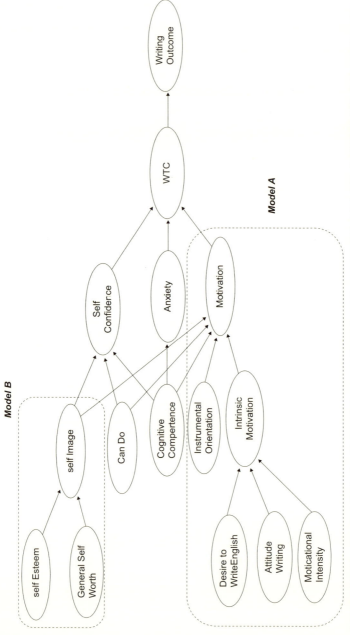

Figure 3. The Hypothesized Motivation Model: Measurement Model A and Measurement Model B. Attitude Writing: Attitude Toward Learning to Write English; WTC: Willingness to Communicate in L2 Writing; Can Do: Eiken Can Do Questionnaires.

Procedures and Schedule for Gathering Data   73

Table 11. *Overview of the Study*

Participants	Time	Instrument
232 second-year students	1st week (April, 2010 and 2011)	Eiken Placement Test
204 second-year and third-year students	2nd and 3rd weeks (April, 2010 and 2011)	Background Questionnaire, Affective Orientation Questionnaire
204 second-year and third-year students	2nd week (April, 2010 and 2011)	Eiken Can-do Questionnaires
204 second-year and third-year students	12th week (July, 2010 and 2011)	Eiken Can-do Questionnaires
179 second-year and third-year students	1st week-28th week (April-December, 2010 and 2011)	Classroom Can-do Questionnaires
179 second-year and third-year students	1st week-28th week (April-December, 2010 and 2011)	Essay Assignments, Writing Grades
204 second-year and third-year students	27th week (December, 2010 and 2011)	Eiken Can-do Questionnaires
179 second-year and third-year students	(November, 2011)	Classroom Can-do Questionnaires

CHAPTER 4
PRELIMINARY ANALYSES

The purpose of this chapter is to examine the validity and reliability of the ten affective orientation variables questionnaires and the EIKEN Can-Do Questionnaires and convert the Likert scale scores to interval measures using the Rasch rating scale model as implemented in WINSTEPS version 3.64.2 (Linacre & Wright, 2007). For each construct, the following analyses are reported: Rating scale category structure, Rasch descriptive statistics for the items, PCA of the item residuals, and Rasch item and person reliability and separation statistics. In addition, a Wright map is shown for each variable. The original sample size was 204, however, the sample size was decreased to 168 participants because 36 participants did not complete the questionnaires.

Desire to Write English

The category structure of the six original categories for Desire to Write English was examined. The original 6-point scale was collapsed to a 5-point scale, as points 1 (*Strongly disagree*) and 2 (*Disagree*) did not separate clearly and they did not show a clear difference between the two. As shown in Table 12, the resulting 5-point scale met all the criteria for proper scale functioning set by Linacre (1999).

Table 12. *Category Structure Statistics for Desire to Write English (5-point scale)*

	Count (%)	Infit MNSQ	Outfit MNSQ	Andrich threshold	Category measure
1 Disagree	59 (6)	1.06	1.10	None	(-3.36)
2 Slightly disagree	129 (13)	1.04	1.05	-2.15	-1.62
3 Slightly agree	273 (27)	.97	1.00	-.99	-.15
4 Agree	330 (33)	.95	.92	.57	1.59
5 Strongly agree	217 (22)	1.00	.99	2.47	3.67

The Rasch descriptive statistics for the six items designed to measure Desire to Write English are shown in Table 13. The items displayed adequate fit to the Rasch model as they all met the .60 to 1.40 criterion set by Wright and Linacre (1994) for rating scale models. Point-measure correlations were also acceptable, as they were all between .62 and .76.

The Rasch PCA of item residuals was run to check the degree of unidimensionality formed by the six items. As shown in Table 14, the Rasch model accounted for 58.0% of the variance, which exceeded the 50% criterion. The variance explained by the items (29.2%) was less than four times the variance explained by the first contrast (14.7%), but the eigenvalue of the first contrast was 2.1, which was well below the 3.0 criterion. This indicated that there was little unexplained variance to indicate the presence of a second factor in the data. Thus, it can be concluded that the data are fundamentally unidimensional.

The Wright map for the items measuring Desire to Write English and the participants

Table 13. *Rasch Descriptive Statistics for the Desire to Write English Items*

Item	Measure	SE	Infit MNSQ	Infit ZSTD	Outfit MNSQ	Outfit ZSTD	Pt-measure correlation
DWE3	1.16	.10	1.28	2.5	1.28	2.4	.68
DWE2	1.02	.10	.79	-2.1	.81	-1.8	.76
DWE5	.35	.10	1.29	2.5	1.29	2.5	.68
DWE1	-.58	.11	.93	-.6	1.03	.3	.62
DWE4	-.58	.11	.84	-1.5	.82	-1.6	.75
DWE6	-1.38	.12	.78	-2.1	.77	-1.8	.70

Table 14. *Rasch Standardized Residual Variance Results for Desire to Write English*

	Eigenvalue	Percent
Total raw variance in observations	14.3	100.0
Raw variance explained by measures	8.3	58.0
Raw variance explained by persons	4.1	28.7
Raw Variance explained by items	4.2	29.2
Raw unexplained variance (total)	6.0	42.0
Unexplained variance in first contrast	2.1	14.7

76   CHAPTER 4 PRELIMINARY ANALYSES

are shown in Figure 4. The items are well spread out and well centered on the participants with their difficulty estimates ranging from -1.30 to 1.06. Given the relative position of the participants to the items, the items were generally easy to endorse for many of the participants. The empirical item hierarchy indicates that the easiest item to endorse was item DWE6, which is an abstract idea that does not involve any work. On the other hand, item DWE1 concerns the current classes and shows a willingness to do the coursework. Item DWE4 might have been interpreted as a class assignment given its proximity to item DWE1. Items DWE5 and DWE2 are specific and concrete, there is work involved, and the work is over and above the coursework. Item DWE3, concerning taking the course even if it is not required, is the most difficult item to endorse and likely can be endorsed strongly only by individuals with exceptionally strong motivation. If the items contain an expression such as, *would like to be able to write*, they are generally easier to endorse, while if the item concerns extra work, such as *write English outside of the class,* they are more difficult to endorse.

The Rasch item reliability (item separation) estimate was .98 (8.04), which is excellent. The Rasch person reliability (person separation) estimate was .78 (1.90), which is fair. The mean person ability estimate of .92 (*SD* = 1.57) was higher than mean difficulty estimate (.00; *SD* = .92), which indicates the items measuring DWE were generally easy to endorse for many of the participants.

Attitude Toward Learning to Write English

The category structure of the six original categories for Attitudes toward Learning to Write English was examined (see Table 15). The original 6-point scale was collapsed to a 5-point scale, as points 1 (*Strongly disagree*) and 2 (*Disagree*) did not separate clearly and they did not show a clear difference between the two. As shown in Table 15, the resulting 5-point scale met the criteria for proper scale functioning.

The Rasch descriptive statistics for the six items designed to measure Attitude Toward Learning to Write English are shown in Table 16. The items displayed adequate fit to the Rasch model, as they all met the .60 to 1.40 criterion for rating scale items, except for

Attitude Toward Learning to Write English   77

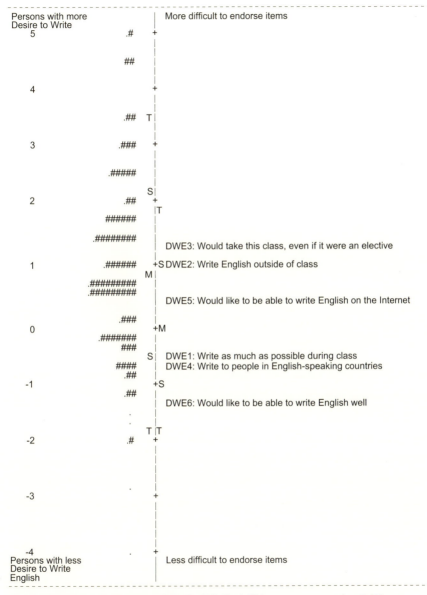

Figure 4. Wright map for Desire to Write English. Each '#' is two persons and each '.' is one person. M = Mean; S = 1 SD; T = 2 SD.

78 CHAPTER 4 PRELIMINARY ANALYSES

Table 15. *Category Structure Statistics for Attitude Toward Learning to Write English (5-point scale)*

	Count (%)	Infit MNSQ	Outfit MNSQ	Andrich threshold	Category measure
1 Stronglydisagree	70 (7)	1.26	1.22	None	(-3.93)
2 Slightly disagree	273 (27)	.87	.86	-2.75	-1.76
3 Slightly agree	374 (37)	.91	.90	-.66	.16
4 Agree	207 (21)	1.03	1.06	1.09	1.79
5 Strongly agree	84(8)	.98	1.02	2.32	3.60

Table 16. *Rasch Descriptive Statistics for the Attitude Toward Learning to Write English Items*

Item	Measure	SE	Infit MNSQ	Infit ZSTD	Outfit MNSQ	Outfit ZSTD	Pt-measure correlation
ALWE3	.80	.11	1.89	6.5	1.86	6.3	.45
ALWE2	.26	.11	.76	-2.4	.75	-2.5	.73
ALWE1	.20	.11	.69	-3.2	.71	-2.9	.72
ALWE4	-.06	.10	1.06	.6	1.03	.4	.71
ALWE6	-.23	.10	.64	-3.9	.64	-3.9	.78
ALWE5	-.98	.10	.97	-.2	.99	-.1	.67

item ALWE 3, which had an Infit MNSQ statistic of 1.89. Point-measure correlations were also acceptable, as they were all between .45 and .78.

The Rasch PCA of item residuals was run to check the degree of unidimensionality formed by the six items. As shown in Table 17, the Rasch model accounted for 49.7% of the variance, which nearly met the 50% criterion. The variance explained by the items (8.2%) was less than four times the variance explained by the first contrast (14.1%), but the eigenvalue of the first contrast was 1.7, which was well below the 3.0 criterion and nearly equal to the 1.5 criterion defined as excellent by Linacre (2009). This small amount of variance in the first contrast indicated that there was little unexplained variance to indicate the presence of a second factor in the data. Thus, it can be concluded that the data are fundamentally unidimensional.

The Wright map for the items measuring Attitude Toward Learning to Write English and the participants are shown in Figure 5. The items are well spread out and well centered

Table 17. *Rasch Standardized Residual Variance Results for Attitude Toward Learning to Write English*

	Eigenvalue	Percent
Total raw variance in observations	11.9	100.0
Raw variance explained by measures	5.9	49.7
Raw variance explained by persons	4.9	41.5
Raw Variance explained by items	1.0	8.2
Raw unexplained variance (total)	6.0	50.3
Unexplained variance in first contrast	1.7	14.1

on the participants, as their difficulty estimates range from -.90 to .75. Given the relative position of the participants to the items, the items were generally easy to endorse for many of the participants.

The empirical item hierarchy indicates that items ALWE5 and ALWE6, which concern a sense of achievement, are the easiest items to endorse. On the other hand, items ALWE4, ALWE2, and ALWE1 concern the sense enjoyment gained when actually writing. As such, these items are somewhat more difficult to endorse. Item ALWE3 was the most difficult item to endorse and was the only item to compare writing with another skill. Items that were easier to endorse concerned feeling a sense of

enjoyment in writing class, while more difficult to endorse items concerned more challenging aspects of writing.

The Rasch item reliability (item separation) estimate was .96 (4.65), which is excellent. The Rasch person reliability (person separation) estimate was .76 (1.77), which is fair. The mean person ability estimates of .03 (SD = 1.33) was almost equal to the mean item difficulty estimate (.00; SD = .54), which indicates the ALWE items were not difficult to endorse; thus, the participants had good level of Attitude Toward Learning to Write English.

Motivational Intensity to Write English

The category structure of the six original categories for Motivational Intensity to Write English was examined. The original 6-point scale was collapsed to a 5-point scale, as points 1 (*Strongly disagree*) and 2 (*Disagree*) did not separate sufficiently and they did not show a

80 CHAPTER 4 PRELIMINARY ANALYSES

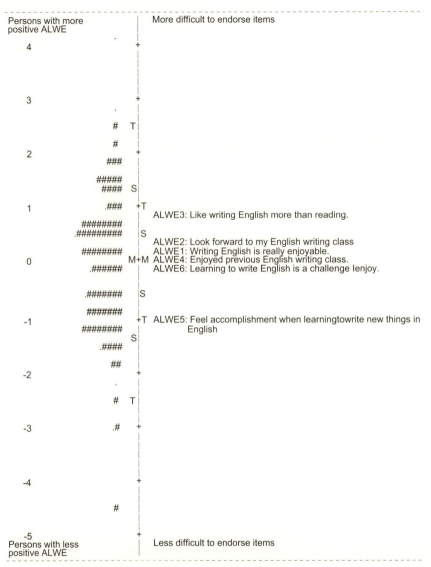

Figure 5. Wright map for Attitude Toward Learning to Write English. Each '#' is two persons and each "." Is one person. M = Mean; S = 1 SD; T = 2 SD.

Motivational Intensity to Write English   *81*

clear difference between the two. As shown in Table 18, the resulting 5-point scale met all the criteria for proper scale functioning.

The Rasch descriptive statistics for the six items designed to measure Motivational Intensity are shown in Table 19. The items displayed adequate fit to the Rasch model, as they all met the .60 to 1.40 criterion, except for item M12, which had an Infit MNSQ statistic of 1.45. Therefore, item M12 was deleted from the study. Point-measure correlations were also acceptable, as they were between .71 and .79.

The Rasch PCA of item residuals was run to check the degree of unidimensionality formed by the six items. As shown in Table 20, the Rasch model accounted for 64.4% of the variance, which exceeded the 50% criterion. The variance explained by the items (28.5%) was less than four times the variance explained by the first contrast (11.4%), but the eigenvalue of the first contrast was 1.9, which was well below the 3.0 criterion. This indicated that there was little unexplained variance to indicate the presence of a second factor in the data. Thus, it can be concluded that the data are fundamentally unidimensional.

Table 18. *Category Structure Statistics for Motivational Intensity (5-point scale)*

	Count (%)	Infit MNSQ	Outfit MNSQ	Andrich threshold	Category measure
1 Stronglydisagree	26 (3)	1.22	1.26	None	(-4.67)
2 Slightly disagree	100 (10)	1.08	1.20	-3.47	-2.54
3 Slightly agree	336 (33)	.91	.94	-1.58	-.09
4 Agree	327 (32)	.83	.83	1.38	2.54
5 Strongly agree	219(22)	1.10	1.11	3.67	4.84

Table 19. *Rasch Descriptive Statistics for the Motivational Intensity Items*

Item	Measure	SE	Infit MNSQ	Infit ZSTD	Outfit MNSQ	Outfit ZSTD	Pt-measure correlation
MI5	1.97	.13	1.01	.1	1.13	1.1	.78
MI6	-.07	.13	.96	-.3	.95	-.4	.79
MI3	-.82	.13	.80	-1.9	.84	-1.3	.76
MI1	-.96	.13	.91	-.8	.95	-.4	.75
MI4	-1.24	.14	.74	-2.6	.74	-2.2	.77

82   CHAPTER 4 PRELIMINARY ANALYSES

Table 20. *Rasch Standardized Residual Variance Results for Motivational Intensity*

	Eigenvalue	Percent
Total raw variance in observations	16.8	100.0
Raw variance explained by measures	10.8	64.4
Raw variance explained by persons	6.1	35.9
Raw Variance explained by items	4.8	28.5
Raw unexplained variance (total)	6.0	35.6
Unexplained variance in first contrast	1.9	11.4

The Wright map for the items measuring Motivational Intensity and the participants are shown in Figure 6. The items are well spread out and well centered on the participants, as their difficulty estimates range from -1.18 to 1.88. Given the relative position of the participants to the items, the items were generally easy to endorse for many of the participants.

The empirical item hierarchy indicates that items MI4, MI1, and MI3, which involve working hard in writing class, were the easiest items to endorse. Item MI6 might indicate humility about the possibility of improvement or an actual belief that the writing curriculum will not produce improvements. Finally, the two most difficult items to endorse, MI5 and MI2 indicate that the participants are not competing with their classmates when engaging in class writing activities. Items such as like MI5 and MI2 that concern competition with classmates were more difficult to endorse, while items that concerned self-improvement were generally easier to endorse.

The Rasch item reliability (item separation) estimate was .99 (8.54), which was excellent. The Rasch person reliability (person separation) estimate was .83 (2.24), which was good. The mean person ability estimate of 1.66 (SD = 2.11) was higher than mean item difficulty estimate (.00; SD = 1.17), which indicates that the items measuring Motivational Intensity were easy to endorse for many of the participants.

Instrumental Orientation for Writing in English

The category structure of the six original categories for Instrumental Orientation was examined. The original 6-point scale was collapsed to a 5-point scale, as points 1 (*Strongly disagree*) and 2 (*Disagree*) did not separate sufficiently in the initial analysis. Outfit mean-

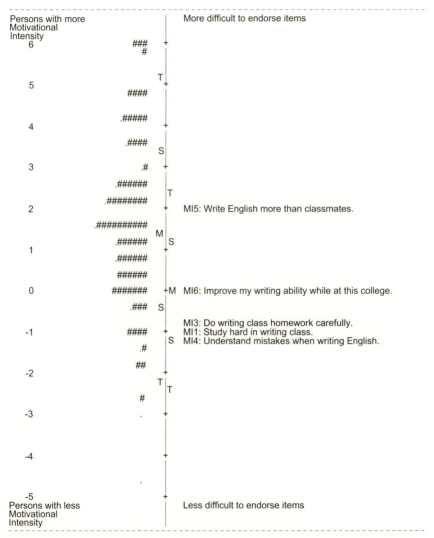

Figure 6. Wright map for Motivational Intensity to Write English. Each '#' is two persons and each "." Is one person. M = Mean; S = 1 SD; T = 2 SD.

84   CHAPTER 4 PRELIMINARY ANALYSES

squares should be less than 2.0 (Linacre, 1999). As shown in Table 21, the resulting 5-point scale met all the criteria for proper scale functioning.

The Rasch descriptive statistics for the four items designed to measure Instrumental Orientation are shown in Table 22. The items displayed adequate fit to the Rasch model, as they all met the .60 to 1.40 criterion, except for item IO5, which had an Infit MNSQ statistic of 1.44. Point-measure correlations were also acceptable as they were all between .66 and .88. Therefore, item IO5 was kept in this study. Items IO1 and IO6 were deleted from the study because they misfit in point-measure correlations.

The Rasch PCA of item residuals was run to check the degree of unidimensionality formed by the four items. As shown in Table 23, the Rasch model accounted for 68.2% of the variance, which exceeded the 50% criterion. The variance explained by the items (25.3%) was less than four times the variance explained by the first contrast (14.7%), but the eigenvalue of the first contrast was 1.8, which was well below the 3.0 criterion. This indicated that there was little unexplained variance to indicate the presence of a second factor in the data. Thus, it can be concluded that the data are fundamentally unidimensional.

Table 21. *Category Structure Statistics for Instrumental Orientation (5-point scale)*

	Count (%)	Infit MNSQ	Outfit MNSQ	Andrich threshold	Category measure
1 Disagree	35 (5)	.93	.95	None	(-4.72)
2 Slightly disagree	107 (16)	.93	.90	-3.53	-2.58
3 Slightly agree	209 (31)	.91	.89	-1.56	-.31
4 Agree	206 (31)	.92	1.21	.88	2.56
5 Strongly agree	115 (17)	1.28	1.22	4.21	5.33

Table 22. *Rasch Descriptive Statistics for the Instrumental Orientation Items*

Item	Measure	SE	Infit MNSQ	Infit ZSTD	Outfit MNSQ	Outfit ZSTD	Pt-measure correlation
IO4	1.32	.13	.85	-1.4	.83	-1.6	.87
IO3	1.02	.13	.72	-2.8	.72	-2.8	.88
IO2	-.69	.14	.97	-.3	1.01	.1	.79
IO5	-1.65	.14	1.44	3.4	1.61	3.9	.66

Table 23. *Rasch Standardized Residual Variance Results for Instrumental Orientation*

	Eigenvalue	Percent
Total raw variance in observations	12.6	100.0
Raw variance explained by measures	8.6	68.2
Raw variance explained by persons	5.4	42.9
Raw Variance explained by items	3.2	25.3
Raw unexplained variance (total)	4.0	31.8
Unexplained variance in first contrast	1.8	14.7

The Wright map for the items measuring Instrumental Orientation and the participants are shown in Figure 7. The items are well spread out and well centered on the participants, as their difficulty estimates range from -1.63 to 1.23. Given the relative position of the participants to the items, the items were generally easy to endorse for many of the participants.

The empirical item hierarchy indicates that item IO5 was the easiest item to endorse. This item concerns the positive relationship between writing well and being an educated person. Item IO2 was considerably more difficult to endorse; it suggests that improvements in English writing ability are not seen as having a strong relationship to getting a good job. Finally, getting a higher position in Japanese society and earning more money were not seen to be the outcomes of writing English more skillfully, and as such, they are the two most difficult items to endorse.

The Rasch item reliability (item separation) estimate was .99 (8.48), which was excellent. The Rasch person reliability (person separation) estimate was .83 (2.21), which was good. The mean person ability estimate of 1.08 (*SD* = 2.64) was higher than mean item difficulty estimate (.00; *SD* = 1.22), which indicates the items measuring Instrumental Orientation were generally not difficult to endorse for the participants.

L2 Writing Anxiety

The category structure of the six original categories for L2 Writing Anxiety was examined. The original 6-point scale was collapsed to a 5-point scale, as points 1 (*Strongly dis-*

86 CHAPTER 4 PRELIMINARY ANALYSES

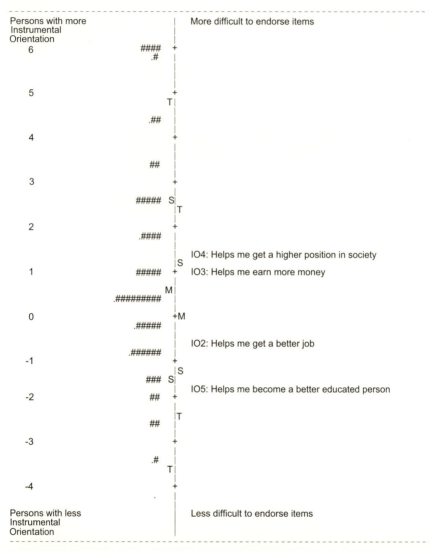

Figure 7. Wright map for Instrumental Orientation for Writing in English. Each '#' is three persons and each "." is one or two persons. M = Mean; S = 1 SD; T = 2 SD.

agree) and 2 (*Disagree*) did not separate sufficiently. Outfit mean-squares should be less than 2.0 (Linacre, 1999). Category characteristic curves for this item with ordered thresholds. The thresholds curves now operated correctly. As shown in Table 24, the resulting 5-point scale met the criteria for proper scale functioning.

The Rasch descriptive statistics for the six items designed to measure L2 Writing Anxiety are shown in Table 25. The items displayed adequate fit to the Rasch model, as they all met the .60 to 1.40 criterion. Point-measure correlations were also acceptable as they ranged between .71 and .83.

The Rasch PCA of item residuals was run to check the degree of unidimensionality formed by the six items. As shown in Table 26, the Rasch model accounted for 67.0% of the variance, which exceeded the 50% criterion. The variance explained by the items (17.3%) was less than four times the variance explained by the first contrast (12.2%), but the eigenvalue of the first contrast was 2.2, which was well below the 3.0 criterion. This in-

Table 24. *Category Structure Statistics for L2 Writing Anxiety (5-point scale)*

	Count (%)	Infit MNSQ	Outfit MNSQ	Andrich threshold	Category measure
1 Stronglydisagree	139 (14)	1.00	.99	None	(-3.58)
2 Slightly disagree	218 (22)	.92	.84	-2.34	-1.65
3 Slightly agree	254 (25)	.83	.78	-.78	-.05
4 Agree	243 (24)	.98	.96	.64	1.65
5 Strongly agree	154 (15)	1.36	1.28	2.48	3.68

Table 25. *Rasch Descriptive Statistics for the L2 Writing Anxiety Items*

Item	Measure	SE	Infit MNSQ	Infit ZSTD	Outfit MNSQ	Outfit ZSTD	Pt-measure correlation
ANX1	.92	.11	1.34	2.9	1.22	1.8	.76
ANX4	.64	.11	.95	-.4	.89	-.9	.80
ANX6	.50	.11	.89	-1.0	.85	-1.4	.83
ANX5	.39	.11	.78	-2.1	.76	-2.4	.83
ANX3	-.55	.11	1.04	.4	1.06	.6	.76
ANX2	-1.90	.12	1.06	.5	.96	-.3	.71

88 CHAPTER 4 PRELIMINARY ANALYSES

Table 26. *Rasch Standardized Residual Variance Results for L2 Writing Anxiety*

	Eigenvalue	Percent
Total raw variance in observations	18.2	100.0
Raw variance explained by measures	12.2	67.0
Raw variance explained by persons	8.9	49.2
Raw Variance explained by items	3.3	17.9
Raw unexplained variance (total)	6.0	33.0
Unexplained variance in first contrast	2.2	12.2

dicated that there was little unexplained variance to indicate the presence of a second factor in the data. Thus, it can be concluded that the data are fundamentally unidimensional.

The Wright map for the items measuring L2 Writing Anxiety and the participants are shown in Figure 8. The items are well spread out and well centered on the participants, as their difficulty estimates ranged from -1.83 to .81. Given the relative position of the participants to the items, the items were generally easy to endorse for many of the participants, which indicates that they generally felt anxious about writing.

The empirical item hierarchy indicated that items ANX2 and ANX3 were the easiest items to endorse. In both cases, they indicate anxiety about writing skills and one of the key skills underlying good writing, grammatical knowledge. Items ANX6, ANX4, ANX5, and ANX1 were grouped closely together.

Items ANX4 and ANX5 concern evaluation by others (i.e., classmates and teachers) when they write English. Items ANX6 and ANX1 concern a sense of anxiety when actually participating in class writing activities. A comparison of items ANX2 and ANX1 indicates that actually writing is less anxiety provoking than imaginary and fanciful writing. This is a reasonable outcome if anxiety is in part caused by fear of negative evaluation by peers and teachers (Park & Lee, 2005). The Rasch item reliability (item separation) estimate was .99 (8.42), which was excellent. The Rasch person reliability (person separation) estimate was .85 (2.40), which was good. The mean person ability estimate of .13 (SD = 1.89) was almost equal to mean item difficulty estimate (.00; SD = .96), which indicates the L2 Anxiety items were well targeted on this group of participants.

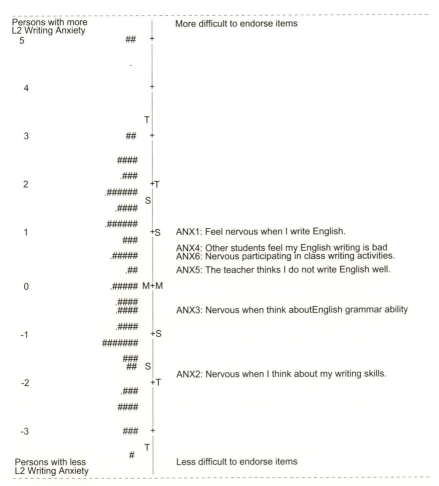

Figure 8. Wright map for L2 Writing Anxiety. Each '#' is two persons and each "." Is one person. M = Mean; S = 1 SD; T = 2 SD.

L2 Writing Self-Confidence

The category structure of the eight original categories for L2 Writing Self-Confidence was examined. As shown in Table 27, the 6-point scale met all the criteria for proper scale

90   CHAPTER 4 PRELIMINARY ANALYSES

Table 27. *Category Structure Statistics for L2 Writing Self-Confidence (6-point scale)*

	Count (%)	Infit MNSQ	Outfit MNSQ	Andrich threshold	Category measure
1 Strongly disagree	376 (28)	1.00	.99	None	(-5.12)
2 Disagree	388 (29)	.92	.83	-3.93	-2.96
3 Slightly disagree	360 (27)	.97	.97	-1.92	-.89
4 Slightly agree	174 (13)	.95	.96	.15	1.11
5 Agree	40 (3)	1.35	1.38	2.13	2.91
6 Strongly agree	6 (0)	1.37	1.45	3.56	(4.81)

functioning.

The Rasch descriptive statistics for the six items designed to measure L2 Writing Self-Confidence are shown in Table 28. The items displayed adequate fit to the Rasch model, as they all met the .60 to 1.40 criterion. Point-measure correlations were also acceptable and ranged between .70 and .83.

The Rasch PCA of item residuals was run to check the degree of unidimensionality formed by the eight items. As shown in Table 29, the Rasch model accounted for 66.1% of the variance, which exceeded the 50% criterion. The variance explained by the items (24.0%) was approximately four times the variance explained by the first contrast (7.3%), and the eigenvalue of the first contrast was 1.7, which was well below the 3.0 criterion.

Table 28. *Rasch Descriptive Statistics for the L2 Writing Self-Confidence Items*

Item	Measure	SE	Infit MNSQ	Infit ZSTD	Outfit MNSQ	Outfit ZSTD	Pt-measure correlation
SC5	1.70	.14	1.11	.9	.88	-.6	.70
SC3	1.00	.13	.70	-2.8	.64	-2.8	.79
SC1	.36	.12	1.12	1.0	1.13	1.1	.72
SC7	.10	.12	.96	-.3	.98	-.1	.78
SC8	.08	.12	1.26	2.1	1.25	2.0	.74
SC6	-.81	.12	.87	-1.1	.89	-1.0	.82
SC4	-1.06	.12	1.08	.8	1.07	.7	.83
SC2	-1.37	.11	.92	-.7	.93	-.6	.82

Table 29. *Rasch Standardized Residual Variance Results for L2 Writing Self-Confidence*

	Eigenvalue	Percent
Total raw variance in observations	23.6	100.0
Raw variance explained by measures	15.6	66.1
Raw variance explained by persons	9.9	42.0
Raw Variance explained by items	5.7	24.0
Raw unexplained variance (total)	8.0	33.9
Unexplained variance in first contrast	1.7	7.3

This indicated that there was little unexplained variance to indicate the presence of a second factor in the data. Thus, it can be concluded that the data are fundamentally unidimensional.

The Wright map for the items measuring L2 Writing Self-Confidence and the participants are shown in Figure 9. The items are well spread out and well centered on the participants, as their difficulty estimates range from -1.35 to 1.79.

Given the relative position of the participants to the items, the items were generally difficult to endorse for many of the participants. The empirical item hierarchy indicates that the easiest items to endorse, items SC2, SC4, and SC6, concern writing about common topics and short assignments (i.e., 1 page). Somewhat more difficult to endorse items, SC1, SC8 and SC7, concern writing for an on-line audience outside of the classroom in the form of e-mail or blogs. The most difficult to endorse items, SC5 and SC3, concern writing on an academic topic or writing longer texts (i.e., 5 pages) in English. These are unrealistic classroom tasks because the participants' proficiency is limited to the A1 to B1 CEFR levels.

The Rasch item reliability (item separation) estimate was .98 (7.62), which was excellent. The Rasch person reliability (person separation) estimate was .88 (2.69), which was good. The mean person ability estimate of -2.54 (*SD* = 2.19) is considerably lower than mean item difficulty estimate of .00 (*SD* = .98), which indicates that the Self-Confidence items were quite difficult to endorse for the majority of participants, partly because the self-effacing (*enryo*) nature of Japanese exists to some degree. Japanese in general are reluctant to admit to being good at something, even when they are actually very good at it

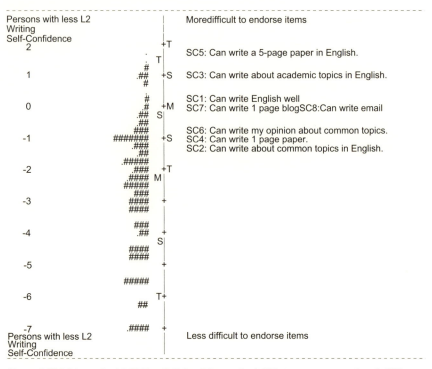

Figure 9. Wright map for L2 Writing Self-Confidence. Each '#' is two persons and each "." Is one person. M = Mean; S = 1 SD; T = 2 SD.

(Sato, 2010).

Willingness to Communicate in L2 Writing

The category structure of the six original categories for Willingness to Communicate in Writing was examined. As shown in Table 30, the 6-point scale met the criteria for proper scale functioning.

The Rasch descriptive statistics for the eight items designed to measure Willingness to Communicate in Writing are shown in Table 31. The items displayed adequate fit to the Rasch model, as they all met the .60 to 1.40 criterion. Point-measure correlations were also acceptable and ranged between .75 and .87.

Table 30. *Category Structure Statistics for Willingness to Communicate in Writing (6-point scale)*

	Count (%)	Infit MNSQ	Outfit MNSQ	Andrich threshold	Category measure
1 Strongly disagree	83 (6)	1.23	1.22	None	(-4.92)
2 Disagree	165 (12)	.96	.94	-3.67	-2.98
3 Slightly disagree	394 (29)	.86	.86	-2.20	-1.04
4 Slightly agree	366 (27)	.99	1.00	.12	.89
5 Agree	265 (20)	.88	.89	1.65	2.94
6 Strongly agree	71 (5)	1.33	1.24	4.11	(5.27)

Table 31. *Rasch Descriptive Statistics for the Willingness to Communicate in Writing Items*

Item	Measure	SE	Infit MNSQ	Infit ZSTD	Outfit MNSQ	Outfit ZSTD	Pt-measure correlation
WTC1	.87	.11	1.36	3.0	1.33	2.7	.81
WTC7	.33	.11	.96	-.3	.97	-.2	.81
WTC4	.25	.11	.95	-.5	.95	-.4	.81
WTC5	.13	.11	.82	-1.7	.80	-1.9	.83
WTC6	-.09	.11	1.34	2.9	1.34	2.9	.75
WTC3	-.17	.11	.81	-1.9	.79	-2.0	.85
WTC8	-.57	.11	.92	-.7	.96	-.4	.82
WTC2	-.75	.11	.72	-2.8	.71	-2.9	.87

The Rasch PCA of item residuals was run to check the degree of unidimensionality formed by the eight items. As shown in Table 32, the Rasch model accounted for 66.4% of the variance, which exceeded the 50% criterion. The variance explained by the items

Table 32. *Rasch Standardized Residual Variance Results for Willingness to Communicate in Writing*

	Eigenvalue	Percent
Total raw variance in observations	23.8	100.0
Raw variance explained by measures	15.8	66.4
Raw variance explained by persons	11.4	47.7
Raw Variance explained by items	4.5	18.7
Raw unexplained variance (total)	8.0	33.6
Unexplained variance in first contrast	2.2	9.4

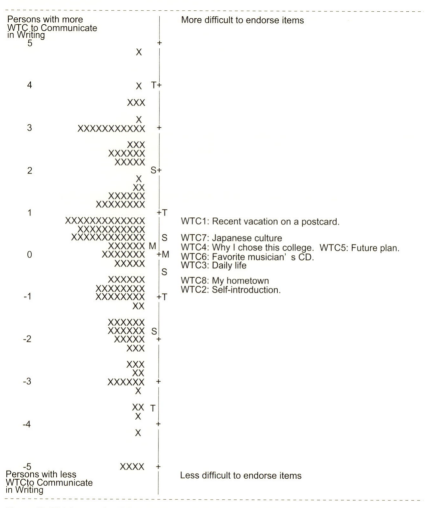

Figure 10. **Wright map for Willingness to Communicate in L2 Writing. Each '#' is 2 persons. M = Mean; S = 1 SD; T = 2 SD.**

(18.7%) was less than four times the variance explained by the first contrast (9.4%), but the eigenvalue of the first contrast was 2.2, which was well below the 3.0 criterion. This indicated that there was little unexplained variance to indicate the presence of a second factor in the data. Thus, it can be concluded that the data are fundamentally unidimensional.

The Wright map for the items measuring Willingness to Communicate and the participants are shown in Figure 10. The items are well spread out and well centered on the participants, as their difficulty estimates range from -.75 to .86. Given the relative position of the participants to the items, the items were generally easy to endorse for many of the participants. The empirical item hierarchy indicates that items WTC2, WTC8, and WTC3, which concern personal topics (i.e., self-introduction, hometown, and daily life) that are extremely familiar to the students, are the easiest to endorse. Topics that are somewhat more abstract and less central to the students' lives in terms of well-developed schemata, items WTC7, WTC6, WTC5, and WTC4, are somewhat more difficult to endorse. Item WTC1, writing on a postcard, was the most difficult item to endorse, possibly because this is the most public type of writing listed and the participants might not be familiar with writing postcards.

The Rasch item reliability (item separation) estimate was .94 (4.08), which was very good. The Rasch person reliability (person separation) estimate was .93 (3.52), which was also very good. The mean person ability estimate of .08 (*SD* = 2.19) was nearly equivalent to the mean item difficulty estimate of .00 (*SD* = .49), which indicates that the L2 WTC writing items were well targeted on the participants.

Self-Esteem

The category structure of the ten original categories for Self-Esteem was examined. As shown in Table 33, the resulting 6-point scale met the criteria for proper scale functioning.

Table 33. *Category Structure Statistics for Self-Esteem (6-point scale)*

	Count (%)	Infit MNSQ	Outfit MNSQ	Andrich threshold	Category measure
1 Strongly disagree	107 (8)	.94	.93	None	(-5.51)
2 Disagree	197 (15)	.92	.89	-4.28	-3.48
3 Slightly disagree	505 (38)	.94	.94	-2.63	-1.24
4 Slightly agree	382 (28)	1.08	1.09	.11	1.28
5 Agree	114 (8)	.98	.97	2.51	3.44
6 Strongly agree	39 (3)	1.20	1.22	4.29	(5.50)

96   CHAPTER 4 PRELIMINARY ANALYSES

The Rasch descriptive statistics for the six items designed to measure Self-Esteem are shown in Table 34. The items displayed adequate fit to the Rasch model, as they all met the .60 to 1.40 criterion, except for item SE2, which had an Infit MNSQ statistic of 1.41. This slight degree of misfit was not considered problematic enough to delete the item. Point-measure correlations were also acceptable and ranged between .73 and .85.

The Rasch PCA of item residuals was run to check the degree of unidimensionality formed by the ten items. As shown in Table 35, the Rasch model accounted for 66.6% of the variance, which exceeded the 50% criterion. The variance explained by the items (18.6%) was less than four times the variance explained by the first contrast (7.0%), but the eigenvalue of the first contrast was 1.7, which was well below the 3.0 criterion. This in-dicated that there was little unexplained variance to indicate the presence of a second fac-

Table 34. *Rasch Descriptive Statistics for the Self-Esteem Items*

Item	Measure	SE	Infit MNSQ	Infit ZSTD	Outfit MNSQ	Outfit ZSTD	Pt-measure correlation
SE5	1.00	.12	.83	-1.6	.81	-1.6	.83
SE6	1.00	.12	1.31	2.6	1.29	2.2	.77
SE8	.60	.12	.91	-.8	.92	-.7	.82
SE10	.25	.12	1.06	-.5	1.02	-.2	.81
SE3	-.22	.12	.75	-2.5	.75	-2.4	.84
SE1	-.56	.12	.76	-2.3	.75	-2.4	.85
SE4	-.57	.12	.89	-1.0	.86	-1.3	.83
SE2	-1.51	.12	1.41	3.3	1.47	3.7	.73

Table 35. *Rasch Standardized Residual Variance Results for Self-Esteem*

	Eigenvalue	Percent
Total raw variance in observations	24.0	100.0
Raw variance explained by measures	16.0	66.6
Raw variance explained by persons	11.5	48.0
Raw Variance explained by items	4.5	18.6
Raw unexplained variance (total)	8.0	33.4
Unexplained variance in first contrast	1.7	7.0

tor in the data. Thus, it can be concluded that the data are fundamentally unidimensional.

The Wright map for the items measuring Self-Esteem and the participants are shown in Figure 11. The items are well spread out and well centered on the participants, as their difficulty estimates range from -1.37 to .99. Given the relative position of the participants to the items, the items were generally easy to endorse for many of the participants. The empirical item hierarchy indicates that the participants do not consider themselves to be inferior to their peers, as shown by item SE2, the easiest item to endorse. Items SE1, SE4, and SE3 indicate that they have a positive sense of themselves, but they do not go so far as to consider themselves a success (item SE6) or to express respect for themselves (item SE5). It is possible that those two statements are too strong in the context of Japanese society

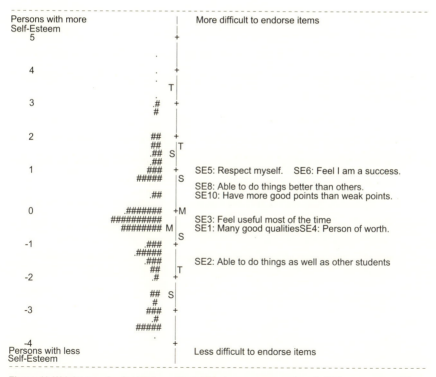

Figure 11. Wright map for Self-Esteem. Each '#' is two persons and each "." Is one person. M = Mean; S = 1 SD; T = 2 SD. The bottom of the Wright map has been truncated.

98   CHAPTER 4 PRELIMINARY ANALYSES

where self-praise is not traditionally seen in a positive light.

The Rasch item reliability (item separation) estimate was .98 (6.35), which was excellent. The Rasch person reliability (person separation) estimate was .91 (3.22), which was very good. The mean person ability estimate of -.64 (SD = 2.25) was lower than the mean item difficulty estimate (.00; SD = .82), which indicates the Self Esteem items were slightly difficult to endorse for a number of the participants.

Cognitive Competence

The category structure of the seven original categories for Cognitive Competence was examined. As shown in Table 36, the resulting 6-point scale met all the criteria for proper scale functioning set by Linacre (1999).

The Rasch descriptive statistics for the six items designed to measure Cognitive Competence are shown in Table 37. The items displayed adequate fit to the Rasch model, as they all met the .60 to 1.40 criterion. Point-measure correlations were also acceptable and ranged between .66 and .82.

The Rasch PCA of item residuals was run to check the degree of unidimensionality formed by the seven items. As shown in Table 38, the Rasch model accounted for 57.0 % of the variance, which exceeded the 50% criterion. The variance explained by the items (26.7%) was approximately four times the variance explained by the first contrast (10.4%), and the eigenvalue of the first contrast was 1.7, which was well below the 3.0 criterion. This indicated that there was little unexplained variance to indicate the presence of

Table 36. *Category Structure Statistics for Cognitive Competence (6-point scale)*

	Count (%)	Infit MNSQ	Outfit MNSQ	Andrich threshold	Category measure
1 Strongly disagree	93 (8)	1.09	1.13	None	(-4.11)
2 Disagree	170 (14)	.78	.76	-2.78	-2.43
3 Slightly disagree	363 (31)	.86	.85	-1.87	-.98
4 Slightly agree	386 (33)	.87	.89	-.26	.78
5 Agree	123 (10)	1.27	1.22	1.87	2.52
6 Strongly agree	41 (3)	1.36	1.35	3.05	(4.33)

Table 37. *Rasch Descriptive Statistics for the Cognitive Competence Items*

Item	Measure	SE	Infit MNSQ	Infit ZSTD	Outfit MNSQ	Outfit ZSTD	Pt-measure correlation
CC1	.74	.10	.69	-3.2	.68	-3.2	.79
CC3	.71	.10	.64	-3.8	.64	-3.7	.82
CC5	.46	.10	1.31	2.6	1.33	2.8	.66
CC6	.22	.10	1.36	3.0	1.35	2.9	.73
CC4	.00	.10	.72	-2.8	.71	-2.8	.76
CC7	-.78	.10	.81	-1.8	.80	-1.8	.69
CC2	-1.34	.10	1.40	3.3	1.38	3.1	.60

Table 38. *Rasch Standardized Residual Variance Results for Cognitive Competence*

	Eigenvalue	Percent
Total raw variance in observations	16.3	100.0
Raw variance explained by measures	9.3	57.0
Raw variance explained by persons	4.9	30.3
Raw Variance explained by items	4.4	26.7
Raw unexplained variance (total)	7.0	43.0
Unexplained variance in first contrast	1.7	10.4

a second factor in the data. Thus, it can be concluded that the data are fundamentally unidimensional.

The Wright map for the items measuring Cognitive Competence and the participants are shown in Figure 12. The items are well spread out and well centered on the participants, as their difficulty estimates range from -1.42 to .77. Given the relative position of the participants to the items, the items were generally easy to endorse for many of the participants. The empirical item hierarchy indicates that the participants have positive feelings about school (item CC2) and that they feel they are doing reasonably well at school (items CC7 and CC4). Doing the schoolwork easily (item CC5) and working quickly (item CC6) were more difficult to endorse, suggesting that they feel a sense of effort where their schoolwork is concerned.

The most difficult item to endorse, item CC1, indicates that they do not perceive them-

100   CHAPTER 4 PRELIMINARY ANALYSES

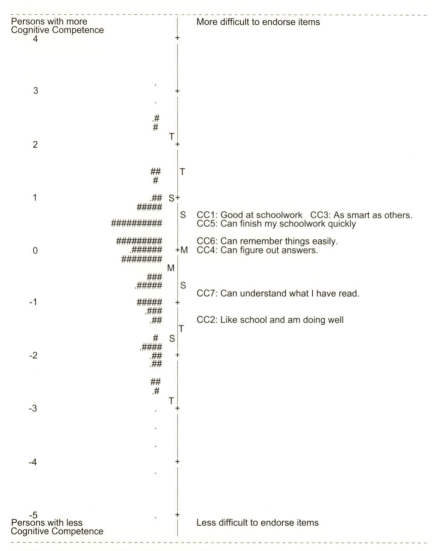

Figure 12. Wright map for Cognitive Competence. Each '#' is two persons and each ".". Is one person. M = Mean; S = 1 SD; T = 2 SD.

selves as being good at schoolwork. This could be in part because of the ranking system in Japanese education. They are aware that they are not attending an elite university and this might be reflected in their slightly negative evaluation of themselves as students.

The Rasch item reliability (item separation) estimate was .98 (6.62), which was excellent. The Rasch person reliability (person separation) estimate was .83 (2.21), which was good. The mean person ability estimate of -.34 (SD = 1.45) was lower than mean item difficulty estimate (.00; SD = .73), which indicates that items measuring Cognitive Competence were slightly difficult to endorse for many of the participants.

General Self-Worth

The category structure of the seven original categories for General Self-Worth was examined. The original 6-point scale was collapsed to a 5-point scale, as points 1 (*Strongly disagree*) and 2 (*Disagree*) did not separate sufficiently. Outfit mean-squares should be less than 2.0 (Linacre, 1999). Category characteristic curves for this item with ordered thresholds. The thresholds curves now operated correctly. They did not show a clear difference between the two. As shown in Table 39, the resulting 5-point scale met all the criteria for proper scale functioning set by Linacre (1999).

The Rasch descriptive statistics for the seven items designed to measure General Self-Worth are shown in Table 40. The items displayed adequate fit to the Rasch model, as they all met the .60 to 1.40 criterion. Point-measure correlations were also acceptable and ranged between .66 and .78.

Table 39. *Category Structure Statistics for General Self-Worth (5-point scale)*

	Count (%)	Infit MNSQ	Outfit MNSQ	Andrich threshold	Category measure
1 Stronglydisagree	189 (16)	1.09	1.06	None	(-3.69)
2 Slightly disagree	346 (29)	.92	.91	-2.48	-1.66
3 Slightly agree	349 (30)	.94	.90	-.69	.09
4 Agree	193 (16)	.92	.91	.93	1.67
5 Strongly agree	99 (8)	1.21	1.21	2.23	(3.50)

102   CHAPTER 4 PRELIMINARY ANALYSES

Table 40. *Rasch Descriptive Statistics for the General Self-Worth Items*

Item	Measure	SE	Infit MNSQ	Infit ZSTD	Outfit MNSQ	Outfit ZSTD	Pt-measure correlation
GSW1	1.16	.11	1.02	.2	.95	-.3	.72
GSW5	.45	.11	.94	-.5	.91	-.7	.71
GSW7	.24	.11	.77	-2.2	.79	-2.0	.78
GSW6	.21	.11	.99	.0	1.02	.2	.73
GSW4	-.16	.10	.80	-2.0	.83	-1.6	.76
GSW3	-.19	.10	1.12	1.2	1.11	1.0	.76
GSW2	-1.72	.11	1.36	3.1	1.26	2.1	.66

The Rasch PCA of item residuals was run to check the degree of unidimensionality formed by the seven items. As shown in Table 41, the Rasch model accounted for 60.3% of the variance, which exceeded the 50% criterion. The variance explained by the items (27.7%) was less than four times the variance explained by the first contrast (10.7%), but the eigenvalue of the first contrast was 1.9, which was well below the 3.0 criterion. This indicated that there was little unexplained variance to indicate the presence of a second factor in the data. Thus, it can be concluded that the data are fundamentally unidimensional.

The Wright map for the items measuring General Self-Worth and the participants are shown in Figure 13. The items are well spread out and well centered on the participants, as their difficulty estimates range from -1.70 to 1.06. Given the relative position of the participants to the items, the items were generally easy to endorse for many of the participants. The empirical item hierarchy indicates that item GSW2, the easiest item to endorse,

Table 41. *Rasch Standardized Residual Variance Results for General Self-Worth*

	Eigenvalue	Percent
Total raw variance in observations	17.6	100.0
Raw variance explained by measures	10.6	60.3
Raw variance explained by persons	5.7	32.6
Raw Variance explained by items	4.9	27.7
Raw unexplained variance (total)	7.0	39.7
Unexplained variance in first contrast	1.9	10.7

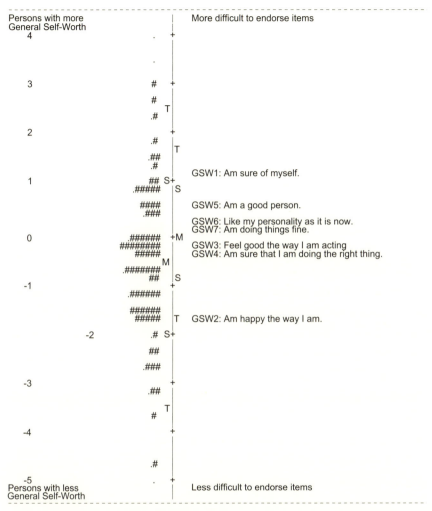

Figure 13. Wright map for General Self-Worth. Each '#' is two persons and each "." is one person. M = Mean; S = 1 SD; T = 2 SD.

shows that they are satisfied with the status quo, or present condition. More difficult to endorse items, such as items GSW3 and GSW4, show that they are less confident about their present behaviors and actions. These items are somewhat more concrete than item GSW2. Items GSW6 and GSW5, the next most difficult items to endorse, are strong posi-

104   CHAPTER 4 PRELIMINARY ANALYSES

tive statements about one's personality that would likely be difficult for most people, and particularly persons in late adolescence, to endorse. The item hierarchy shows that while the participants were generally happy with who they are, they did not have strong confidence in themselves.

The Rasch item reliability (item separation) estimate was .98 (7.59), which was excellent. The Rasch person reliability (person separation) estimate was .84 (2.30), which was good. The mean person ability estimate of -49 (SD = 1.62) was lower that mean item difficulty estimate (.00; SD = .82), which indicates the items measuring General Self-Worth were slightly difficult to endorse for the participants.

EIKEN Can-Do Questionnaires (April, July, and December)

The category structure of the EIKEN Can-Do Questionnaires was examined. As shown in Table 42, the 4-point scale met the criteria for proper scale functioning. The data here are a combination of all three Eiken Can-Do Questionnaires. Item EIKEN 24, *Can write dates and days of the week*, was deleted because the infit MNSQ statistic was 1.63 and the outfit MNSQ statistic was 2.62. I Item EIKEN 24 was inappropriate for the university participants.

The Rasch descriptive statistics are shown in Table 43. The items displayed adequate fit to the Rasch model as they all met the .60 to 1.40 criterion. Point-measure correlations were all acceptable and ranged between .66 and .84.

The Wright map for the items on the EIKEN Can-Do Questionnaires and the participants are shown in Figure 14. The items are well spread out and well centered on the par-

Table 42. *Category Structure Statistics for the EIKEN Can-Do Questionnaires*

	Count (%)	Infit MNSQ	Outfit MNSQ	Andrich threshold	Category measure
1 Cannotdo at all	493 (4)	1.20	1.17	None	(-5.34)
2 Can do slightly	3344 (29)	1.08	1.16	-4.23	-1.89
3 Can do fairly well	4146 (36)	.92	.96	.51	2.12
4 Can do very well	3681 (32)	.89	.90	3.72	4.85

EIKEN Can-Do Questionnaires(April, July, and December)   105

Table 43. *Rasch Descriptive Statistics for the EIKEN Can-Do Questionnaires*

Item	Measure	SE	Infit MNSQ	Infit ZSTD	Outfit MNSQ	Outfit ZSTD	Pt-measure correlation
EIKEN 1	3.18	.10	1.04	.7	1.04	.6	.72
EIKEN 6	2.97	.10	1.27	3.9	1.27	3.1	.73
EIKEN 2	2.65	.10	.92	-1.3	.89	-1.4	.76
EIKEN 5	2.63	.09	1.12	1.8	1.15	1.9	.72
EIKEN 3	2.42	.09	.93	-.1.0	.96	-.4	.75
EIKEN 4	2.26	.09	1.01	.2	1.03	.4	.75
EIKEN 11	1.26	.09	1.26	3.7	1.33	4.2	.73
EIKEN 8	.85	.09	.89	-1.7	.90	-1.4	.80
EIKEN 10	.81	.09	.81	-3.2	.80	-2.9	.84
EIKEN 7	.78	.09	.76	-4.1	.77	-3.5	.82
EIKEN 9	.38	.09	.75	-4.3	.71	-4.2	.82
EIKEN 12	-.22	.09	1.24	3.6	1.17	1.9	.75
EIKEN 18	-.67	.09	1.14	2.1	1.05	.5	.77
EIKEN 15	-.91	.09	.77	-3.9	.78	-2.2	.81
EIKEN 16	-1.11	.10	.97	-.5	.93	-.6	.78
EIKEN 13	-1.20	.10	.66	-6.0	.63	-3.5	.82
EIKEN 17	-1.27	.10	1.18	2.6	1.17	1.3	.72
EIKEN 19	-1.57	.10	1.05	.8	1.17	1.3	.75
EIKEN 14	-1.95	.10	.63	-6.4	.52	-3.7	.81
EIKEN 23	-2.46	.11	1.42	5.2	1.44	2.2	.66
EIKEN 20	-2.80	.11	.79	-3.1	.61	-2.2	.76
EIKEN 21	-3.00	.11	1.08	1.1	.95	-.1	.69
EIKEN 22	-3.07	.11	1.14	1.7	1.15	.7	.67

ticipants, as their difficulty estimate ranged from -2.96 to 3.23. Given the relative position of the participants to the items, the items were generally divided into four EIKEN levels, ranging from EIKEN fourth level to EIKEN second level. The empirical item hierarchy indicates that items EIKEN 20, 21, 22, 23, which measure fourth level objectives, are easiest to endorse. Items EIKEN 13, 14, 15, 16, 17, 18, 19, which measure third level objectives, are somewhat more difficult to endorse. Finally, items EIKEN 1, 2, 3, 4, 5, 6, which concern the second level objectives, were the most difficult items to endorse. The Rasch

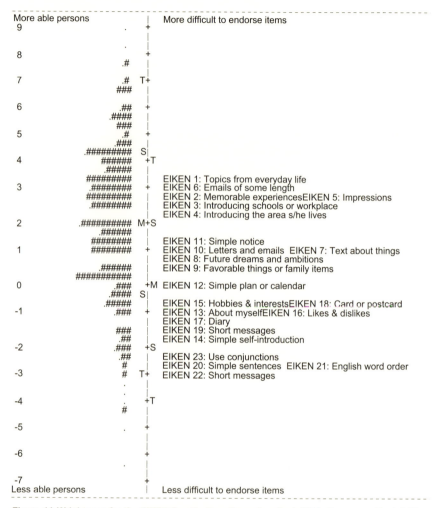

Figure 14. Wright map for the EIKEN Can-Do Questionnaires. Each "#" is 3 persons. Each "." is 1 to 2 persons. M = Mean; S = 1 SD; T = 2 SD.

item reliability (item separation) estimate was 1.00 (19.72), which was excellent. The Rasch person reliability (person separation) estimate was .96 (4.81), which was also excellent. The Rasch mean person ability estimate was 2.03 (SD = 2.48), which also indicated the mean item difficulty estimate, because person ability and item difficulty are conjointly estimated and placed on a single numerical scale.

The Rasch PCA of item residuals was run to check the dimensionality formed by the 23 items; however, the results were not satisfactory, because the variance in first contrast was over the 3.0 criterion. Items 5,10, 13, 22, 23, and 24 were removed because they were either redundant or misfitting. For example, item 22 *short messages* and item 23 *use conjunctions* were redundant because these items were very easy for many participants. The results improved considerably.

As shown in Table 44, the Rasch model accounted for 71.0 % of the variance, which exceeded the 50% criterion. The variance explained by the items (33.4%) was approximately six times the variance explained by the first contrast (5.6%), but the eigenvalue of the first contrast was 3.5, which slightly exceeded the 3.0 criterion.

The items with positive and negative residual loadings were inspected (see Table 45). As EIKEN 5, 10, 13, 22, 23, and 24 had been removed from the study, the residual loading showed good statistical fit.

In this chapter, I described the validity and reliability of the ten affective orientation variables questionnaires and the EIKEN Can-Do Questionnaires, using the Rasch analysis. In the next chapter, the results for three research questions are presented.

Table 44. *Rasch Standardized Residual Variance Results for the EIKEN Can-Do Questionnaires*

	Eigenvalue	Percent
Total raw variance in observations	62.1	100.0
Raw variance explained by measures	44.1	71.0
Raw variance explained by persons	23.4	37.6
Raw Variance explained by items	20.7	33.4
Raw unexplained variance (total)	18.0	29.0
Unexplained variance in first contrast	3.5	5.6

108   CHAPTER 4 PRELIMINARY ANALYSES

Table 45. *Winsteps Output for Residual Loadings for Each Eiken Item*

Item	Residual loading	Measure	Infit MNSQ	Outfit MNSQ
EIKEN 1	.52	3.05	1.00	.99
EIKEN 2	.62	2.51	.90	.87
EIKEN 3	.60	2.28	.91	.92
EIKEN 4	.50	2.11	1.00	1.02
EIKEN 6	.33	2.84	1.30	1.28
EIKEN 7	.42	.60	.75	.75
EIKEN 8	.32	.67	.90	.91
EIKEN 9	.25	.20	.76	.72
EIKEN 11	.09	1.10	1.26	1.30
EIKEN 12	.03	-.41	1.23	1.17
EIKEN 14	-.23	-2.17	.64	.53
EIKEN 15	-.38	-1.12	.79	.82
EIKEN 16	-.45	-1.32	.98	.93
EIKEN 17	-.53	-1.48	1.19	1.19
EIKEN 18	-.54	-.87	1.15	1.07
EIKEN 19	-.52	-1.75	1.05	1.18
EIKEN 20	-.58	-3.03	.85	.64
EIKEN 21	-.43	-3.22	1.18	1.13

CHAPTER 5

RESULTS

In this chapter, I present the results for research questions 1, 2, and 3, which are answered using quantitative analyses.

Research Question 1: Writing Performance and Affective Orientation Variables

Research Question 1 asked about the relationship between teacher ratings of the students' writing performances, as measured by six essay writing assignments, the students' self-assessed writing ability using the Eiken Can-Do Questionnaires, and ten affective orientation variables: Desire to Write English, Attitude Toward Learning to Write English, Motivational Intensity (Intrinsic Motivation), Instrumental Orientation for Writing in English (Extrinsic Motivation), L2 Writing Anxiety, L2 Writing Self-Confidence, Willingness to Communicate in L2 Writing, Self-Esteem, Cognitive Competence, and General Self-Worth. The relationships among the above variables were investigated using structural equation modeling. Two models were tested to answer Research Question 1. In the first model, Complete Structural Model A, the outcome variable was the Eiken Can-Do Questionnaire results, and in the second model, Complete Structural Model B, the outcome variable was the estimated writing ability of the participants based on their performance on six essays.

Research Question 1 was answered in four stages. In the first stage, Measurement Model A, which consists of six variables, was tested. Desire to Write English, Attitude Toward Learning to Write English, and Motivational Intensity were first-order latent variables that defined Intrinsic Motivation. Intrinsic Motivation and Instrumental Orientation for Writing in English (Extrinsic Motivation), predicted the second-order latent variable of Moti-

110   CHAPTER 5 RESULTS

vation. In the second stage, Measurement Model B, which consists of three variables Self-Esteem, General Self-Worth, and Self-Image, was tested. This model was tested because three variables—Self-Esteem, General Self-Worth, and Self-Image—contained similar elements in each item. Measurement Models A and B are shown together in Figure 3 in Chapter 3.

In the third stage, Measurement Model C was tested. Measurement Model C included both Measurement Model A and Measurement Model B and the five affective orientation variables, Cognitive Competence, Motivation, L2 Writing Anxiety, L2 Writing Self-Confidence, and Willingness to Communicate in L2 Writing. Lastly, in the fourth stage, the Structural Model, Writing Outcome was added and the entire model was tested. The measurement models tested are detailed in Table 46.

Table 47 shows the Pearson correlation coefficients among the Affective Orientation Variables, the Eiken Can-Do Questionnaire, and the Writing Outcome. These correlational analyses show how each affective variable correlate in this study, for example, Self Esteem and Cognitive Comptence correlate at .668, which are relatively high.

Table 46. *Measurement Models Tested*

Model	Variables
A. Motivation	Desire to Write English
	Attitude Toward Learning to Write English
	Motivational Intensity
	Intrinsic Motivation
	Instrumental Orientation for Writing in English
B. Self	Self-Image
	Self-Esteem
	General Self-Worth
C. Affective Orientations	L2 WTC Writing
	L2 Self-Confidence
	L2 Writing Anxiety
	Motivational Intensity
	Instrumental Orientation for Writing in English
	Cognitive Competence
	Eiken Can-Do Questionnaire

Table 47. *Pearson Correlations among Affective Orientation Variables, Eiken Can-Do and Writing* Outcome (*N* = 164)

Subscale	1	2	3	4	5	6	7	8	9	10	11	12	13	14	15
1. Anxiety	—														
2. CC	-.253	—													
3. GSW	-.085	.475	—												
4. SC	-.333	.436	.115	—											
5. WTC	-.073	.220	.049	.359	—										
6. ALWE	.052	.198	.186	.201	.284	—									
7. DWE	.087	.306	.249	.310	.280	.608	—								
8. IO	.263	.144	.079	-.042	.068	.230	.383	—							
9. MI	.191	.210	.257	.175	.282	.736	.750	.356	—						
10. SE	-.209	.668	.741	.303	.126	.146	.285	.104	.212	—					
11. Writing	.064	.309	-.061	.311	.208	-.312	.305	-.128	.245	.168	—				
12. Eiken April	-.307	.412	.120	.594	.327	.232	.319	.125	.235	.309	-.353	—			
13. Eiken July	-.162	.351	.141	.401	.324	.297	.388	.167	.351	.252	-.286	.643	—		
14. Eiken Dec	-.265	.386	.096	.515	.303	.256	.365	.175	.238	.233	-.417	.578	.651	—	
15. Difference	.479	.574	.707	.171	.622	.853	.678	.567	.926	.248	.527	.000	.805	.000	—

Note. All coefficients are significant at p < .01

CC=Cognitive Competence, GSW=General Self-Worth, SC=Self-Confidence, WTC=Willingness to Communicate in L2 Writing, ALWE=Attitude Toward Learning to Write English, DWE=Desire to Write English, IO=Instrumental Orientation, MI=Motivational Intensity, SE=Self Esteem, Writing=Writing Outcome, Eiken April=Eiken Can-Do Questionnaire April, Eiken July=Eiken Can-Do Questionnanire July, Eiken Dec=Eiken Can-Do Questionnaire December

Research Question 2: The Relationship between Each Variable in Structural Equation Models

In the following sections, I present the results of the structural equation models. Research Question 2 asked the relationship between each variable in Structural Equation Models. The four measurement models were evaluated using EQS, Build 6.0 (Bentler, 2007). Kline (2005) suggested that a sample size in excess of 200 is advisable and in the current study, the original sample size of 204 slightly exceeded that number; however, the sample size decreased to 168 participants because 36 questionnaires were incomplete: be-

112   CHAPTER 5 RESULTS

cause those participants were absent from the classes or they did not submit the question-naire.

The Measurement Models

An important first step in the analysis of full latent variable models is to test the validity of the measurement models (Byrne, 2006). Four measurement models were tested, based on the hypothesized model presented in Chapter 3 (Figure 3).

The hypothesized model was based on Gardner's (1985) model, MacIntyre's (1994) WTC model (Figure 1), and Yashima's (2002) model (Figure 2). Measurement Models A and B were based on Gardner's model, and Measurement Model C was based on MacIntyre's WTC model and Yashima's model.

Measurement Model A: Motivation

Measurement Model A consisted of Desire to Write English, Attitude Toward Learning to Write English, Motivational Intensity, Instrumental Orientation, Intrinsic Motivation and Motivation (Figure 15).

The items measuring Desire to Write English, Attitude Toward Learning to Write English, Motivational Intensity, Intrinsic Motivation, Instrumental Orientation, and Motivation were examined to ensure that the residuals were small and symmetrically distributed around the mean. The residuals were not sufficiently symmetric around the zero midpoint with 79.84% falling in the ±0.1 range. This result indicated that the model had a degree of misfit given the 90% criterion proposed by Byrne (2006, p. 93). Four cases were deleted because they increased kurtosis to 9.275; thus the N-size for this analysis was 164. Multivariate kurtosis was 6.491 (Mardia's coefficient = 32.941), which exceeded the < 5.0 criterion. Measurement Model A fit the data poorly. The chi-square value of 412.057 (df = 202) was significant, and the chi- squared / df ratio was 2.039, which is close to the 2.0 criterion proposed by Byrne (2006) and Tabachnick and Fidell (2004, p. 698). Both CFI (.888) and IFI (.890) indicated poor model fit. SRMR failed to meet the < .08 criterion at .083, and the RMSEA statistic was inadequate at .080 (90% CI = .069, .091); however,

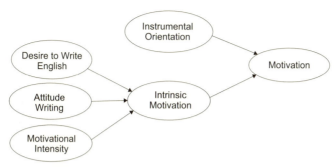

Figure 15. **Measurement Model A: Motivation. Attitude Writing = Attitude Toward Learning to Write English.**

the reliability coefficient was relatively good at .931. This model also displayed a linear dependency problem. To resolve this problem, item parceling was used and the modified model was run again. Item parceling was adopted for three reasons: (a) the sample sizes are relatively small, (b) each variable is unidimensional, and (c) individual item scores are statistically less reliable than aggregated scores (Little et al., 2002).

Measurement Model A': Motivation with Item Parceling

Three variables, Desire to Write English, Attitude Toward to Learning to Write English, and Motivational Intensity, were selected for parceling. Little et al. (1999) maintained that three indicators per construct is an optimal number and parceling techniques can reduce the number of indicators to this optimum number while reducing the sample variability to a level at which the construct representation will likely be accurate (e.g., Kishton & Widaman, 1994; Marsh, Hau, Balla, & Grayson, 1998).

When the items were parceled, multicollinearity and singularity problems appeared: Multicollinearity and singularity occur when variables in a correlation matrix are too highly correlated (Tabachnick & Fidell, 2001, p. 82). With multicollinearity, correlations are in excess of .90. In this study, when the correlations between each variable and items were checked, a relatively high correlation (.87) was found between L2 Writing Anxiety item 4, *I feel nervous that other students will feel that my English writing ability is bad*, and L2 Writing Anxiety item 5, *I feel nervous that the teacher will think that I do not write English well.*

114 CHAPTER 5 RESULTS

In addition, L2 Writing Self-Confidence item 7, *I can write a 1-page blog every week about my daily activities in English*, and L2 Writing Self-Confidence item 8, *I can write an email message in English to a native speaker of English*, were highly correlated at .93. These correlation coefficients indicated that the variables were redundant; therefore, L2 Writing Anxiety item 4 and L2 Writing Self-Confidence item 7 were removed from the analysis. L2 Writing Anxiety item 5 was retained and L2 Writing Anxiety item 4 was deleted because the former assessed the teachers' perception, which is more important when considering the construct being measured. L2 Writing Self-Confidence item 8 was retained and L2 Writing Self-Confidence item 7 was deleted because the former contained a higher frequency of occurrence, which implied that L2 Writing Self-Confidence item 8 was more established in the classroom, because writing an email to native speakers is more common than writing a 1-page blog every week.

In this section, the results for the revised model A prime (denoted A') are reported. Measurement Model A' consisted of Desire to Write English items, Attitude Toward Learning to Write English items, Motivational Intensity items, Intrinsic Motivation items, and Instrumental Orientation for Writing in English items (Figure 16). First, Desire to Write English items 1-6 were parceled into three sets: The first set was made up of items DWE 1 and DWE 3, the second set was made up of items DWE 2 and DWE 4, and the third set was made up of items DWE 5 and DWE 6. Attitude Toward Learning to Write English, Motivational Intensity, and Instrumental Orientation, all of which had six items, were similarly parceled. Cases 64 and 114 made the kurtosis higher at 15.8941, so they were deleted from the analysis, leaving an *N*-size of 166. As a result of the deletions, the multivariate kurtosis was 3.810, which met the 5.0 criterion. The residuals were nearly symmetric around the zero midpoint with 94.45% falling in the ±0.1 range. This result indicated that the model was well specified based on the 90% criterion (Byrne, 2006, p. 174).

Model fit was relatively good. The Chi-Square ratio of 2.133 almost met the 2.00 criterion (Byrne, 2006). Although CFI (.974) and IFI (.974) indicated good model fit and SRMR was below the .08 criterion at .048, RMSEA was inadequate at .083; (90% CI = .046, .119); however, the reliability coefficient was relatively good at .921.

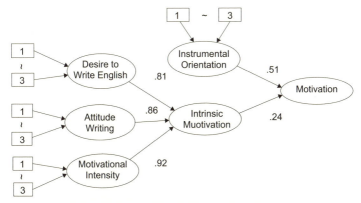

Figure 16. **Factor Loadings for Items in Measurement Model A': Motivation with Item Parceling. Attitude Writing = Attitude Toward Learning to Write English. The four factors are measured by three item parcels each; only the first and last item parcels are shown.**

As shown in Table 49, Model A' was superior to Model A in terms of the reliability coefficient (rho), multivariate kurtosis, the chi-square ratio, fit to the data, and the distribution of the residuals. However, Measurement Model A' encountered a linear dependency problem; no clear reason for the problem could be identified. The case-item ratio was around 13.6, while the case-parameter ratio was approximately 6.5; therefore, the *N*-size was likely too small to run this model. To address the problem, the three intrinsic motivation subscales, Desire to Learn English, Attitude Toward Learning to Write English, and Motivational Intensity, were collapsed into a single scale, which was labeled Intrinsic Motivation, with a total of eight parceled items. Item ALWE 3, *I like writing English more than reading English*, was deleted because it was a redundant with other ALWE items and because it made a comparison between writing and reading skills. Furthermore, item ALWE3 misfit the Rasch model. Because this item was a potential contributor to the linear problems in the model, it was deleted. With these changes in place, the model ran without the linear dependency problem and exhibited adequate fit statistics (Table 49).

The process used for collapsing the three intrinsic motivation subscales was as follows: The Intrinsic Motivation subscale correlated with Attitude at $r = .176$, The Internal Motivation subscales (Desire, Attitude, and Intensity) correlated moderately at .388 (Desire is correlated with Attitude), .429 (Desire is correlated with Intensity), and .459 (Attitude is correlated with Intensity) (Table 48); therefore, it was decided to treat the three extrinsic motivation subscales as subcomponents of the Motivational Intensity subscale instead of as three distinct subscales.

Four cases, 64, 114, 118, and 124, increased the multivariate kurtosis to 8.151, which exceeded the < 5.0 criterion. All four cases were deleted, leaving the N-size at 162. After deleting the four cases, Multivariate kurtosis was still high at 6.833. The Chi-Square ratio of 1.771 met the 2.0 criterion (Byrne, 2006). CFI (.924) and IFI (.925) indicated good fit, and RMSEA for this model was .069, which was below the .08 criterion, and the 90% confidence interval ranged from .056 to .081, which was nearly within the desired range of .050-.080. The reliability coefficient was good at .930. Revised Measurement Model A '

Table 48. *Inter-Item Correlations for Motivation Subscales*

Measure	1	2	3	4
1. Desire to Write English	—			
2. Attitude toward Learning to Write English	.388	—		
3. Motivational Intensity	.429	.459	—	
4. Intrinsic Motivation	.247	.176	.263	—

Note. All coefficients are significant at $p < .01$.

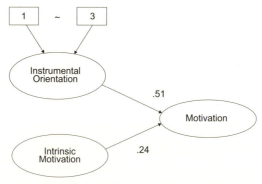

Figure 17. Revised Measurement Model A': Motivation with Item Parceling. Instrumental Orientation was measured with three item parcels; only the first and last item parcels are shown.

The Measurement Models   *117*

Table 49. *Summary of Fit Indices for Model A and Model A'*

	Model A	Model A'
Reliability coefficient (rho)	.931	.921
Multivariate kurtosis		
Mardia's coefficient	32.941	7.481
Normalized estimate	6.491	3.810
Residuals		
Average absolute standardized residuals	.059	.027
Average off-diagonal absolute standardized residuals	.064	.034
Model χ^2		
Model estimation method	ML	ML
Independence model χ^2 (df = 231)	2114.516	809.876
χ^2(df = 202, 18)	412.057	38.396
Probability value for the χ^2 statistic	< .001	<. 001
χ^2/df ratio	2.039	2.133
Fit Indices		
Comparative fit index (CFI)	.888	.974
Incremental fit index (IFI)	.890	.974
Standardized root mean square residual (SRMR)	.083	.048
Root mean square error of approximation (RMSEA)	.080	.083
RMSEA 90% confidence interval	[.069, .091]	[.046,.119]

Note. ML = maximum likelihood.

consisted of Instrumental Orientation, Intrinsic Motivation and Motivation (Figure 17). This model was created by combining three subscales (Desire to Write English, Attitude Toward Learning to Write English and Motivational Intensity) into one (Intrinsic Motivation).

Measurement Model B: Self Variables

Second, Measurement Model B, which included items measuring Self-Esteem, General Self-Worth, and the latent variable, Self-Image, was tested (Figure 18).

Case 157 substantially increased kurtosis at 10.275, so that person was deleted from this analysis. The kurtosis after deleting this participant was 5.425, which was slightly higher than the < 5.0 criterion. The resulting *N*-size for this analysis was 161. The residuals were

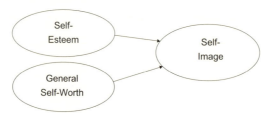

Figure 18. **Measurement Model B: Self Variables.**

almost symmetric around the zero midpoint with 95.43% falling in the ±0.1 range. This result indicated that the model was reasonably well specified (Byrne, 2006, p. 93).

This model fit the data relatively well. Multivariate kurtosis was 8.025, which did not exceed the < 5.0 criterion. One reason why the kurtosis was still high is because the data include participants who increased the kurtosis; however, the Chi-Square/*df* ratio (2.209) was close to the 2.0 criterion (Byrne, 2006). Although CFI (.925) and IFI (.926) indicated good fit, and SRMR was below the .08 criterion at .051, RMSEA for this model was slightly high at .085, and the RMSEA 90% Confidence Interval ranged from .071 to .099, which is above the desired range of .050-.080. The reliability coefficient was reasonably good at .945. Model B was inadequate for these reasons, which implies the necessity of item parceling.

In the next section, the results for revised model B prime (denoted B') with item parceling are reported.

Measurement Model B': Self Variables with Item Parceling

In this section, the results for the revised model B prime (denoted B') are reported. Items measuring Self-Esteem, General Self-Worth, and Self Image were examined (Figure 19). Self-Esteem items 1-10 were parceled into four groups: items SE 1, SE 2, which misfit the Rasch model, and SE 3 were PSE 1, which was named Parceled Self Esteem 1; items SE 4, SE 5, and SE 6 were PSE2; items SE 7 and SE 8 were PSE3; and items SE 9 and SE 10 were PSE4. The items measuring General Self-Worth were parceled into two groups: items GSW 1, GSW 2, GSW 3, and GSW 4 were PGSW 1; and items GSW 5, GSW 6, and GSW 7 were PGSW 2. Cases 43 and 124 were deleted because they increased the kur-

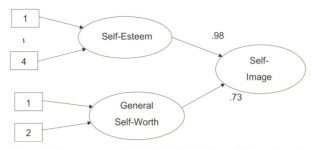

Figure 19. **Measurement Model B': Self Variables with Item Parceling. Self-Esteem consists of four item parcels; only the first and last items are shown.**

tosis to 6.281. After deleting the two cases, the kurtosis was 5.763 and the *N*-size was 159. The residuals were almost symmetric around the zero midpoint with 100.00% falling in the ±1 range, which indicated that the model was very well specified (Byrne, 2006, p. 174).

This model fit the data relatively well. Multivariate kurtosis was 2.773, which is relatively good according to Ullman (2001) and Schumacker and Lomax's (2004) 2.0 criterion. The Chi-Square / df ratio of 1.781 met the 2.0 criterion (Byrne, 2006). CFI (.992) and IFI (.992) indicated very good fit. SRMR was below the .08 criterion at .019 and RMSEA for this model was acceptable at .069, and the RMSEA 90% Confidence Interval ranged from .000 to .125. The reliability coefficient was good at .941.

As shown in Table 50, although the reliability coefficients (rho) are almost the same for the two models, the kurtosis was smaller in Model B' compared to that of Model B. The chi-square statistic and the CFI, IFI, SRMR, and RMSEA fit statistics improved in Model B' as a result of item parceling.

As Table 50 shows, Model B' displayed better fit indices than Model B. Therefore, in the next section, as I could assume that item parceling was necessary, Measurement Model C was not tested; instead, I proceeded directly to Measurement Model C': Affective Orientations with item parceling.

120 CHAPTER 5 RESULTS

Table 50. *Summary of Fit Indices for Model B and Model B'*

	Model B	Model B'
Reliability coefficient (rho)	.945	.941
Multivariate kurtosis		
Mardia's coefficient	31.566	4.217
Normalized estimate	8.025	2.773
Residuals		
Average absolute standardized residuals	.037	.013
Average off-diagonal absolute standardized residuals	.042	.018
Model χ^2		
Model estimation method	ML	ML
Independence model χ^2 (df = 136)	2008.737	824.200
χ^2(df = 116, 8)	256.251	14.251
Probability value for the χ^2 statistic	<.000	<.000
χ^2/df ratio	2.209	1.781
Fit Indices		
Comparative fit index (CFI)	.925	.992
Incremental fit index (IFI)	.926	.992
Standardized root mean square residual (SRMR)	.051	.019
Root mean square error of approximation (RMSEA)	.085	.069
RMSEA 90% confidence interval	[.071, .099]	[.000,.125]

Note. ML = maximum likelihood.

Measurement Model C': Affective Orientations with Item Parceling

First, Instrumental Orientation, Intrinsic Motivation, Motivation, Self-Esteem, General Self-Worth, Self-Image, Cognitive Competence, L2 Writing Self-Confidence, L2 Writing Anxiety, Willingness to Communicate in L2 Writing, and the Eiken Can-Do Questionnaires were examined in Measurement Model C' as shown in Figure 20. How the items in each variable were parceled is shown in Appendix X.

The data fit this model relatively well. Multivariate kurtosis was 9.083, which was high based on the < 5.0 criterion; however, the Chi-Square ratio of 1.500 met the 2.0 criterion (Byrne, 2006). CFI (.924) and IFI (.925) indicated good fit. SRMR was below the .08 criterion at .076, and RMSEA was below the .08 criterion at .055. The RMSEA 90% Confidence interval ranged from .047 to .061, which exemplified relatively good fit. The reli-

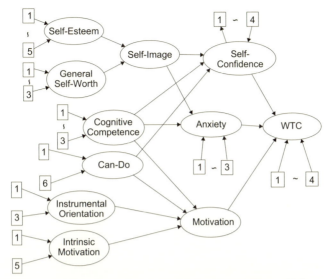

Figure 20. **Measurement Model C': Affective Orientations with Item Parceling. The nine latent variables consist of 3-6 item parcels; only the first and last item parcels are shown.**

ability coefficient was good at .957.

Two variables, Self-Esteem and General Self-Worth, were highly correlated at .95; thus, this was a case of multicollinearity that might invalidate the measurement model. The results for Measurement Model C' are displayed in Table 51.

The Structural Models

Based on the results shown in the previous section for Models A, A', B, B', and C', the structural model was respecified in the following ways. Namely, the measurement model was respecified in Complete Structural Model C' with Writing Outcome and Complete Structural Model D Without Anxiety and Writing Outcome.

Complete Structural Model C' with Writing Outcome

Complete structural model C' was tested to obtain a more robust model. This model

122 CHAPTER 5 RESULTS

featured the addition of the final writing outcome after Willingness to Communicate in L2 Writing. The Can-Do Questionnaires were made up of three measurement variables, Can-Do April, Can-Do July and Can-Do December, while Intrinsic Motivation was made up of three measurement variables, Desire to Write English, Attitude Toward Learning to Write English, and Motivational Intensity (Figure 20). The residuals were not sufficiently symmetric around the zero midpoint with 75.84% falling in the ±1 range; thus, the model misfit (Byrne, 2006, p. 93).

This model did not fit the data well. Multivariate kurtosis was high at 10.286; however, the Chi-Square ratio of 2.685 was very good. CFI (.882) and IFI (.884) indicated poor fit, SRMR was above the .08 criterion at .125, and RMSEA for this model was inadequate at .100. The 90% for Confidence Interval RMSEA was .084-.117, while the reliability coeffi-

Table 51. *Summary of Fit Indices for Model C'*

	Model C'
Reliability coefficient (rho)	.957
Multivariate kurtosis	
Mardia's coefficient	79.260
Normalized estimate	9.083
Residuals	
Average absolute standardized residuals	.005
Average off-diagonal absolute standardized residuals	.046
Model χ^2	
Model estimation method	ML
Independence model χ^2 (df = 136)	5204.885
χ^2(df = 677)	1015.200
Probability value for the χ^2 statistic	.000
χ^2/df ratio	1.500
Fit Indices	
Comparative fit index (CFI)	.924
Incremental fit index (IFI)	.925
Standardized root mean square residual (SRMR)	.076
Root mean square error of approximation (RMSEA)	.055
RMSEA 90% confident interval	[.047,.061]

Note. ML = maximum likelihood.

cient rho was reasonably good at .817.

As for the measurement equation with standard errors and test statistics, the structural equation model, the Complete Structural Model C with Writing Outcome, describes the influence of the 15 variables on F15 Writing Outcome (i.e., writing proficiency in spring and fall term). First, two variables were strong predictors of Willingness to Communicate in L2 Writing. Among them, L2 Writing Self-Confidence yielded a relatively strong effect, with a standardized regression weight of $\beta = .24$. The other variable Motivation's direct effect was relatively strong with a standardized regression weights of $\beta = .48$. L2 Writing Anxiety had a nonsignificant negative relationship with Willingness to Communicate in L2 Writing. The path from Willingness to Communicate in L2 Writing to Writing Outcome was not significant.

Second, the Eiken Can-Do Questionnaire was a strong predictor of L2 Writing Self-Confidence at $\beta = .71$, and it had a small direct effect on Motivation at $\beta = .22$. Again,

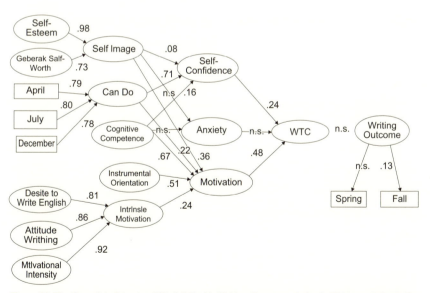

Figure 21. The Complete Structural Model C' with Writing Outcome. Attitude Writing = Attitude Toward Learning to Write English. WTC = Willingness to Communicate in L2 Writing. Can Do = Eiken Can-Do Questionnaire. Numerical values indicate that path coefficients were significant at p < .01. $\chi2$ = 2.685, CFI = .882, RMSEA = .100. 90% CI = .084-.117.

124   CHAPTER 5 RESULTS

four variables had direct effects on Motivation: the first was Self-Image at β = .36, which is moderate, the second was Can-Do at β = .22, which is small and the third was Intrinsic Motivation at β =.24, which is also small. Instrumental Orientation was a strong predictor of Motivation at β = .51.

L2 Writing Anxiety did not work well in this model, as the paths from Self-Image, Cognitive Competence, and Willingness to Communicate in L2 Writing to L2 Writing Anxiety were not significant. Lastly, I provide the information on how Writing Outcome behaved in this model. The path from Writing fall semester to Writing Outcome was weak but significant at β = .13. Figure 21 features the addition of the the final Writing Outcome after Willingness to Communicate in L2 Writing.

The last model, Complete Structural Model D Without Anxiety and Writing Outcome, which does not include L2 Writing Anxiety and Writing Outcome (Figure 22), was tested next.

Complete Structural Model D Without Anxiety and Writing Outcome

Because the variables L2 Writing Anxiety and Writing Outcome did not work well in Complete Structural Model C', Complete Structural Model D was tested. In this model, Writing Outcome, which consists of spring term and fall terms, was excluded from the model. L2 Writing Anxiety was also excluded because it did not produce any statistically significant results. The residuals were not sufficiently symmetric around the zero midpoint with 78.20% falling in the ±1 range; thus, the model misfit (Byrne, 2006, p. 93). This model fit the data well. Multivariate kurtosis was relatively high at 9.359. The Chi-Square ratio of 2.573 nearly met the 2.0 criterion (Byrne, 2006). Although CFI (.924) and IFI (.926) indicated good fit, and SRMR was close to the .08 criterion at .081. RMSEA was inadequate at .097, the 90% Confidence Interval ranged from .075-.118, which is above the desired range of .050-.080, while the reliability coefficient was reasonably good at .840. This model fit better than the previous model, the complete structural model C' with Writing Outcome.

The structural equation model, Complete Structural Model D without Anxiety and Writing Outcome, describes the influence of the 13 variables on Willingness to Commu-

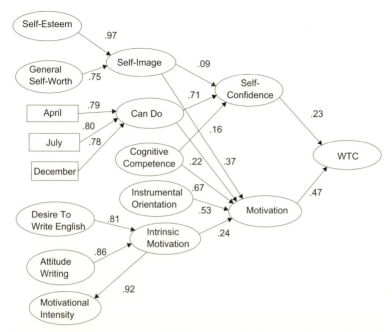

Figure 22. **Results for re-specified revised model of the Complete Structural Model D without Anxiety and Writing Outcome. Attitude Writing = Attitude Toward Learning To Write English. WTC = Willingness to Communicate in L2 Writing. Can Do = Eiken Can-Do Questionnaire. Numerical values indicate that path coefficients were significant at p < .01. χ2 = 2.573, CFI = .927, RMSEA = .097. 90% CI = .075-.118.**

nicate in L2 Writing. First, two variables, L2 Writing Self-Confidence and Motivation, were predictors of Willingness to Communicate in L2 Writing. L2 Writing Self-Confidence yielded a relatively small effect with a standardized regression weight of $\beta = .23$. Motivation had a moderately large direct effect with a standardized regression weight of $\beta = .47$.

Second, Can-Do July was a strong predictor of Self-Confidence at $\beta = .71$, while Can-Do July had a weak direct effect on Motivation at $\beta = .22$. Again, three variables had relatively weak direct effects on Motivation: The first one was Self-Image at $\beta = .37$, the second was Can-Do July at $\beta = .22$, and the third was Intrinsic Motivation at $\beta = .24$.

Third, Instrumental Orientation was a relatively strong predictor of Motivation at $\beta =$

126   CHAPTER 5 RESULTS

.53. Furthermore, Attitude toward Learning to Write English was a strong predictor of Intrinsic motivation at β = .86, while Motivational Intensity was a stronger predicator of Intrinsic Motivation at β = .92.

Fourth, Motivation was a weak predictor of Intrinsic Motivation at β = .24, Self-Image at β =.37, and Can-Do July at β =.22 (Figure 22). Can-Do July played an important role with regard to L2 Writing Self-Confidence and Motivation, which implies that Can-Do July affected Self-Confidence and Motivation indirectly through Willingness to Communicate in L2 Writing.

Lastly, Cognitive Competence was a weak predictor of Self-Confidence at β = .16.while the Can-do Questionnaires was a relatively strong predictor of Self-Confidence at β =. 71, which shows that Cognitive Competence is related to internal scholastic ability. However, the Can-do Questionnaires are related to writing performance, though the relationship between WTC in L2 writing and Writing Outcome was not statistically significant (Figure 21). β =. 97 from Self-Esteem to Self-Image is a violation of linearity and shows that two variables are virtually identical, after item parceling was conducted (Figure 22).

Research Question 2 asked about the relationship between teacher ratings of the students' writing performances, as measured by six essay writing assignments, the students' self-assessed writing ability using the Eiken Can-Do Questionnaires, and ten affective orientation variables. The variables L2 Writing Anxiety and Writing Outcome (Spring and Fall) did not produce any statistically significant results in Complete Structural Model C', so Complete Structural Model D was tested. As Complete Structural Model D shows, the relationships between the 13 variables and Eiken Can-Do Questionnaires were assessed as detailed in this section. The variables L2 Writing Anxiety and Writing Outcome (Spring and Fall) were deleted, yielding a well-fitting model with reasonable statistics.

Next, I present the results of Research Questions 3, which dealt with the relationship between perceived writing performance and actual proficiency.

Research Question 3: The Transition of Perceived Writing Performance and Students' Writing Ability

Reseach Question 3 asked about the relationship between Perceived Writing Performance, as measured by the Eiken Can-Do Questionnaires, and the students' writing proficiency, as measured by essay writing performance over one year.

The preliminary data analysis results of writing assignment grades were arrived using multi-faceted Rasch analysis using the FACETS 3.71.3 software (Linacre, 2006) (see Figure 23). As Figure 23 shows, the difficulty levels of Essays 1, 2, 3, 4, and 5 were almost the same; however, Essay 6 was more difficult. Rater 4 was the most severe rater, while Rater 2 was the most lenient.

As Table 52 shows, the difficulty level of the essay assignments was displayed. essay number 4, *What are the merits and demerits of the Japanese school system ?*, was the easiest one to endorse, while essay number 6, *What effects have computers had on society,* was the most difficult one to endorse for the participants.

As Table 53 shows, the difficulty level of rating criteria was displayed. Item number 1, Contents was the easiest one to endorse, while item number 4 Grammar was the most difficult one to endorse for the participants.

As Table 54 shows, the difficulty level of raters of writing assignments was displayed. Rater 2 was the most lenient one for the participants, while Rater 4 was the most severe one for them.

The results indicated that the gap between Eiken April and Eiken July (perceived writing performance) was greater (change = 8.43) than the gap between Eiken July and Eiken December (change = 3.81). Although the change was not linear, the mean displayed a gradual increase over one academic year from April (63.84) to the mean of Eiken July (72.27) and finally Eiken December (76.08) (Table 55).

Possible reasons for the transition of the Eiken Can-Do results over the academic year are that the students might have enjoyed completing the self-evaluation and they might have realized that their writing ability had improved after completing the writing assign-

```
+--------+----------+-----------+-------------------------------------+--------------+---------+
| Measr  | +Raters  | -Students | -Essay                              | -Item        | Scale   |
+--------+----------+-----------+-------------------------------------+--------------+---------+
|  3  +  |     +    |     +     |  +                                  |  +           |  + (5)  |
|        |    4     |     .     |                                     |              |         |
|        |          |     .     |                                     |              |    4    |
|        |    1     |     .     |                                     |              |         |
|        |          |     *.    |                                     |              |         |
|  2  +  3 |    +    |     +     |                                     |  +           |  +      |
|        |          |     .     |                                     |              |         |
|        |    2     |     **    |                                     |              |         |
|        |          |    ***.   |                                     | Grammar      |         |
|        |          |     *.    |                                     |              |         |
|        |          |     *.    |                                     |              |  ---    |
|  1  +  |     +    |     *.    |  +                                  |  +           |  +      |
|        |          |     **.   |                                     |              |         |
|        |          |    ****   |                                     |              |         |
|        |          |    ***    |                                     | Vocabulary   |         |
|        |          |   *****.  |                                     |              |         |
|        |          |    ***    |                                     |              |         |
|        |          |    ***.   |  Essay 6                            |              |         |
|        |          |   *****.  |                                     |              |         |
|  0     |          |     *.    |  Essay 1  Essay 3  Essay 5          |              |         |
|        |          |   *****   |  Essay 2  Essay 4                   |              |    3    |
|        |          |   *****   |                                     |              |         |
|        |          |     *     |                                     |              |         |
|        |          |  ******   |                                     | Organization |         |
|        |          |  ******.  |                                     | Mechanics    |         |
|        |          |    **     |                                     |              |         |
|        |          |    ***.   |                                     |              |         |
| -1  +  |     +    |     *     |  +                                  |  + Contents  |  +      |
|        |          |    **     |                                     |              |         |
|        |          |     *     |                                     |              |         |
|        |          |     *.    |                                     |              |         |
|        |          |    **     |                                     |              |  ---    |
|        |          |     *     |                                     |              |         |
|        |          |    **.    |                                     |              |         |
| -2  +  |     +    |     +     |                                     |  +           |  +      |
|        |          |           |                                     |              |         |
|        |          |     .     |                                     |              |    2    |
|        |          |     .     |                                     |              |         |
|        |          |     .     |                                     |              |         |
| -3  +  |     +    |     +     |  +                                  |  +           |  + (1)  |
+--------+----------+-----------+-------------------------------------+--------------+---------+
| Measr  | +Raters  |  * = 2    | -Essay                              | -Item        | Scale   |
+--------+----------+-----------+-------------------------------------+--------------+---------+
```

Figure 23. Results of the FACETS analysis for the writing assignments.

Research Question 3: The Transition of Perceived Writing Performance and Students' Writing Ability   *129*

Table 52. *The FACETS Output Table for Essays Assignments*

Number	Measure	SE	Infit MNSQ	Infit ZSTD	Outfit MNSQ	Outfit ZSTD	Pt-measure correlation
4	-.10	.05	.75	-7.5	.75	-7.4	.67
2	-.09	.04	1.05	1.4	1.05	1.4	.62
3	-.06	.04	.91	-2.6	.91	-2.4	.65
1	-.01	.04	1.22	5.8	1.23	6.2	.59
5	.02	.04	.95	-1.2	.94	-1.7	.67
6	.22	.04	1.08	2.1	1.07	2.0	.63

Table 53. *The FACETS Output Table for Rating Criteria*

Criterion	Measure	SE	Infit MNSQ	Infit ZSTD	Outfit MNSQ	Outfit ZSTD	Pt-measure correlation
1 Contents	-.97	.04	1.16	4.7	1.14	4.0	.46
5 Mechanics	-.60	.04	1.07	2.2	1.06	1.9	.46
2 Organization	-.52	.04	1.06	1.9	1.06	1.6	.54
3 Vocabulary	.65	.04	.89	-3.4	.89	-3.5	.59
4 Grammar	1.44	.04	.85	-4.8	.89	-4.8	.60

Table 54. The FACETS Output Table for Raters of Writing Assignments

Rater	Measure	SE	Infit MNSQ	Infit ZSTD	Outfit MNSQ	Outfit ZSTD	Pt-measure correlation
2	1.48	.04	1.33	8.3	1.33	8.1	.59
3	1.99	.04	1.26	6.6	1.27	6.8	.59
1	2.39	.03	.76	-9.0	.77	-9.0	.66
4	2.71	.04	1.09	2.4	1.10	2.7	.60

Table 55. *Eiken Can-Do Results' Transition over One Academic Year (April, July and December)*

	Eiken April	Change	Eiken July	Change	Eiken December
Count (*N*)	168		168		168
M	63.84	+8.43**	72.27	+3.81**	76.08
SD	12.91		12.52		11.35

** *p* < .01

130   CHAPTER 5 RESULTS

ments and receiving their course level. As Figure 21 shows, the path from Willingness to Communicate in L2 Writing to Writing Outcome was not significant. I deleted Writing Outcome from the final model in Figure 22.

The results indicated that Eiken Can-Do Questionnaire was a predictor of L2 Writing Self-Confidence (β = .71), Motivation (β = .22), and Willingness to Communicate in L2 Writing through Motivation (β = .47). On the other hand, they were not predictors of Writing Outcome in Figure 21.

In this chapter, the results in this study were presented. Those results are discussed in the next chapter.

CHAPTER 6
DISCUSSION

In this chapter, I summarize the findings for the three research questions, discuss them, and then present the theoretical implications and pedagogical implications. Because the Eiken Can-Do Questionnaires are relatively new, little previous research is available for a comparison. Although Motivation and Willingness to Communicate in L2 Writing have been studied extensively, previous researchers did not focus on Willingness to Communicate in L2 Writing in language classrooms in Japan. Thus, the findings of this study make a contribution to our understanding of the role of the Can-Do Questionnaires and their relationships with several Affective Orientation variables.

Unidimensionality and Item Difficulty in the Rasch Analysis of the Eiken Can-Do Questionnaires

This analysis concerned an investigation of the validity of the writing section of Eiken Can-Do Questionnaires using Rasch analysis. I investigated whether the Eiken Can-Do Questionnaires were utilized effectively by the learners as a self-assessment checklist and whether they were helpful when the learners engaged in classroom tasks.

The writing section of Eiken Can-Do Questionnaires showed a single underlying pattern of the scores; therefore, each of them is likely to measure a unidimensional construct. The point-biserial correlation values and the item fit statistics indicated the unidimensionality when those values were compared with the standards proposed by Wright and Linacre (1994).

The preliminary analyses showed that 18 of the 24 items fit the Rasch model, which indicated that they meaningfully contributed to the measurement of the underlying construct. It is still necessary to confirm the validity of the remaining Eiken Can-Do lists (i.e.

132 CHAPTER 6 DISCUSSION

Listening, Speaking, and Reading) from the same Eiken levels and skill areas in order to validate the whole Eiken Can-Do lists.

The analyses suggested that Eiken Can-Do items properly reflect the students' English proficiency levels, that is, the more proficient students become, the more confident they become. Although it has been reported that Japanese tend to be modest and that high proficiency L2 learners assess their ability more critically (Matsuno, 2009), Eiken Can-Do items successfully differentiated the participants based on language proficiency and learning experience.

This analyses provided a clearer understanding of factors affecting students' responses to Eiken Can-Do Questionnaires. The findings can contribute to a better understanding of self-assessment in Japanese EFL writing classrooms, and because they can help learners identify attainable learning objectives, this can lead the learners to become more goal-oriented and autonomous, which are important factors in the process of achieving high levels of English proficiency.

The Relationship Among the Eiken Can-Do Questionnaires, Affective Orientation Variables and Writing Outcomes

The first and second research question concerned the structural relationships among Eiken Can-Do Questionnaires, affective orientation variables and Writing Outcome. The Complete Structural Model D without Anxiety and Writing Outcome (Figure 22) is an extension of Gardner's (1985) model, MacIntyre's (1994) WTC model (Figure 1) and Yashima's (2002) model (Figure2) in that they include the motivational, self, and affective orientation variables; however, the model underwent considerable revision when the Eiken Can-Do Questionnaires were added. The Eiken Can-Do Questionnaire July was a strong predictor of Self-Confidence at $\beta = .71$. It suggests that the more confident the learners are when they do self-assessments, the stronger self-confidence the learners have. The Eiken Can-Do Questionnaire July had a weak direct effect on Motivation at $\beta = .22$, which suggests that more confident the learners are, more motivated the learners are. This model differs from the previous model, the Complete Structural Model C' with Writing Outcome (Figure 21) in that it includes the Eiken Can-Do Questionnaires. In the model, three factors yielded good statistical results. Self-Confidence (β = .71,) and Motivation (β = .22) acted as two direct predictors of the Eiken Can-Do Questionnaires, while Willingness to Communicate in L2 Writing predicted the Eiken Can-Do Questionnaires indirectly through Self-Confidence and Motivation.

Moreover, the first-order factor of Cognitive Competence was Self-Confidence. The Complete Structural Model D without Anxiety and Writing Outcome (Figure 22) indicated that Cognitive Competence was a weak predictor of Self-Confidence at β = .16. It suggests that the more competent learners are, the stronger their self-confidence. Cognitive Competence did not directly or indirectly affect the Eiken Can-Do Questionnaires in this study, which was in contrast to the results reported by Sitzmann et al. (2010) in which the relationship between self-assessment and cognitive learning was moderate. However, these two instruments differ in that the Eiken Can-Do Questionnaires are self-assessments while the Cognitive Competence instrument is not. Harter (1982) stated that Cognitive Competence concerns academic performance and involves self-perceptions of doing well at schoolwork, being smart, and feeling good about one's classroom performance. It seems logical because learners' cognitive competence, an internally-focused construct, would have little or no relationship with learners' self-confidence, an externally focused construct.

Second, the Complete Structural Model D without Writing Outcome (Figure 22) indicated that Instrumental Orientation was a strong negative predictor (β = -.53) of Motivation, while Intrinsic Motivation was a relatively weak positive predictor (β = .24). This finding was in line with the models of Gardner et al. (1997) and Gardner and Lambert (1959), in which Intrinsic Motivation was a weak predictor of Motivation (β =. 21 in the former and β = .25 in the latter).

Third, Self-Image was a moderately strong predictor of Motivation (β =.37), indicating that the more learners have a better self-image in studying, the more motivated the learners are. Self-Image only weakly predicted L2 Writing Self-Confidence (β = . 09), which contravened the findings of Christou et al. (2001) and Hein and Hagger (2006), who found Self-Image to be a strong predictor of Motivation. However, those two studies addressed general self-confidence whereas the current study dealt with Self-Confidence in L2

134   CHAPTER 6 DISCUSSION

Writing and the current study was conducted in Japan and the former was done in the United States.

The results of the present study shed light on how L2 Writing Anxiety played a role in the motivational preferences of Japanese university students (Figure 21): L2 Writing Anxiety was not a significant predictor of Self-Image, Cognitive Competence, and Willingness to Communicate in L2 Writing. L2 Writing Anxiety is asynchronous, meaning there is a time lag in which the student can revise, whereas speaking is much more a synchronous activity in which little time is available for revision. Thus, there is less anxiety and nervousness when writing than when speaking (Palacious, 1998; Price, 1991). Further studies and replications are needed to confirm the stability of this path.

Fourth, the Eiken Can-Do Questionnaires predicted Motivation (β = .22), and indirectly predicted Willingness to Communicate in L2 Writing with β = .10 (i.e., .47 x .22) through Motivation, suggesting that the more positive the learners are when they are assessed using Eiken Can-Do questionnaires, the more they are motivated and more willing to communicate in L2 writing. These relationships have been investigated in speaking contexts as well (e.g., Gardner et al., 1997; Yashima, 2002), in which similar results were found. Therefore, the finding in the current study is in line with studies in the different contexts of Canada and Japan.

The results of the present study indicated that the Eiken Can-Do Questionnaires were weak predictors of Motivation (β = .22) and Motivation was a relatively strong predictor of Willingness to Communicate in Writing (β = .47). Moreover, the construct measured by the Eiken Can-Do Questionnaires had an indirect effect (β = .10) on Willingness to Communicate in L2 Writing; no previous studies have identified a relationship between the two variables, Can-Do and Willingness to Communicate in L2 Writing, because Can-Do, especially, the Eiken Can-Do Questionnaires, is relatively new with little extant research. This indirect effect between the Eiken Can-do Questionnaires and Willingness to Communicate in Writing is noteworthy.

Fifth, as shown in Figure 24, the Eiken Can-Do Questionnaires were strong predictors of L2 Writing Self-Confidence (β = .71) and Cognitive Competence was a weak predictor of L2 Writing Self-Confidence (β = .16); furthermore, L2 Writing Self-Confidence predicted Willingness to Communicate in L2 Writing (β = .23). Moreover, the paths by which the Eiken Can-Do Questionnaires indirectly predicted WTC through Self-Confidence and Motivation were statistically significant at β = .16 and β = .10, respectively (shown with dashed lines in Figure 24). It suggests that greater L2 Writing Self-Confidence is associated with greater Willingness to Communicate in L2 Writing. Again, the finding is consistent with previous research by Clément, Dörnyei, and Noels (1994) who stated that Self-Confidence was a cognitive component made up of the learners' self-evaluation of their proficiency.

Furthermore, this finding stated above is consistent with previous research by Clément and Kruidenier (1985), who reported that Self-Confidence was a significant predictor of achievement. Gardner, Tremblay, and Masgoret (1997) reported that the path from Self-Confidence to Willingness to Communicate was significant. Clément and his associates found that indices of Self-Confidence correlate significantly with measures of L2 proficien-

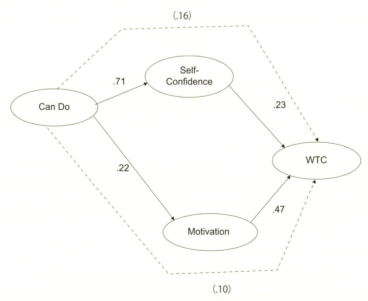

Figure 24. Model of direct effects and indirect effects. Direct effects are shown with solid lines and indirect effects with dashed lines. Values in parentheses indicate indirect effect coefficients.

136 CHAPTER 6 DISCUSSION

cy in the L2 (Clément, Dörnyei, & Noels, 1994; Clément, Gardner, & Smythe, 1980; Clément & Kruidenier, 1985). Again, MacIntyre, Dörnyei, Clément, and Noels (1998) suggested that Self-Confidence significantly contributes to the learner's Willingness to Communicate in a foreign language, which is consistent with this study's findings. Therefore, theoretically and practically, the Eiken Can-Do Questionnaires or Classroom Can-Do Questionnaires have a certain relationship with Motivation, Self-Confidence and Willingness to Communicate in L2 Writing.

Sixth, Cognitive Competence did not predict the Eiken Can-Do Questionnaire variable directly, which is not consistent with findings by Sitzmann et al. (2010), who reported a moderately strong relationship between self-assessment and cognitive learning (i.e., cognitive competence). Pearson correlations among the Affective Orientation Variables, Eiken Can-Do, and Writing Outcome (Table 47) also show that Cognitive Competence has a relatively strong correlation with the Eiken Can-Do Questionnaire April (.412), the Eiken Can-Do Questionnaire July (.351), and the Eiken Can-Do Questionnaire December (.386). This finding is inconsistent with past research in which the strongest predictors of Willingness to Communicate were two individual characteristics, communication anxiety and perceived communication competence (Baker & MacIntyre, 2000; MacIntyre, Clément, Baker, & Conrad, 2001; McCroskey & Richmond, 1991).

Seventh, consistent with Hui et al. (2011) and Tanaka et al. (2002), in which Cognitive Competence directly affected Motivation, a weak positive relationship (β = .22) was found between Cognitive Competence and Motivation in the current study. The weakness of this relationship is reasonable because Cognitive Competence is related to the internal scholastic ability while Motivation consists of both an internal component (Intrinsic Motivation) and an external component (instrumental orientation, which has a relationship with jobs or language acquisition processes).

Lastly, although Takemura (2008) found that learners who assessed themselves highly tended to perform the writing task more successfully than their peers who gave themselves lower assessments, in this study, no statistically significant relationship was found between Eiken Can-Do Questionnaires and Writing outcomes, which led to the deletion of the writing outcomes variable from the final model, the Complete Structural Model D without Anxiety and Writing Outcome (Figure 22). One reason why this happened in this study is that the data collection period was just one year, which might have been too short to discern any relationship between Eiken Can-Do Questionnaires and Writing Outcome. Another reason should be that this might be the limit of the positive aspects in Eiken Can-Do Questionnaires or Classroom Can-Do Questionnaires, because the students might have realized their actual writing proficiency after completing the six writing tasks in one academic year.

To sum up, based on the findings of the present study, a new model—one grounded in a motivational perspective—emerged that included the Eiken Can-Do Questionnaires. The model is shown in Figure 22, the Complete Structural Model D without Anxiety and Writing Outcome. It is an extension of the models presented by Gardner (1985a), MacIntyre (1994), and Yashima (2002) in that it included all the motivational, self, and affective orientation variables in one model. The Complete Structural Model D without Anxiety and Writing Outcome in Figure 22 differs from their models in that it includes the Eiken Can-Do Questionnaires. L2 Writing Self- Confidence and Motivation are two immediate precursors of Eiken Can-Do Questionnaires. At the next level, Willingness to Communicate in L2 Writing affected Eiken Can-Do Questionnaires indirectly through Self-Confidence and Motivation.

The Transition in the Students' Self-Perceived Writing Ability and Writing Ability Over One Academic Year

The third research question concerned the transition in the students' self- perceived writing ability and writing ability over one academic year. I hypothesized that the participants' self-perceived writing ability (as measured by the Eiken Can-Do Questionnaires) would increase gradually over one academic year; however, the gap between the Eiken Can-Do Questionnaire April and the Eiken Can-Do Questionnaire July was bigger than the gap between the Eiken Can-Do Questionnaire July and the Eiken Can-Do Questionnaire December. It suggests that the students might have realized that it had become more difficult to successfully complete the writing assignments toward the end of the fall semes-

138 CHAPTER 6 DISCUSSION

ter.

The results of this study indicated that the students conducted six writing assignments and received grades, which led to the result that the gap between the Eiken Can-Do Questionnaire April and the Eiken Can-Do Questionnaire July was bigger than the gap between the Eiken Can-Do Questionnaire July and the Eiken Can-Do Questionnaire December. By doing the self-assessment check, the students could understand their short-term and long-term objectives in English learning. This should be a substructure of lifelong learning. The Council of Europe (2001) argued that the main potential for self-assessment is in its use as a tool for motivation and awareness raising.

As Ross (1998) stated, self-assessment has frequently been viewed as being opposed to the concerns of traditional educational measurement because self-assessment often introduces a large number of unwanted measurement facets. Moral reasons, such as the sharing of power between teacher and learner, as well as motivational ones, such as the excitement of self-discovery, are often used to justify self-assessment practices against the accusation of lack of reliability (Davies et al., 1999). Despite these drawbacks, there are advantages to using self-assessment including its potential to increase student and teacher motivation. This finding is consistent with Little (2005), who stated that CEFR's Can-Do statements should help to develop learners' autonomy, self-regulation, and metacognitive strategies.

Again, Cognitive Competence did not work well in the final model, the Complete Structural Model D without Anxiety and Writing Outcome in Figure 22, which implied that it was not a predictor of the Eiken Can-Do Questionnaires. The Eiken Can-Do Questionnaires were predictors of L2 Writing Self-Confidence, Motivation, and Willingness to Communicate in L2 Writing that are affective factors, while the Eiken Can-Do Questionnaires were not predictors Cognitive Competence and Writing Outcome which implied the limit of the positivism of self-evaluation, Eiken Can-Do questionnaires.

Therefore, it should be noted that it is important to develop students' Self-Confidence, raise their Motivation, and impel their Willingness to Communicate in L2 Writing by encouraging students to learn English more in the classroom. The rationale is that higher levels of Self-Confidence, Motivation, and Willingness to Communicate in L2 Writing could lead to the higher level of the realization of what they can do and what they cannot do regarding English learning process.

Theoretical Implications

First, Can-Do Questionnaires have appeared occasionally in research to date, but in general they were neither the main focus nor investigated in a Japanese EFL context. Gardner et al. (1997), for example, utilized a small sample in Canada to gain insights into the relationship between affective variables and Can-Do. However, it revealed the positive relationship between Motivation, Self-Confidence, and Can-Do, and the results were preliminary and cannot be generalized to Japanese contexts, especially because the Can-Do was not the center of the research. One of the major implications in this convergent Can-Do study is that the Complete Structural Model D without Anxiety and Writing Outcome in Figure 22 can serve as a productive framework from which to study instructor conceptions about the Eiken Can-Do Questionnaires in more detail. This study thus moves research towards a diverse configuration of communication.

Second, in this study, the Eiken Can-Do Questionnaires constituted an important addition to WTC-Writing models. The Eiken Can-Do Questionnaires had an indirect impact on Willingness to Communicate in L2 Writing (β = .10) through Motivation, suggesting that the Eiken Can-Do Questionnaires positively affected actual behavior of Willingness to Communicate in L2 Writing. As the theory by Gardner et al. (1997) did not show enough positive statistical relationships between the Can-Do Questionnaire and Willingness to Communicate, the finding in this study could contribute to research on Willingness to Communicate in the SLA field.

Lastly, through this convergent study, it could be theorized that with an aggregable attitude to the subjective norm, students are more likely to have greater Motivation, Self-Confidence, and Willingness to Communicate in L2 Writing if the Eiken Can-Do Questionnaires and Classroom Can-Do Questionnaires are distributed in any place, though this is a modest indirect support at β = .10. This finding can contribute to the enhancement and spread of Can-Do Questionnaires in the future.

140   CHAPTER 6 DISCUSSION

Pedagogical Implications

First, it is noteworthy that the Eiken Can-do Questionnaires were found to be significant predictors of Motivation, Self-Confidence, and Willingness to Communicate in L2
Writing, and the pedagogical implication of the indirect impact of the Eiken Can-Do
Questionnaires on Willingness to Communicate in L2 Writing is of paramount importance. It suggests that the potential application of various teachers' strategies to distribute
the Eiken Can-Do Questionnaires or Classroom Can-Do Questionnaires could trigger
learners' stronger Motivation, Self-Confidence and Willingness to Communicate in L2
Writing.

Second, Can-Do Questionnaires have a potential usefulness in the classroom. In this
study, the Eiken Can-do Questionnaires had a direct impact on Motivation (β = .22) and
Self-Confidence (β = .71). This finding corresponds with the Council of Europe's (2001)
assertion that any Can-Do Questionnaires positively affected greater motivation. Developing students' motivation is important because if the students feel they are learning efficiently, they will be more motivated to continue learning. By having students complete the
Eiken Can-Do Questionnaires and Classroom Can-Do Questionnaires several times in
one academic year, teachers can determine the learners' perceived level of proficiency.
Completing self-assessments as an external measure (i.e., the Eiken Can-Do Questionnaires) a few times in one academic year and completing self-assessment as an internal
measure (Classroom Can-Do Questionnaires) is one way to increase learners' motivation,
autonomous learning and metacognitive awareness toward English learning as the CEFR
states (The Council of Europe, 2001).

Third, Can-Do Questionnaires should be used in multiple ways. In this study, I used
the Eiken Can-Do Questionnaires and Classroom Can-Do Questionnaires so that I could
investigate the effectiveness of triangulation in using Can-Do Questionnaires in the classroom. The participants experienced the self-assessment at least four times in the academic
year, which is found to be effective with a view to the relationship between Motivation and
Self-Confidence, Willingness to Communicate in L2 Writing. This finding corresponds to

Green's (2011) theory, in which regarding developing more concrete versions of CEFR's or the Eiken Can-Do Questionnaires, when applied to a classroom, CEFR should consist of three layers: (a) abstract, which is made up of can-do objectives, (b) elaboration, which refers to reference level descriptions, and (c) concrete, which concerns classroom and real-life tasks undertaken by language learners. He also emphasized the necessity of linking the interpretation of Can-Do Questionnaires to specific learning contexts.

Fourth, the relative effectiveness of developing Classroom Can-Do Questionnaires is potentially of interest to practitioners who are looking for concrete ways to enhance students' motivation. Practitioners who are looking for ways to enhance learners' motivation might want to add extra activities to make this treatment more powerful. For example, activities could be planned to help students to develop more detailed proximal classroom objectives, that is, Classroom Can-Do Questionnaires. A brief instruction to how to develop Classroom Can-Do Questionnaires might also be integrated into the classroom to raise students' Motivation and Self- Confidence, and Willingness to Communicate in L2 Writing.

Lastly, I suggest that practitioners who know how to develop Classroom Can-Do Questionnaires could hold a workshop in a conference which aims to introduce the likely effectiveness of distributing the Eiken Can-Do Questionnaires, which are external measures, and Classroom Can-Do Questionnaires, which are internal measures. The implication of this study is that for researchers and practitioners, to connect the proximal objectives in the classroom to their distal objectives in the future seems to be an important aspect for the success of English as a lifelong learning endeavor.

In the final chapter, summary of the findings, the limitations of the study, suggestions for future research, and final conclusions are presented.

CHAPTER 7
CONCLUSION

In this chapter, I briefly summarize the findings of the study, list the limitations of the study, make suggestions for future research, and provide final comments.

Summary of the Findings

This study produced three main findings. This study shed light on the participants' encounter with the Eiken Can-Do Questionnaires and the Classroom Can-Do Questionnaires, topics that have not been studied much in the second language acquisition field.

First, Rasch Analysis was conducted to check each variable's unidimensionality. The point-biserial correlation values and the item fit statistics indicated the unidimensionality when those values were compared with the standards proposed by Wright and Linacre (1994). The results showed that 18 of the 24 items fit the Rasch model and meaningfully contributed to the measurement of the underlying construct.

I found that the Eiken Can-Do items adequately reflected the students' English proficiency levels, that is, the more proficient students become, the more confident they become. Although it has been reported that Japanese tend to be modest and that high level L2 learners assess their ability more critically (Matsuno, 2009), it can be assumed that these Eiken Can-Do items successfully differentiated the participants based on language proficiency and learning experience. In this sense, as the Eiken Can-Do Questionnaires were recommended by Yoshida (2006), I found STEP (2006) was adequate and proper in itemizing each Can-Do Questionnaire.

Second, the Complete Structural Model D without Anxiety and Writing Outcome in Figure 22 provided sufficient fit of the model to the data and showed how these affective variables affect each other. The Eiken Can-Do Questionnaires were predictors of Motivation, and L2 Writing Self-Confidence, which are consistent with Sitzmann et al. (2010) in which they stated that self-assessment's strong correlations were motivation and satisfaction. Motivation was a predictor of Willingness to Communicate in L2 Writing. Therefore, it should be noted that the Eiken Can-Do Questionnaires had an indirect effect with Willingness to Communicate in L2 Writing, which is reasonable, and understandable. It should be point out that being different from Sitzmann et al. (2010) in which they stated that the relationship between self-assessment and cognitive competence was moderate, Cognitive Competence did not directly or indirectly affect the Eiken Can-Do Questionnaires.

Third, this study showed that data from Eiken Can-Do Questionnaires and Classroom Can-Do Questionnaires, distributed a few times over one academic year in the classroom can be used as a tool to predict L2 Writing Self-Confidence, Motivation, and Willingness to Communicate in English. Motivation in turn increases their Willingness to Communicate in English. CEFR (1996) maintained that the Can-Do Questionnaires should be presented in a way to stimulate students' motivation. Contemporary language learning pedagogy has placed substantial emphasis on students' interactions in communicative tasks in the classroom, with an attempt to enhance students' communicative competence. In communicative language classes, it is essential that students engage in communicative activities; their success largely depends on their degree of motivation to learn English and their Willingness to Communicate. Therefore, in this sense, the result of this study that the Eiken Can-Do questionnaires directly predicted Motivation and Self-Confidence, and indirectly predicted Willingness to Communicate in L2 writing, is an important contribution to the field.

Lastly, it is noteworthy that students could initially set their lifetime achievement goals by obtaining the Eiken Can-Do Questionnaires in the classroom and gradually narrow down their goals to class or semester goals, by obtaining the Classroom Can-Do questionnaires, then to writing goals in each classroom. The result implies that through having Eiken Can-Do questionnaires and Classroom Can-Do Questionnaires to achieve their future goals, their English classes and their future learning objectives were connected. Through the process of setting lifetime goals by external Eiken Can-Do Questionnaires and gradu-

144   CHAPTER 7 CONCLUSION

ally narrowing them down to classroom-based internal Classroom Can-Do Questionnaires in each class, it is assumed that learners perceived the proximal goals to be the instrument to realize the distal goals (Miller & Brickman, 2004).

Limitations

There are five primary limitations to this study. First, the period of study was short, ranging from one year to one year and a half. Though the English ability does not improve much over such a short period of time in developing the Classroom Can-Do Questionnaires, the school curriculum and timetable did not allow the researcher to have the same students for a longer period. For findings to be more conclusive, the study concerns need to be investigated over a longer period.

The second limitation of this study is that I did not include a qualitative element. Time constraints precluded the collection of interview and observation data that could likely support the empirical data used in this study.

Third, the results of this study might not be generalizable to other EFL contexts in Japan and elsewhere. This is because the core participants in this study were Japanese students studying at Music College and a prestigious university in the Tokyo metropolitan area. Though efforts were made to collect additional data from participants at various academic levels, that is, various proficiency levels for cross validation, all additional participants also came from the Tokyo area, many of whom were also drawn from competitive universities. Overall, their general cognitive ability, motivation to learn English and their English proficiency level are mostly higher than average.

Fourth, as a large portion of this study is based on self-reported questionnaires, participants' responses might have been affected by various problems that can afflict questionnaire data. For example, responses might have been influenced by social desirability. That is students might have responded in a way that is socially desirable in a Japanese context, rather than expressed their true feelings and motivation. In addition, a possible Hawthorne effect needs to be acknowledged; some participants might have worked harder because they realized that they were research participants. Another possibility is the halo effects; some students might have responded positively to please their teacher because the researcher taught the classes, did the survey, examined the effects of the Eiken Can-Do Questionnaires and the Classroom Can-Do Questionnaires. As current ethical standards require that research participants should be both willing and informed, Hawthorn and halo effects are unavoidable and inevitable to some degree.

Lastly, through the Structural Equation Modeling analysis, item parceling technique has been adopted, which is a procedure for combining individual items and using these combined items as observed variables. Bandalos (2002) pointed out that one advantage of parceling is that parcel solutions typically result in better model fit than solutions produced by the item level. Furthermore, many scales have 50 or 100 items. Modeling this many items with moderate sample sizes (e.g., n = 200) can work poorly (Anglim, 2014). Little et al. (2002) also suggested that parcels are preferred when the sample size is relatively small, which is the case in this study. Parceling permitted me to use structural equation modeling as it solved the linear dependency problem and produced acceptable statistical results.

Suggestions for Future Research

This study attempted to reveal a quantitative effect of the Eiken Can-Do Questionnaires and Classroom Can-Do Questionnaires in the Japanese EFL context. The key findings of this study, I hope, will be applied to further enhance learners' motivation in learning English. For further studies, I would like to suggest the following issues be investigated.

The first suggestion is that, as the number of participants in this study is 168, which is relatively small especially for Structural Equation Modeling, this study is still tentative and explanatory, and should be tested with a larger N-size.

Second, the structural equation model presented in this study presented the dynamic interaction of a full range of ten affective orientation variables as well as Can-Do Questionnaires to represent the complex evolving nature of learners' motivational psychology. As mentioned above, the analytic results of structural equation modeling might need further empirical exploration, especially with regard to the path from the Can-Do questionnaires to Willingness to Communicate in L2 Writing, for further evidence to support the

146 CHAPTER 7 CONCLUSION

stability of the implied causal relationships. Future researchers need to see whether the model can be improved, either by re-specification or by using improved affective orientations variables.

Third, the participants are the students from the Music College and the Faculty of Management in a prestigious university, I would like to collect data next time from students whose major is English, because I imagine that the result of the Structural Equation Modeling might be different from this study, especially with regard to the Extrinsic Motivation (Instrumental Orientation for Writing in English) and Intrinsic Motivation. It would be of interest to compare the differential impact of affective motivational variables on Can-Do Questionnaires, according to age group, to explore the similarities and differences in the nature of their motivation.

Fourth, although I am the first researcher who included the Eiken Can-Do Questionnaires in Structural Equation Modeling and examined the validity of the writing section of the Eiken Can-Do Questionnaires, it would also be of interest to test the listening, reading and speaking items of the Eiken Can-Do Questionnaires in the future. Likewise, in the Rasch analysis as well, I would like to investigate items from sections other than the writing section of the Eiken Can-Do Questionnaires and would like to check the predictive ability of the respective sections.

Fifth, future researchers should collect more holistic data by adopting a mixed method design. Future researchers can explore these methods in a wider context, especially using qualitative methods such as students' observation in the classroom and stimulated recall interviews as mentioned above after developing the Classroom Can-Do Questionnaires for the targeted students, which should help my understanding of the effect of using the Can-Do Questionnaires more.

Sixth, in this study, the relative effects of distributing the Can-Do Questionnaires were examined over one academic year. A longer longitudinal study could be conducted to explore the effectiveness of these treatments on enhancing other motivational variables and Willingness to Communicate in L2 Writing. It would be also interest to examine whether increase in the Eiken Can-Do Questionnaires is related to increase fluency, accuracy and complexity in L2 writing outcomes. In this sense, integrating the Writing outcomes into the Eiken Can-Do Questionnaires could also be of interest. In that cases, a new better approach to examine the writing outcomes should be included, though in this study, Jacobs et al. (1981)'s rating criteria has been adopted to assess the students' essay writing outcomes.

Seventh, as the next step, it would also be interest to explore whether these treatments have differential effects on gender, high/ low motivational learners or high/ low L2 Willingness to Communicate learners, as individual differences factor in examining the effectiveness of Can-Do Questionnaires. It might be of interest to connect the Eiken Can-Do Questionnaires or the Classroom Can-Do Questionnaires with investigation of learners' learning strategies use, for example, to explore the interaction between motivational factors and learners' strategy use.

Eighth, it would be useful to conduct post hoc research to investigate whether the paths from other variables, such as Willingness to Communicate in L2 Writing and Anxiety to Writing Outcome are statistically significant.

Ninth, the analytic results of Structural Equation Modeling might entail further empirical exploration and replication. In particular, the path from the Eiken Can-Do Questionnaires and Motivation, Self-Confidence, and Willingness to Communicate in L2 Writing, which was tested for the first time in this study, needs further evidence for stability of the limited causal relationship to be supported.

Final Conclusions

First, despite these limitations mentioned above, this study proposed a new model including the Can-Do Questionnaires for the classroom context in which motivational, self, and affective orientation variables were integrated and then provided empirical support for the model. Using Gardner's (1985) socio educational model, MacIntyre's (1994) Willingness to Communicate model and Yashima's (2002) model, this research demonstrated that within the EFL context in Japan, the Eiken Can-Do Questionnaires play a significant role by making the students more willing to communicate in English. Here, the role of the teacher is highlighted as the most influential factor that can provide care to the students in

148   CHAPTER 7 CONCLUSION

self-assessing and promote a deeper understanding of its use in and out of the classroom.

Second, the CEFR is influential in the current English educational context in Japan. As such, MEXT (2013) adopted the Can-Do Questionnaires as one standard of English learning; therefore, teachers should use a Can-Do Questionnaire in their classrooms and provide students with the opportunity to develop greater self-awareness and critical reflection skills (O'Farrell, 2015).

Third, researchers need both top-down approach (external measure) and bottom-up approach (internal measure) when they try to increase the students' English proficiency. It is important to develop the subordinate, classroom based detailed Can-Do Questionnaires or classroom objectives to increase learners' motivation.

Fourth, as an effective tool to increase the learners' motivation, I assume any Can-Do Questionnaires can give students the precious opportunity of reflection, or rather metacognitive awareness and self-efficacy, because any Can-Do Questionnaires contains very positive and bright features in themselves.

Fifth, through the Can-Do triangulation, or by providing several Can-Do Questionnaires in the classroom, we can recognize English as a life-long learning. Therefore, although Japanese university students sometimes are too modest to use English efficiently in front of the native speakers or the people from other countries, we teachers should let them increase the students' motivation, and self-efficacy in English learning process by providing the positive and constructive Can-Do Questionnaires in this global age.

Lastly, I sincerely hope that the participants in this study identified their own learning objectives and paths to success in English learning even after they graduate from their university by developing their self-assessment skills.

REFERENCES

Aida, Y. (1994). Examination of Horwitz, Horwitz and Cope's construct of foreign language anxiety: The case of students of Japanese. *Modern Language Journal, 78,* 155-168.

Ajzen, I. (1988). *Attitudes, personality and behavior.* Chicago, IL: Dorsey Press.

Alderson, J. C. (2000). *Assessing reading.* Cambridge: Cambridge University Press.

Alderson, J. C. (n.d.). Waystage and threshold. Or does the emperor have any clothes? Unpublished article.

Alderson, J. C. (2005). *Diagnosing foreign language proficiency: The interface between learning and assessment.* London, England: Continuum.

Alderson, J. C., Figueras, N., Kuijper, H., Nold, G., Takala, S. & Tardieu, C. (2004). The development of specifications for item development and classification within the Common European Framework of Reference for Languages: learning, teaching, assessment. Reading and listening. Final report of the Dutch CEF construct project. Unpublished document.

Ames, C., & Archer, J. (1988). Achievement goals in the classroom: Student learning strategies and motivation processes. *Journal of Educational Psychology, 80,* 260-267.

Andrich, D. (1978). A rating formulation for ordered response categories. *Psychometrika, 43,* 561-573.

Anglim, J. (2014). Jeromy Anglim's Blog: Psychology and Statistics: Item parceling in confirmatory factor analysis. http://jelomyanglim. blogspot.jp/ 2009/09/item-parceling in confirmatory factor analysis.

Apple, M. T. (2016). A Rasch model analysis of the "Four L2 anxieties." In Q. Zhang (Ed.), *Pacific Rim Objective Measurement Symposium (PROMS) 2015 Conference Proceedings.* 51-70. doi:10.1007/978-981-10-1687-5_4

Arbuckle, J. L., & Wothke, W. (1996). *AMOS 4.0 User's guide.* Chicago, IL: Small Waters.

Aspinwall, L. G., & Taylor, S. E. (1992). Individual differences, coping and psychological adjustment: A longitudinal study of college adjustment and performance. *Journal of Personality and Social Psychology, 63,* 989-1003.

Bailey, K. (1998). *Learning about language assessment: Dilemmas, decisions, and directions.* Cambridge, England: Cambridge University Press.

Baker, S. C., & MacIntyre, P. D. (2000). The role of gender and immersion in communication and second language orientations. *Language Learning, 50*(2), 311-341. doi: 10.1111/0023-8333.00224.

Ballmann, J. M., & Mueller, J. J. (2008). Using self-determination theory to describe the academic motivation of allied health professional-level college student. *Journal of Allied Health, 37,* 90-96.

Bandalos, D. L. (2002). The effects of item parceling on goodness-of-fit and parameter estimate bias in structural equation modeling. *Structural Equation Modeling, 9*(1), 78-102. doi:10.1207/S15328007SEM0901_5.

Bandalos, D. L., & Finney, S. J. (2001). Item parceling issues in structural equation modeling. In G. A. Marcoulides & R. E. Schumacker (Eds.), *New development and techniques in structural equation modeling* (pp. 269-296). Mahwah, NJ: Erlbaum.

Bandura, A. (1997). *Self-efficacy: The exercise of control.* New York, NY: W. H. Freeman.

Bandura, A. (1982). Self-efficacy mechanism in human agency. *American Psychologist, 31,* 122-144.

Beglar, D. (2009a). [Background Questionnaire]. Unpublished, untitled work.

Beglar, D. (2009b). [Affective Orientation Questionnaire] Unpublished, untitled work.

Benson, P. (2001). *Teaching and researching autonomy in language learning.* Harlow, England: Longman.

Benson, P. (2006). Autonomy in language teaching and learning. *Language Teaching, 40,* 21-40. doi:org/10.1017/s0261444806003958.

Blanche, P., & Merino, B. (1989). Self-assessment of foreign language skills: Implications for teachers and researchers. *Language Learning, 39*(3), 313-338.

Blascovich, J., & Tomoka. J. (1993). Measures of self-esteem. In J. P. Robinson, P. R. Shaver, & L. S. Wrightsman (Eds.), *Measures of personality and social psychological attitudes* (pp. 115-160). Ann Arbor, MI: Institute for Social Research.

Bransford, J. D., Brown, A. L., & Cocking R. R. (1999). *How people learn: Brain, mind, experience and school.* Washington, DC: National Academy Press.

Brantmeier, C., & Vanderplank, R. (2008). Descriptive and criterion-referenced self-assessment with L2 readers. *System, 36,* 456-477. doi:10.1016/j.system.2012.01.003.

Brickman, S. J., & Miller, R. B. (2001). The impact of sociocultural knowledge on future goals and self-regulation. In D. McInerny & S. Van Etten (Eds.), *Research on sociocultural influences on motivation and learning* (pp. 119-137). Greenwich, CT: Information Age.

British Council (2011). Retrieved May 5th, 2011from http:/ www.teachingenglish.org.uk/ think/knowledge-wiki/metacognitiveawareness.

British Council (2015). CEFR and British Council. Retrieved March 2nd, 2016 from https://www.britishcouncil.jp/sites/default/files/pro-ee-lesson-level-cefr-jp.pdf.

Brown, D. (2000). *Principles of language learning and teaching.* New York, NY: Longman.

Brown, J. D. (2001)... *Using surveys in language programs.* Cambridge, England: Cambridge University Press.

Brunelle-Joiner, K. M. (1999). Effects of an extended orientation program on personal resiliency and adjustment to college as it relates to academic performance and retention. *Dissertation Abstracts International, Section A: Humanities and Social Sciences, 60,* 354.

Burgoon, J. K. (1976). The unwillingness to communicate scale: Development and validation. *Communication Monographs, 43,* 60-69.

Business Japanese Test (2009). Retrieved August 9th, 2010 from http://www.kanken.or.jp/ bjt/evaluation/evaluation.html.

Byrne, B. M. (2006). *Structural equation modeling with EQS: Basic concepts, applications and programming* (2nd ed.). Mahwah, NJ: Erlbaum.

Cattell, R. B., & Burdsal, C. A. (1975). The radical parcel double factoring design: A solution to the item vs. parcel controversy. *Multivariate Behavioral Research, 10,* 165-179.

Chastain, K. (1975). Affective and ability factors in second language acquisition. *Language Learning, 25,* 153-161.

Cheng, Y-S., Horwitz, E. K., & Schallert, D. L. (1999). Language anxiety: Differentiating writing and speaking components. *Language Learning, 49*(3),417-446.

Cheng, Y-S. (2004). A measure of second language writing anxiety: Scale development and preliminary validation. *Journal of Second Language Writing, 13*, 313-335. doi:10.1016/j.jslw.2004.07.001.

Christou, C., Phillipou, G., & Menon, M. E. (2001). Preservice teachers' self-esteem and mathematics achievement. *Contemporary Educational Psychology, 26*, 44-60. doi:10.1006/ceps.1999.1028.

Church, M. A., Elliot, A. J., & Gable, S. L. (2001). Perceptions of classroom environment, achievement goals, and achievement outcomes. *Journal of Educational Psychology, 93*(1), 43-54. doi:10.1037/10022-0663.93.1.43.

Clément, R. (1980). Ethnicity, contact, and communicative competence in a second language. In H. Giles, W. P. Robinson, & P. M. Smith (Eds.), *Language: Social psychological perspectives* (pp. 147-154). Oxford, England: Pergamon.

Clément, R. (1986). Second language proficiency and acculturation: An investigation of the effects of language status and individual characteristics. *Journal of Language and Social Psychology, 5*, 271-290. doi:10.1177/0261927x3022002003.

Clément, R., Baker, S. & MacIntyre, P. D. (2003). Willingness to communicate in a second language: The effects of context, norms and vitality. *Journal of Language and Social Psychology, 22*(2), 190-209. doi:10.1177/026927X03252758.

Clément, R., Dörnyei, Z., & Noel, K. A. (1994). Motivation, self-confidence, and group cohesion in the foreign language classroom. *Language Learning, 44*, 417-448.

Clément, R., Gardner, R. C., & Smythe, P. C. (1977). Motivational variables in second language acquisition: A study of Francophones learning English. *Canadian Journal of Behavioral Science, 12*, 293-302.

Clément, R., & Kruidenier, B. G. (1985). Aptitude, attitude, and motivation in second language proficiency: A test of Clément's model. *Journal of Language and Social Psychology, 4*, 21-37.

Clute, S. P. (1984). Mathematics anxiety, instructional method, and achievement in a survey course in college mathematics. *Journal for Research in Mathematics Education, 15*, 50-58.

Collet. P., & Sullivan, K. (2010). Considering the use of can-do statements to develop learners' self-regulative and metacognitive strategies. In M. G. Schmidt, N. Nagamuma, F.

O'Dwyer, A. Imig, & K. Sakai (Eds.), *Can-do statements in language education in Japan and beyond–Applications of the CEFR* (pp. 167-183). Tokyo: Asahi Press.

Coombe, C., & Canning, C. (2010). *Using self-assessment in the classroom: Rationale and suggested techniques.* Retrieved December 31, 2010 from http://www.philselfsupport.com/self-assessmenttechniques.htm.

Coopersmith, S. (1981). *Self-esteem inventories,* Palo Alto, CA: Consulting Psychologists.

Council of Europe (2010). www.coe.int/portfolio (August 9, 2010).

Council of Europe (2001). *Common European framework of reference for languages: Learning, teaching, assessment.* Cambridge: Cambridge University Press.

Cresswell, J. W. (2009). *Research design: Qualitative, quantitative and mixed methods approaches.* Los Angeles, CA: Sage.

Cresswell, J. W., & Plano-Clark, V. L. (2007). *Designing and conducting mixed methods research.* London, England: Sage.

Dalgas-Perish, P. (2006). Effects of a self-esteem intervention program on school-age children. *Pediatric Nursing, 32,* 341-348.

Deci, E. L., & Ryan, R. M. (1985). *Intrinsic motivation and self-determination in human behavior.* New York, NY: Plenum Press.

Dickinson, L. (1987). *Self-instruction in language learning.* Cambridge, England: Cambridge University Press.

Dörnyei, Z. (2001). *Teaching and researching motivation.* London, England: Longman.

Douglas, D. (2000). *Assessing language for specific purposes.* Cambridge, England: Cambridge University Press.

Dupeyrat, C., & Marine, C. (2005). Implicit theories of intelligence, goal orientation, cognitive engagement, and achievement: A test of Dweck's model with returning to school adults. *Contemporary Educational Psychology, 30,* 43-59. doi:10.1016/j.cedpsych.2004.01.007.

Dweck, C. (1986). Motivational processes affecting learning. *American Psychologist, 41,* 1040-1048.

Eiken Can-Do List (2006). Retrieved September 11th, 2009 from http://www.eiken.or.jp/about/cando/cando.html.

REFERENCES

Elliot, A. J. (1999) Approach and avoidance motivation and achievement goals. *Educational Psychologist, 34,* 169-189.

Elwood, J. A. (2011). *Enriching structural models of L2 willingness to communicate: The role of personality, ego permeability, and perceived distance.* Doctoral Dissertation. Temple University, Tokyo.

English Quest Group (2011). Retrieved February 6th, 2011 from http:/eq-g.com/article/exam-hikaku.

Epstein, S. (1973). The self-concept revisited or a theory of a theory. *American Psychologist, 28,* 405-416.

ETS (2006). Kyusyu Industrial University Can-Do research. *TOEIC Bridge Newsletter, 9,* August, 2006.

ETS (2008). Can-Do Guide Executive Summary: Listening and Reading. Retrieved January 5, 2017 from http://www. ets.org/Media/Tests/…/TOEIC_Can_Do.pdf

Falchikov, N., & 'Boud, D. (1989). Student self-assessment in higher education: Meta-analysis. *Review of Educational Research, 59,* 395-430.

Fukuda, H. (2007). Fukugengo syugi niokeru gengoishiki kyoiku. *Ibunka Communication Kenkyuu, 19,* 101-119.

Fushino, K. (2008). *Measuring Japanese University students' readiness for second- language group work and its relation to willingness to communicate.* Doctoral Dissertation, Temple University, Tokyo.

Gardner, R. C. (1958). *Social factors in second-language acquisition.* Unpublished master's thesis, McGill University, Montreal.

Gardner, R. C. (1960). *Motivational variables in second-language acquisition.* Unpublished doctoral dissertation, McGill University, Montreal.

Gardner, R. C. (1985a). *Social psychology and second language learning.* London, England: Edward Arnold.

Gardner, R. C. (1985b). *The attitude/motivation test battery: Technical report.* Research Bulletin No.10 by the Language Research Group, Department of Psychology, University of Western Ontario.

Gardner, R. C. (2000). Correlation, causation, motivation, and second language acquisition. *Canadian Psychology, 41*, 10-24.

Gardner, R. C. (2010). *Motivation and second language acquisition: The socio-educational model*. New York, NY: Peter Lang. doi:978-1- 4331-0459-6

Gardner, R. C., Day, J. B., & MacIntyre, P. D. (1992). Integrative motivation, induced anxiety, and language learning in a controlled environment. *Studies in Second Language Acquisition, 14*(2), 197-214.

Gardner, R. C., & Glisman, L. (1982). On "Gardner on affect": a discussion of validity as it relates to the Attitude/Motivation Test Battery: A response from Gardner. *Language Learning, 32,* 191-200.

Gardner, R. C., Lalonde, R. N., Moorcroft, R., & Evers, F. T. (1987). Second language attrition: The role of motivation and use. *Journal of Language and Social Psychology, 6*, 29-47.

Gardner, R. C., & Lambert, W. (1959). Motivational variables in second language acquisition. *Canadian Journal of Psychology, 13*, 266-272.

Gardner, R. C., & Lambert, W. E. (1972). *Attitudes and motivation in second language learning*. Rowley, MA: Newbury House.

Garner, R. C., & MacIntyre, P. D. (1993a). An instrumental motivation in language study: Who says it isn't effective? *Studies in Second Language Acquisition, 13*(1), 57-72.

Gardner, R. C., & MacIntyre, P. D. (1993b). On the measurement of affective variables in second language learning. *Language Learning, 43,* 157-194.

Gardner, R. C., Tremblay, P. F., & Masgoret, A-M. (1997). Towards a full model of second language learning: An empirical investigation. *The Modern Language Journal, 81,* 345-362.

Gardner, R. C., & Smythe, P. C. (1975). *Second language acquisition: A social psychological approach*. (Research Bulletin No. 332). London, Ontario: University of western Ontario, Department of Psychology.

Gliksman, L., Gardner, R. C., & Smythe, P. C. (1982). The role of the integrative motive on students' participation in the French classroom. *The Canadian Modern Language Review, 38,* 625-647.

Green, A. (2011). From common European framework to classroom application: The English profile solution. *Proceedings of the 16th conference of Pan-Pacific Association of Applied Linguistics. 1-5.*

Hagtvet, K. A., & Nasser, F. M. (2004). How well do item parcels represent conceptually defined latent constructs? A two-faceted approach. *Structural Equation Modeling, 11*(2), 168-193. doi:10.1207/s15328007sem1102_2.

Hall, R. J., Snell, A. F., & Foust, M. S. (1999). Item parceling strategies in SEM: Investigating the subtle effects of unmodeled secondary constructs. *Organizational Research Methods, 2,* 233-256.

Hardré, P. L., Crowson, H. M., Debacker, T. K., & White, D. (2007). Predicting the academic motivation of rural high school students. *The Journal of Experimental Education, 75*(4), 247-269. doi:10.3200/JEXE.75.4.247-269.

Harter, S. (1982). The perceived competence scale for children. *Child Development, 53,* 87-97.

Harter, S. (1983). Developmental perspectives on the self-system. In M. Hetherington (Ed.), *Handbook of child psychology: Social and personality development (Vol. 4)* (pp. 275-385). New York, NY: Wiley.

Hashimoto, Y. (2002). Motivation and willingness to communicate as predictors of reported L2 use: The Japanese ESL context. *Second Language Studies, 20*(2), 29-70.

Heckhausen, H. (1991). *Motivation and action.* New York, NY: Springer.

Hein, V., & Hagger, M. S. (2007). Global self-esteem, goal achievement orientations, a self-determined behavioral regulations in a physical education setting. *Journal of Sports Sciences, 25,* 149-159. doi:10.1080/02640410600598315.

Hiromori, Y. (2009). Ehime University ban eigounyou nouryoku handan kijyun (Can-do List) no seichika to datousei no kensyou. *ARELE (Annual Review of English Language Education in Japan), 20,* 281-290.

Hishimura, E. S., Foster, J. E., Miyamoto, R. H., Nishimura, S. T., Andrade, N. N., Nahulu, L. B., et al. (2001). Association between measures of academic performance and psychological adjustment for Asian/Pacific Islander adolescents. *School Psychology International, 22,* 303-320. doi:10.1177/0143034301223007.

Horwitz, E. K., Horwitz, M. B., & Cope, J. (1986). Foreign language classroom anxiety. *Modern Language Journal, 70,* 125-132.

Hu, L. & Bentler, P. M. (1999). Cutoff criteria for fit indexes in covariance structure analysis: Conventional criteria versus new alternatives. *Structural Equation Modeling, 6,* 1-55.

Hui, E. K. P., Sun, R. C. F., Sau-Yan Chow, S., & Ho-Tat Chu, M. (2011). Explaining Chinese students' academic motivation: Filial piety and self-determination. *Educational Psychology, 31.* 377-392. doi:10.1080/01443410.2011.599309.

Ja, R., Huai, L-L., & Guo, W. (2007). The relationship between achievement-motivation and self-esteem of junior high school students. *China Journal of Health Psychology, 15,* 642-644. doi:10.1016/j.sbspro.2011.11.308.

Jacobs, H., Zingraf, S., Wormuth, D., Hartfiel, V., & Hughey, J. (1981). *Testing EFL composition: A practical approach.* Rowley, MA: Newbury House.

Japan Language Proficiency Test (2010). http://www.jlpt.jp/about/points.html (August 8th, 2010).

Keddle, J. S. (2004). The CEFR and the secondary school syllabus. In K. Morrow (Ed.), *Insights from the Common European Framework* (pp. 125-140). Oxford, England: Oxford University Press.

Kenny, D. A. (2014). Retrieved September 6, 2014 from http: davidakenny.net/cm/pathanal.htm.

Kim, S., & Hagtvet, K. A. (2003) The impact of misspecified item parceling on representing latent variables in covariance structure modeling: A simulation study. *Structural Equation Modeling, 10*(1), 101-127. doi:10.1207/s15328007sem1001_5.

Kishton, J. M., & Widaman, K. F. (1994). Unidimensional versus domain representative parceling of questionnaire items: An empirical example. *Educational and Psychological Measurement, 54,* 757-765.

Kline, R. (2005). *Principles and practices of structural equation modeling* (2nd ed.), New York, NY: The Guilford Press.

Koike, I. (2008). Global jidainiokeru Nihonjin no Eigo communication nouryoku no totatumokuhy ou no National standard kawo mezashite. *Meikai University Applied Lin-*

guistics Kenkyu, 10, 55-65.

Koike, I. (2009). CEFR tonihonno Eigokyoikunokadai. *ELEC Eigo Tembo, 117,* 14-19.

Koike, I. (2010). *English skills: What do companies really need?* Tokyo: Asahi.

Kyusyu Industrial University (2009). http://www.ip.kyusan-u.ac.jp/gp/cando.html (August 25th, 2009)

Linacre, J. M. (1999). Investigating rating scale category utility. *Journal of Outcome Measurement, 3*(2), 103-122.

Linacre, J. M. (2004). Winsteps (Version 3.51) [Computer software]. Chicago, IL: MESA Press.

Linacre, J. M. (2006). A user's guide to FACETS. Chicago: MESA Press.

Lincoln, Y., & Guba, E. (1985). *Naturalistic inquiry.* Beverly Hills, CA: Sage.

Little, D. (2005). The Common European Framework and the European Language Portfolio: Involving learners and their judgments in the assessment process. *Language Testing, 22,* 321-336. doi:10.1191/0265532205lt311oa.

Little, T. D., Lindenberger, U., & Nesselroade, J. R. (1999). On selecting indicators for multivariate measurement and modeling with latent variables: When "good" indicators are bad and "bad" indicators are good. *Psychological Methods, 4*(2), 192-211.

Little, T. D., Cunningham, W. A., Shabar, G., & Widaman, K. (2002). To parcel or not to parcel: Exploring the question, weighing the merits. *Structural Equation Modeling, 9*(2), 151-173. doi:10.1207/S15328008SEM0902_1.

Little, T. D. (2013). *Longitudinal structural equation modeling.* New York, NY: The Guilford Press.

Liu, M. (2011). Predicting effects of personality traits, self-esteem, language class risk-taking and sociability on Chinese university EFL Learners' performance in English. *Journal of Second Language Teaching and Research, 1,* 30-57.

MacIntyre, P. D. (1994). Variables underlying willingness to communicate: A causal analysis. *Communication Research Reports, 11,* 135-142.

MacIntyre, P. D. (2002). Motivation, anxiety and emotion in second language acquisition. In P. Robinson (Ed.), *Individual differences and instructed language learning* (pp. 45-68). Philadelphia, PA: Benjamins.

MacIntyre, P. D., Babin, P. A., & Clément, R. (1999). Willingness to communicate: Antecedents & consequences. *Communication Quarterly, 47*, 215-229.

MacIntyre, P. D., Clément, R., Baker, S. C., & Conrod, S. (2001). Willingness to communicate, social support and language learning orientations of immersion students. *Studies in Second Language Acquisition, 23*, 369-388. doi:10.1017/so272263101003035.

MacIntyre, P. D., Dörnyei, Z., Clément, R., & Noels, K. (1998). Conceptualizing willingness to communicate in a L2: A situational model of L2 confidence and affiliation. *Modern Language Journal, 82*, 545-562.

MacIntyre, P. D., & Gardner, R. C. (1991). Methods and results in the study of anxiety in language learning: A review of the literature. *Language Learning, 41*, 85-117.

MacIntyre, P. D., & MacMaster, K., & Baker, S. (2001). The convergence of multiple models of motivation for second language learning: Gardner, Pintrich, Kuhl and McCroskey. In Z. Dörnyei & R. Schmidt (Eds.), *Motivation and second language acquisition* (pp. 462-492). Honolulu, HI: University of Hawaii Press.

Mardia, K. V. (1970). Measures of multivariate skewness and kurtosis applications. *Biometrika 57,* 519-530.

Marsh, H. W., Hau, K-T., Balla, J. R., & Grayson, D. (1998). Is more ever too much? The number of indicators per factor in confirmatory factor analysis. *Multivariate Behavioral Research, 33,* 181-220.

Matsuno, S. (2009). Self, peer, and teacher-assessments in Japanese university EFL writing classrooms. *Language Testing, 26,* 75-100. doi:10.1177/0265532208097337.

Masgoret, A-M., Bernaus, M., & Gardner, R.C. (2001) Examining the role of attitudes and motivation outside of the formal classroom: A test of the mini AMTB for children. In Z. Dörnyei & R Schmidt (Eds.), *Motivation and second language acquisition* (pp. 281-295). Honolulu: University of Hawaii, Second Language Teaching and Curriculum Center.

Masgoret, A-M., & Gardner, R. C. (2003) Attitudes, motivation, and second language learning: A meta-analysis of studies conducted by Gardner and associates. *Language Learning, 53*, 167-210. doi:10.1111/1467-9922.00227.

McCroskey, J. C. (1977). Oral communication apprehension: A summary of recent theory and research. *Human Communication Research, 4,* 78-96.

McCroskey, J., & Baer, J. E. (1985). *Willingness to communicate: The construct and its measurement.* Paper presented at the annual convention of the Speech Communication Association, Denver, CO.

McCroskey, J., & Richmond, V. P. (1987). Willingness to communicate and interpersonal communication. In J. McCroskey & J. A. Daly (Eds.), *Personality and interpersonal communication: Vol. 8* (pp. 129-156). Newbury Park, CA: Sage.

McCroskey, J. C., & Richmond, V. P. (1990). Willingness to communicate: Differing cultural perspective. *Southern Communication Journal, 56,* 72-77.

McCroskey, J., & Richmond, V. P. (1991). Willingness to communicate: A cognitive view. In M. Booth-Butterfield (Ed.), *Communication, cognition and anxiety* (pp. 19-37). Newbury Park, CA: Sage.

McMaster University (2011). The importance of self-esteem: Implications for practice. Retrieved November 6th 2011 from http://www.canchild.ca/en/childrenfamilies/self-esteem.asp

Meece, J. L., Wigfield, A., & Eccles, J. S. (1990). Predictors of math anxiety and its consequences for young adolescents' course enrollment intentions and performances in mathematics. *Journal of Educational Psychology, 82,* 60-70.

Miller, R. B., & Brickman, S. J. (2004). A model of future-oriented motivation and self-regulation. *Educational Psychology Review, 16*(1), 9-33. doi:10.1023/B.EDPR.0000 012343.96370.39.

Miller, R. B., DeBaker, T., & Greene, B. (1999). Perceived instrumentality and academics: The link to task valuing. *Journal of Instrumental Psychology, 21,* 388-422.

MEXT (Ministry of Education, Culture, Sports, Science and Technology) (2003). Eigo-gatukaeru Nihonjinno Ikuseinotameno Koudoukeikaku. http://www/mext.go.jp/ b_menu/houdou/15/03/03033101.htm (August 23rd, 2008)

MEXT (Ministry of Education, Culture, Sports, Science and Technology) (2008). Daigaku niokeru kyouikunaiyou nadono kaikakujoukyou nituite. Retrieved August 23rd, 2009 from http://www/mext.go.jp/b_menu/houdou20/06/08061617/001.htm

MEXT (Ministry of Education, Culture, Sports, Science and Technology)(2013). Can-Do list no katachideno gakusyuutoutatumokuhyou no tebiki September 15, 2014 from http://www.mext.go.jp/a_menu/kokusai/.../1332306_4.pdf

Milanovic, M. (Ed.). (2002). *Studies in language testing 7.* Cambridge, England: Cambridge University Press.

Miller, R. B., Greene, B. A., Montalvo, G. P., Ravindran, B., & Nicholls, J. D. (1996). Engagement in academic work: The role of learning goals, future consequences, pleasing others, and perceived ability. *Contemporary Educational Psychology, 21,* 388-422.

Moritz, C. (1995). Self-assessment of foreign language proficiency: A critical analysis of issues and a study of cognitive orientations of French learners. Unpublished PhD dissertation, Cornell University.

Mullan, E., Markland, D., & Ingledew, D. K. (1997). A Graded conceptualization of self-determination in the regulation of exercise behavior: Development of a measure using confirmatory factor analytic procedures. *Personality and Individual Differences, 23,* 745-752.

Naganuma, N., & Miyajima, M. (2006). Seisen academic can-do framework kouchikuno kokoromito sonokadaito tenbou. *Seisen University Kiyou, 54,* 43-61.

Naganuma, N. (2008). Can-do syakudoha ikani eigokyouikuwo henkakushiuruka: Can-Do kenkyu no houkousei. *ARCLE REVIEW, 2,* 55-77.

Naganuma, N., & Nagasue, A. (2006). *SELHi Jissenn ni motoduku Kasumi Can-do Grade no Kaihatu.* The 45th JACET Zenkoku Taikai Youkou.

Naganuma, N., Okuma, A., Wada, A., Ito, H., Kumagaya, R., & Noguchi H. (2007). *JLPT nihongonoryoku kijyutubun sakuseino kokoromi nihongonoryoku shiken (JLPT) Can-do statements shikoban no bunsekikara.* Nihongokyouikugakkai syuukitaikai.

Naganuma, N., Yoshida, K., Watabe, Y., Negishi, M. & Benesse Cooperation kokusaikyoiku jigyoubu (2005). Gakusei Can-do eigo kyouinishikicyousa karamita nihon, kankoku, cyugoku eigokyouiku no genjoto kongo no kadai. *Higashi Asiakoukou eigokyoiku GTEC cyousa: Koukousei no ishikito koudoukaramiru eigokyouiku no seikato kadai.* B. Cooperation, 11-30.

Nakanishi, C., Hayashi, C., Kobayashi, W., & Sakuma, A. (2010a). Effects of Can-Do lists at college English classes. *Kunitachi College of Music Kenkyu Kiyo, 44,* 71-82.

Nakanishi, C., Hayashi, C., Kobayashi, W., & Sakuma, A. (2010b). Development of Can-Do statements for college students: A preliminary study. *JACET Annual Report, 6,* 14-23.

Negishi, M. (2001). Can-do list no kaihatu—Sono process to tenbou. *Development, 8,* 22-29.

Negishi, M. (2006). GTEC for Students Can-do statements no datousei kensyou kenkyuu gaikann. *ARCLE Review, 1,* 96-103.

Noels, K. A., & Clément, R. (1989). Orientations to learning German: The effects of language heritage on second language acquisition. *Canadian Modern Language Review, 45,* 245-257.

Noel, K. A., Pelletier, L. G., Clément, R., & Vallerand, R. J. (2000). Why are you learning a second language? Motivational orientations and self-determination theory. *Language Learning, 50,* 57-85. doi:10.1111/0023-8333.00111.

Nunan, D. (1988). *The learner centered curriculum.* Cambridge, England: Cambridge University Press.

O'Farrel, C. (2015). Enhancing student learning through assessment: A toolkit approach. September 3, 2015 from http:/ www. Ted.ie/teaching.../assets/.../250309_assessment_toolkit.pd.../

Oka, H., Kawanari, M., Takada, T., Tominaga, Y., & Nakamura, T. (2008). CEFRjapan: Pursuing the standards of "global English communicative competence." Presentation at JACET Zenkokutaikai, 47.

Oscarson, M. (1989a). *Self-assessment of foreign language skills: A survey of research and development work.* Strasbourg: Council of Europe.

Oscarson, M. (1989b). Self-assessment of language proficiency: Rationale and applications. *Language Testing, 6,* 1-13.

Oscarson, M. (1997). Self-assessment of foreign and second language proficiency. In C. Clapham & D. Corson (Eds.), *Language testing and assessment* (pp. 175-187). Dordrecht, Netherlands: Kluwer.

Owens, T. (2001). *Extending self-esteem theory and research.* Cambridge: Cambridge University Press.

Oxford, R. L (1990). *Language learning strategies: What every teacher should know.* New

York, NY: Newbury House.

Palaciou, L. M. (1998). *Foreign language anxiety and classroom environment: A study of Spanish university students.* Unpublished doctoral dissertation, The University of Texas at Austin.

Pajares, F., & Urdan, T. (2002). *Academic motivation of adolescents.* Greenwich, CT: Information Age.

Park, H., & Lee, A, R. (2005). L2 learners' anxiety, self-confidence and oral performance. *Proceeding of the 10th Conference of the Pan-Pacific Association of Applied Linguistics,* 197-208.

Peng, J. E., & Woodrow, L. (2010). Willingness to communicate in English: A model in the Chinese EFL classroom context. *Language Learning, 60*(4), 834-876. doi:10.1111/j.1467-9922.2010.00576.x.

Pepi, A., Faria, L., & Alesi, M. (2006). Personal conceptions of intelligence, self-esteem, and school achievement. *Adolescence, 41*, 615-631. doi:10:1016/j.sbspro.2006.12.164

Phillips, E. (1992). The effects of language anxiety on students' oral test performance and attitudes. *Modern Language Journal, 76*, 14-26.

Prats, D. C. (1990, April). *The effects of forming miniscales on the construct validity of the text anxiety inventory.* Paper presented at the National Council on Measurement in Education, Boston.

Price, M. L. (1991). The subjective experience of foreign language anxiety: Interviews with highly anxious students. In E.K. Horwits and D.J. Young (Eds.), *Language anxiety: From theory and research to classroom implications.* (pp.101-108). Upper Saddle River, NJ: Prentice Hall, Inc.

Randhawa, B. S., & Korpan, S. M. (1973). Assessment of some significant affective variables and the prediction of achievement in French. *Canadian Journal of Behavioral Science, 5*, 24-33.

Rasch, G. (1960). *Probabilistic models for some intelligence and attainment tests.* Chicago, IL: The University of Chicago Press.

Rayle, A. D., Arredondo, P., & Kupius, S. E. R. (2005). Educational self-efficacy of college women: Implication for theory, research and practice. *Journal of Counseling and*

Development, 83, 361-366. doi:10.1022/j.1556-6678.2005.tb00356.x.

Reeve, J., Jang, H., Hardré, P., & Omura, M. (2003). Providing a rational for an uninteresting activity as a motivating strategy to support another's self-determined extrinsic motivation. *Motivation and Emotion, 26*(3), 183-207. doi:10.1023/A:1021711629417.

Richards, J. C., Platt, J., & Platt, H. (1992). *Dictionary of language teaching & applied linguistics.* Essex, England: Longman.

Riessman, C. K. (1993). *Qualitative research method: Narrative analysis.* Newbury Park, CA: Sage.

Roberts, G. C., & Balague, G. (1991). *The development and validation of the perception success questionnaire.* Paper presented to the FEPSAS Congress, Cologne, Germany.

Rogers, C. R., & Dymond, R. F. (Eds.). (1954). *Psychotherapy and personality change: Coordinated studies in the client-centered approach.* Chicago, IL: University of Chicago Press.

Rosenberg, M. (1965). *Society and the adolescent self-image.* Princeton, NJ: Princeton University Press.

Rosenberg, M. (1986). *Conceiving the self.* Maalabar, FL: Krieger.

Ross, S. (1998). Self-assessment in second language testing: A meta-analysis and analysis of experimental factors. *Language Testing, 15,* 1-20.

Rushton, J. P., Brainerd, J. C., & Pressley, M. (1983). Behavioral development and construct validity: The principal of aggregation. *Psychological Bulletin, 94,* 18-38.

Ryan, R. M., & Deci, E. L. (2000). Self-determination theory and the facilitation of intrinsic motivation, social development, and well-being. *American Psychologist, 55,* 68-78. doi:10.1037/0003-066x.55.1.68.

Sakai, K. (2009). Nihon niokeru CEFR jyuyouno jittaito ouyounokanouseinituite: Gengokyouikuseisaku rituannimukete. *ELEC Eigo Tembou, 117,* 20-25.

Sakurai, N. (2005). Gaikokugo gakusyunotameno Europe kyotuusansyou wakugumi: Gakusyuu, kyoujyu, hyouka (CEF) wo sansyoushita Curriculum Kyotuhyouka no saihenseito Nihongojigyou heno Ouyou, Nihongo kyouiku jissen kyouiku Forum. 2009. Retrieved May 30th, 2009 from http://wwwsoc.nii.ac./nkg/kejpnkyu/Fou\rumhoukoku/sakurai.pd#search

Sansone, C., & Morgan, C. (1992). Intrinsic motivation and education: Competence in context. *Motivation and Emotion, 16,* 249-278.

Sasaki, M. (1993). Relationships among second language proficiency, foreign language aptitude, and intelligence: A structural equation modeling approach. *Language Learning, 43*(3), 313-344.

Sato, T. (2010). Validation of the EIKEN Can-do statement measure using Rasch measurement. *The Japan Language Testing Association Journal, 13,* 1-20.

Schumacker, R. E., & Lomax, R. G. (2004). *A beginner's guide to structural equation modeling* (2nd ed.). Mahwah, NJ: Erlbaum.

Schunk, D. H. (1996). Goal and self-evaluative influences during children's cognitive skill learning. *American Educational Research Journal, 33*(2), 359-382.

Scovel, T. (1978). The effect of affect: A review of the anxiety literature. *Language Learning, 28,*129-142.

Situ, Q-M., & Li, J-B. (2007). The relationship between self-esteem and interactive anxiety. *China Journal of Health Psychology, 15,* 1005-1007.

Sitzmann, T., Ely, K., Brown, K. G., & Bauer, K. (2010). Self-assessment of knowledge: A cognitive learning or affective measure? *Academy of Management Learning & Education, 9*(2), 169-191. doi:10.5465/amle.2011.0024A.

Skaalvik, S. M., & Hagtvet, B. (1990). Academic achievement and self-concept. *Journal of Personality and Social Psychology, 58,* 305-315.

Solberg Nes, L., Evans, D. R., & Segerstrom, S. C. (2009). Optimism and college retention: Mediation by motivation, performance, and adjustment. *Journal of Applied Social Psychology, 39,* 1887-1912. doi:10.1111/j.1559-1816.2009.00508.x.

STEP (2006). *The EIKEN Can-Do list.* Tokyo, Japan: The Society for Testing English Proficiency.

STEP (2009). Sample questions of the Eiken placement test B. *Eigo Nouryoku Hantei Test.* Tokyo, Japan: STEP.

Stipek, D. J., & Gralinski, J. H. (1996). Children's beliefs about intelligence and school performance. *Journal of Educational Psychology, 88,* 397-407.

Stringer, R. W., & Heath, N. (2008). Academic self-perception and its relationship to academic performance. *Canadian Journal of Education, 31,* 327-345.

Sullivan, K., & Hall, C. (1997). Introducing students to self-assessment. *Assessment & Evaluation in Higher Education, 22*, 289-306.

Stumph, H., & Stanley, J. C. (2002). Group data on high school Grade point averages and scores on academic aptitude tests as predictors of institutional graduation rates. *Educational and Psychological Measurement, 62*, 1042-1052. doi:10.1177/0013164 402238091.

Tabachnick, B. G., & Fidell, L. S. (2001). *Using multivariate statistics* (4th ed.). New York, NY: Harper Collins.

Tadaki, T. (2007). Common European reference and English education in universities. *Meijo Daigaku Kyoikunenpou, 2,* 42-53.

Takemura, M. (2008). Eiken can-do risutoniyoru writing ginonikansuru datoseino kensyo [Investigation of the validity of the Eiken can-do list for writing ability: using the lists of level pre-2 and level 3] STEP Bulletin, 20, 251-261.

Takeshita, A. (2008). My English no kouchiku nimuketa torikumi—Futukaniokeru Eigo 1-2 no zerokarano kaikaku. *Eigotenbou, 116,* 54-61.

Tanaka, A., Okuno, T., & Yamauchi, H. (2002). Achievement motives, cognitive and social competence, and achievement goals in the classroom. *Perceptual and Motor Skills, 95,* 445-458. doi:10.2466/pms.2002.95.2.445.

Tanaka, S. (2008). Eigo kyouiku niokeru Can-do kenkyu no kouzu.[The structure of Can-do research in English education] *ARCLE Review, 2,* 6-33.

Tremblay, P. F., & Gardner, R. C. (1995). Expanding the motivation construct in language learning. *Modern Language Journal, 79,* 505-518.

Touno, Y. (Ed.). (2013). *Eigo toutatsudo shihyou CEFR-J Guide book.* [CEFR-J Guide book, A resource book for using Can-Do Descriptors for English Language Teaching] Taisyuukanshoten.

Ullman, J. B. (2001). Structural equation modeling. In B. G. Tabachnick & L. S. Fidell, *Using multivariate statistics* (4th ed.) (pp. 653-771). Needham Heights, MA: Allyn & Bacon.

Unrau, N., & Schlackman, J. (2006). Motivation and its relationship with reading achievement in an urban middle school. *The Journal of Educational Research, 100,* 81-101. doi:10.3200/JOER.100.2.81-101.

Ushioda, E. (2007). Motivation, autonomy and sociocultural theory. In P. Benson (Ed.), *Learner autonomy and perspectives* (pp. 5-24). Dublin, Ireland: Authentik.

Usuta, Y. (2009). Eiken can-do risutono supikingubunyaniokeru can-do koumokuno datoseikensyo [Invesitigation of the validity of can-do items for speaking skills in the Eiken Can-do List] *STEP Bulletin, 21,* 262-273.

Vieira, Jr. E. T., & Grantham, S. (2009). Antecedent influence on children's extrinsic motivation to go online. *Journal of Applied Social Psychology, 39,* 707-733. doi:10.1111/j.1559-1816.2009.00457.x.

Watkins, D. (2000). Language learning strategy and personality variables: Focusing on extroversion and introversion. *International Review of Applied Linguistics in Language Teaching (IRAL), 38,* 71-81. doi:10.1515/iral.2000.38.1.71.

Weaver, C. (2010). *Japanese university students' willingness to use English with different interlocutors.* Unpublished doctoral dissertation. Temple University. Tokyo.

Weir, C. J. (2005). Limitations of the Common European Framework for developing comparable examinations and tests. *Language Testing, 22,* 281-300. doi:10.1191/0265532205lt309oa.

Wray, L. D., & Stone, E. R. (2005). The role of self-esteem and anxiety in decision making for self-versus others in relationships. *Journal of Behavioral Decision Making, 18,* 125-144. doi:10.1002/bdm.490.

Wright, B. D., & Linacre, J. M. (1994). Reasonable mean-square fit values. *Rasch Measurement Transactions, 8*(3), *370.*

Wright, B. D., & Masters, G. N. (1982). *Rating scale analysis.* Chicago, IL: MESA Press.

Yashima, T. (2002). Willingness to communicate in a second language: The Japanese EFL context. *The Modern Language Journal, 86,* 54-66. doi:10.1111/1540-4781.00136.

Yamanishi, H., & Hiromori, Y. (2008). Tekisetuna Hyoukawo mezashita Ehime University kyotuu Kyoiku English curriculum kaihatuheno torikumi.[Towards an important assessment: Ehime University's trial to cultivate a common English curriculum]. *Annual Review of English Language Education in Japan, 19,* 263-272.

Yoshida, K. (2006). *The EIKEN Can-Do list.* Tokyo, Japan: The Society for Testing English Proficiency.

Yoshizawa, K. (2009). To what extent can self-assessment of language skill predict language proficiency of EFL learners in school context in Japan? *Gaikokugokyouiku Kenkyu, 17,* 65-82.

Young Learners English Test (2010). Retrieved August 12th, 2010 from www.Cambridgeesol.Org/exams/young-learners/yle.html.

Zhang, L. (2005). Prediction of Chinese life satisfaction: Contribution of collective self-esteem. *International Journal of Psychology, 40,* 189-200. doi:10.1080/00207590444 000285.

APPENDICES

APPENDIX A
STUDENTS' PROFICIENCY LEVEL BY CEFR
(COMMON REFERENCE LEVELS: GLOBAL SCALE)

Independent User	B1	Can understand the main points of clear standard input on familiar matters regularly encountered in work, school, leisure, etc. Can deal with most situations likely to arise whilst traveling in an area where the language is spoken. Can produce simple connected text on topics which are familiar or of personal interest. Can describe experiences and events, dreams, hopes and ambitions and briefly give reasons and explanations for opinions and plans.
Basic User	A2	Can understand sentences and frequently used expressions related to areas of most immediate relevance (e.g., very basic personal and family information, shopping, local geography, employment). Can communicate in simple and routine tasks requiring a simple and direct exchange of information on familiar and routine matters. Can describe in simple terms aspects of his/ her background, immediate environment and matters in areas of immediate need.
Basic User	A1	Can understand and use familiar everyday expressions and very basic phrases aimed at the satisfaction of needs of concrete type. Can introduce him / herself and others and can ask and answer questions about personal details such as where he/she lives, people he/she knows and things he/she has. Can interact in a simple way provided the other person talks slowly and clearly and is prepared to help.

APPENDIX B   CLASS SYLLABUSES IN 2010 AND 2011 ACADEMIC YEARS   *171*

APPENDIX B
CLASS SYLLABUSES IN 2010 AND 2011 ACADEMIC YEARS

A Class (Music College), the first semester of 2010

Class	Activity
1	Orientation; Speaking, Self-introduction; Reading, Unit 1: Should capital punishment be abolished?; Can-do questionnaire 1
2	Writing (composition): Write an essay in support of the abolishment of capital punishment; Listening and Grammar: English Quest Unit 8 (Modification 3)
3	Vocabulary Test 1; Writing (Essay): Should English be taught in primary school?; Should mothers stay at home until their children go to school?; Should the marriage system be abolished?; Should children leave home after reach the age of twenty?; Should university entrance examinations be abolished?
4	Speaking: Presentation; Reading: Is English the world most common language?; Should smoking be banned in public places?
5	Vocabulary Test 2; Reading, Unit 2: How are people today using mobile phones? Listening and Grammar: English Quest Unit 9 (Relative pronoun); Writing (composition): Why are coffee shops so popular in Japan?
6	Reading: The comic café; Green tea is booming.; Writing (Essay): Hot spring (*onsen*) are now popular again; Chinese noodles ("ramen") are booming Why have personal computer spread so quickly?; Why have mobile phones spread so quickly?; Why are karaoke boxes so popular?; Free essay title
7	Vocabulary Test 3; Writing: Continued from 6th class.; Reading: Unit 3: Your eyebrows express more than your eyes; Can-do questionnaire 2
8	Speaking: Presentation; Reading: Mobile Phones may affect your fertility; Hunger Hormone.
9	Vocabulary Test 4; Listening and Grammar: English Quest 10 (Relative adverbs); Writing (composition): Explain the experiment conducted by Pavlov.
10	Writing(Essay): Women can do more things at the same time than men; Free essay title; Reading, Unit 4: What are the merits and demerits of the lifetime employment system?
11	Vocabulary Test 5; Speaking: Presentation; Reading: Abortion: Murder or Freedom?; Euthanasia; Writing (composition): What are the merits and demerits of paper swapping in the classroom?
12	Listening and Grammar: English Quest unit 11 (Comparatives); Can-do questionnaire 3
13	Writing (Essay): What are the merits and demerits of the Japanese school system?; What are the merits and demerits of e-learning?; What are the merits and demerits of living alone?; What are the merits and demerits of living in an apartment(flat) rather than in a house?; Free essay; Can-do interview 1
14	Final examination (60 minutes)

172 APPENDICES

A class (Music College), second semester 2010.

Class	Activity
1	Speaking: (30 seconds) What did you do during the summer holiday?; Reading, Unit 5: Japanese and British university entrance systems; Writing (composition): Comparing co-educational and single-sex schools.
2	Vocabulary Test 7; Reading: Sociology and Anthropology; Japanese and western Employment Systems.
3	Speaking: (30 seconds) What did you do last weekend?; Listening and Grammar: English Quest Unit 12 (Auxiliary verb); Writing (Essay): 1 Compare Japanese and American family life. 2 Compare television news and newspaper news. 3 Compare public school education with private school education. 4 Compare city life and country life. 5 Free essay.
4	Vocabulary Test 8; Writing (Essay): Continued from the 3rd class; Reading: Communism and Capitalism.
5	Speaking: (30 seconds) What is your major?; Speaking: Presentation; Writing (composition): Divide the countries of the world into three groups: those surrounded by the sea, those partly facing the sea, and those that are landlocked.
6	Vocabulary Test 9; Reading: Holy Europe Religious Worlds; Listening and Grammar: English Quest Unit 13 (Conditional clause and Subjunctive)
7	Writing (Essay): Developed, rapidly developing, and still underdeveloped countries. Countries with hot, temperate, and cold climates.; Europe, Asia, Africa and America.; Free essay title; Reading, Unit 7: How to behave at a buffet party.
8	Vocabulary Test 10; Poetry recitation practice: My heart leaps up when I be hold by William Wordsworth; Listening and Grammar: English Quest Unit 14 (Conditional clause and Subjunctive)
9	Speaking: (30 seconds) What do you want to do after graduation?; Poetry recitation practice: My heart leaps up when I behold; Writing (composition): How to succeed in an interview.
10	Vocabulary Test 11; Poetry recitation practice: My heart leaps up when I behold; Reading: How to join in a discussion. How to prevent suicides; Writing (Essay) 1 How to save paper / water / electricity. (Choose one item.) 2 How to succeed in an exam. 3 How to make friends. 4 How to stay fit. (How to stay healthy.) 5 Free essay.
11	Speaking: Presentation; Poetry recitation practice: My heart leaps up when I behold; Reading, Unit 9: The falling birthrate; Listening and Grammar: English Quest Unit 7 (Modification 2)
12	Vocabulary Test 12; Poetry recitation practice: My heart leaps up when I behold; Writing (composition): All Japanese public schools have gone over to a five-day school week. What effects do you think this will have on society?
13	Speaking: Poetry recitation exam; Can-do questionnaire 4; Can-do interview 2; Writing: 1 What effects have computers had on society? 2 What is the influence of the spread of mobile phones on society? 3 How did the Meiji Restoration affect Japanese history? 4 Free essay.
14	Final examination (60 minutes)

APPENDIX B   CLASS SYLLABUSES IN 2010 AND 2011 ACADEMIC YEARS   *173*

B class (Music College), first semester 2010

Class	Activity
1	Orientation; Speaking: Self-introduction; Writing and Reading: Unit 1 Who am I?; Can-do questionnaire 1
2	Writing: Email letter of self-introduction; Writing: Editing the essay; Speaking: Giving feedback to your partner
3	Vocabulary Test 1; Reading: Is English the world's most common language?; Listening and Grammar: English Quest Unit 8 (Modification 3)
4	Speaking: Presentation; Writing and Reading: Unit 2 Special Places; Can-do questionnaire 2
5	Vocabulary Test 2; Writing: Special places and what happened there
6	Writing: Editing the essay; Speaking: Giving feedback to your partner; Listening and Grammar: English Quest Unit 9 (Relative pronoun)
7	Vocabulary Test 3; Speaking: Presentation; Writing and Reading, Unit 3: An Ideal Partner
8	Listening and Grammar: English Quest Unit 10 (Relative adverb); Writing: My Ideal Partner
9	Vocabulary Test 4; Writing: Editing; Speaking: Giving feedback to your partner; Writing and Reading, Unit 4: Snapshot
10	Speaking: Presentation; Listening and Grammar: English Quest Unit 11 (Comparison)
11	Vocabulary Test 5; Reading: The Comic Café; The Green Tea is Booming; Writing and Reading: Unit 4: Snapshot
12	Writing: My favorite photo; Writing: Editing the essay; Speaking: Giving feedback to your partner; Can-do interview 1
13	Vocabulary Test 6; Speaking: Presentation; Reading: Should smoking be banned in public places? Euthanasia; Can-do questionnaire 3
14	Final examination (60 minutes)

174   APPENDICES

B class (Music College), second semester 2010

Class	Activity
1	Speaking: (in 30 seconds) What did you do during the summer holidays?; Writing and Reading, Unit 5: My Seal
2	Vocabulary Test 7; Writing: My personal seal
3	Writing: Editing the essay; Speaking: Giving feedback to your partner; Reading: Sociology and Anthropology
4	Vocabulary Test 8; Speaking: (in 30 seconds) What is your major?; Speaking: Presentation; Listening and Grammar: English Quest Unit 12 (Auxiliary verb)
5	Speaking: (in 30 seconds) What did you do last weekends? Reading: Holy Europe Writing and Reading, Unit 6: It's a party
6	Vocabulary Test 9; Writing: A party notice and a paragraph; Writing: Editing the essay Speaking: Giving feedback to your partner
7	Speaking: Presentation; Poetry recitation practice: My heart leaps up when I behold by William Wordsworth; Listening and Grammar: English Quest Unit 13 (Conditional clause and Subjunctive); Writing and Reading, Unit 7: Thank-you letter
8	Vocabulary Test 10; Poetry recitation practice: My heart leaps up when I behold; Reading: How to join in a discussion; Writing: Thank-you letter
9	Speaking: (in 30 seconds) What do you want to do after graduation?; Poetry recitation practice: My heart leaps up when I behold; Writing Editing the essay; Speaking: Giving feedback to your partner
10	Vocabulary Test 11; Poetry recitation practice: My heart leaps up when I behold; Speaking: Presentation; Listening and Grammar: English Quest Unit 14 (Conditional clause and Subjunctive)
11	Poetry recitation practice: My heart leaps up when I behold; Speaking: What is your favorite music?; Reading: Christmas; Reading and Writing, Unit 8: Movie Review
12	Vocabulary Test 12; Poetry recitation practice: My heart leaps up when I behold; Writing: Movie Review; Can-do questionnaire 4
13	Poetry recitation exam; Writing: Editing the essay; Speaking: Giving feedback to your partner; Review for the final exam
14	Final exam (60 minutes)

APPENDIX B   CLASS SYLLABUSES IN 2010 AND 2011 ACADEMIC YEARS   *175*

B class (Music College), first semester 2011

Class	Activity
1	Orientation; Distribute the Background Questionnaire; Speaking and writing: 30-second Self-Introduction speech; Grammar: Question forms: be, have got, do
2	Listening and speaking: register at the language school; Grammar: Present simple; The Affective Orientation Questionnaire; The Can-do Questionnaire.
3	Writing: email letter of self-introduction; English for everyday life: Making appointments at the dental clinic; Speaking: Pair work
4	Reading and listening: Events in the past; Grammar: Past simple
5	Speaking: Presentation on the email letter of self-introduction; Listening and writing: Understand and re-tell a story.
6	Grammar: Past simple; Reading and listening: events in the past; English for Everyday Life: Responding to news; Speaking: Pair work
7	Writing: A special place and what happened there; Grammar: Present continuous; Reading and listening: Compare regular and current activities.
8	Speaking: presentation on a special place; Mid-term examination (30 minutes); Grammar: comparison between present continuous and present simple; Listening: conversation between taxi drivers and three passengers.
9	Listening: conversation between taxi drivers and three passengers; Grammar: Past continuous; Reading and Writing: Giving directions; Speaking: Pair work
10	Writing: Giving directions; Grammar: be going to; Speaking: Are you going to do these things in the evening?; Listening and writing: Interview about travel on a yacht.
11	Listening and Writing: Complete the summary of Rachel and Stefan's journey; Grammar: Adjectives and adverbs; Reading and listening: At the shops; Speaking: At the shops
12	Grammar: Present perfect; Reading and listening: The lottery; Speaking: Using present perfect; Listening: Understand the news; Writing: Change the newspaper headlines into full sentences.
13	Distribute the Can-do Questionnaire; Final examination
14	Writing: Your favorite photo and why it is important to you.

176   APPENDICES

B class (Music College), second semester 2011

Class	Activity
1	Writing and speaking activity: Presentation on what you did during this summer holiday.
	Listening and writing: Change the newspaper headlines into full sentences; Grammar: Present perfect and past simple
2	English for everyday life: at the doctor's; Grammar: Quantity: Describing a recipe for summer pudding.
3	Writing: My three seals; Grammar: Quantity: countable nouns and uncountable nouns
4	Speaking: Presentation on my three seals; Grammar: Comparatives and superlatives
	Listening and writing: Different kinds of shopping
5	English for everyday life: in a clothes shop; Grammar: Future with will
6	Grammar: First conditional; English for everyday life: Booking a hotel room.
7	Writing: Thank you letter; Grammar: Obligation (must / have to)
8	Speaking: Presentation on thank you letter; Mid-term examination; Listening and speaking: daily journey
9	Poetry recitation practice: My heart leaps up when I behold by W. Wordsworth; Listening and speaking: daily journey
10	Poetry recitation practice: My heart leaps up when I behold by W. Wordsworth; Grammar: Advice (should / shouldn't); English for everyday life: Describing faults
11	Poetry recitation practice: My heart leaps up when I behold by W. Wordsworth; Distribute the Classroom Can-Do Questionnaire; Grammar: Passive; Listening and writing: About the festivals
12	Poetry recitation practice: My heart leaps up when I behold by W. Wordsworth; Grammar: Relative clause; English for everyday life: Asking what things are called
13	Poetry recitation test; Grammar: Present perfect (for and since); Distribute the Can-Do Questionnaire
14	Final examination

APPENDIX B   CLASS SYLLABUSES IN 2010 AND 2011 ACADEMIC YEARS   *177*

C class (Music College), first semester 2011.

Class	Activity
1	Orientation; Distribute the Background Questionnaire; Speaking and Writing: 30-second Self-Introduction speech
2	Vocabulary: Introduction and nationalities; Reading and Listening: Self-Introduction; Reading and Listening: That's life! Episode 1; Distribute the Affective Orientation Questionnaire; Distribute the Can-do Questionnaire.
3	Writing: Email self- introduction letter; Vocabulary: Jobs; Listening: Describe different jobs.
4	Reading and Speaking: My job; Speaking: Presentation on email letter of self- introduction.
5	Reading: A long passage about someone's jobs; Vocabulary: Collocations; Speaking and Listening: Say the sentences with the correct verbs
6	Reading and Listening: That's life! Episode 2; Speaking: Responding to information; Vocabulary: Life events; Speaking and Listening: What happened last year?
7	Writing: A special place and what happened there; Reading and Listening: A famous person's life story (Ray Charles)
8	Speaking: Presentation on a special place; Mid-term examination (30 minutes); Reading: Agatha Christie
9	Vocabulary: At the station; Listening: Conversation at the station; Reading and Listening: That's life! Episode 3
10	Vocabulary: Directions and locations; Listening and Speaking: Describe a route; Reading: The Gardener (a scary story)
11	Vocabulary: The world; Listening: The world; Grammar: Articles with geographical names Reading and Listening: That's life! Episode 4.
12	Speaking: Expressing doubt; Vocabulary: Describing people; Reading and writing: Personality and likes and dislikes.
13	Distribute the Can-do Questionnaire; Final examination (60 minutes)
14	Writing: Your favorite photo and why it is important to you; Conduct interviews

178 APPENDICES

C class (Music College), Second Semester 2011

Class	Activity
1	Writing and speaking: Presentation on what you did during this summer holiday; Vocabulary: TV program; English for everyday life: That's life: Episode 5
2	Vocabulary: Health problems; Reading and writing: advice for travelers
3	Writing: My three seals; Vocabulary: Cooking
4	Speaking: Presentation on my three seals; Reading and speaking: Eat as much as you like; English for everyday life: That's life: Episode 6
5	Vocabulary: Shops; Vocabulary: Money
6	Reading and speaking: What will the future be like?; English for everyday life: That's life :Episode 7
7	Writing: Thank you letter; Vocabulary: Activities
8	Speaking: Presentation on thank you letter; Mid-term examination; Reading and speaking: Dream holidays
9	Poetry recitation practice: My heart leaps up when I behold by W. Wordsworth; Reading and listening: Dream holidays
10	Poetry recitation practice: My heart leaps up when I behold by W. Wordsworth; Vocabulary: In the office; English for everyday life: That's life: Episode 8
11	Poetry recitation practice: My heart leaps up when I behold by W. Wordsworth; Distribute the Classroom Can-Do Questionnaire; Vocabulary: In the home; Reading and writing: I promise to love, honor, and wash up.
12	Poetry recitation practice: My heart leaps up when I behold by W. Wordsworth; Vocabulary: Materials; English for everyday life: That's life: Episode 9
13	Poetry recitation test: My heart leaps up when I behold by W. Wordsworth; Distribute the Can-Do Questionnaire; Writing: Should English be taught in primary school?
14	Final examination

APPENDIX C
BACKGROUND QUESTIONNAIRE (ENGLISH VERSION)
(Adapted from Beglar, 2009)

1   What is your gender? (1) Male (2) Female

2   What is your major? (1) Playing (2) Music culture design (3) Music education

3   What is your nationality? (1) Japanese (2) Chinese (3) Korean (4) Other

4   Have you ever studied in an English-medium school?

5   If your answer to #4 is "yes", which level of school was it? (1) Elementary school (2) Junior high school (3) High school (4) University

6   If your answer to #4 is "yes", how long did you study in an English-medium school? (1) 1 year (2) 2 years (3) 3 years (4) 4years (5) 5 or more years

7   Have you ever lived in a foreign country? (1) yes (2) no

8   If your answer to #7 is "yes", how long did you live overseas in total? (1) less than 6 months (2) 6-12 months (3) 1.0-1.5 years (4) 2-3 years (5) 3 years or more

9   If your answer to #8 was "yes", what kind of country did you live in? (1) An English speaking country (e.g., the US or UK) (2) A country where English is widely used (e.g., India, Singapore) (3) A non-English speaking country (e.g., Thailand, France)

10   What choice was that College of Music when you were applying to universities (1) 1st choice (2) 2nd choice (3) 3rd choice (4) 4th choice (5) 5th choice or lower

APPENDIX D
BACKGROUND QUESTIONNAIRE (JAPANESE VERSION)
(Adapted from Beglar, 2009)

1   性別：(1) 男性　(2) 女性

2   専攻：(1) 演奏　(2) 音楽文化デザイン　(3) 音楽教育

3   国籍：(1) 日本　(2) 中国　(3) 韓国　(4) その他

4   今までに全ての授業が英語で教えられている学校で学んだことがありますか？　(1) ある
    (2) ない

5   4番で「ある」と回答された方、全ての授業が英語で教えられている学校で学んだのはいつ
    のことですか？（回答が複数になる場合は、最後に学んだ学年に当てはまるものを1つ選
    んで下さい。）(1) 小学校の時（それ以前も含む）(2) 中学校の時 (3) 高校生の時 (4) 大
    学に入ってから

6   4番で「ある」と回答された方、全ての授業が英語で教えられている学校で学んだことのあ
    る期間はどのくらいですか？ (1) 1年間 (2) 2年間 (3) 3年間 (4) 4年間 (5) 5年以上

7   今までに外国で生活したことがありますか？ (1) ある　(2) ない

8   7番で「ある」と回答された方、この大学に入学する前にどのくらいの期間外国に住んでい
    ましたか？ (1) 6ヶ月未満 (2) 6ヶ月～1年 (3) 1年～1年半 (4) 1年半～2年 (5) 2
    年～3年 (6) 3年以上

9   8番で「ある」と回答された方、それはどの様なタイプの国でしたか？ (1) 英語圏の国（ア
    メリカ・英国など）(2) 英語が広く用いられている国（インド・シンガポールなど）(3)
    英語を用いない国（タイ・フランス）

10 大学に入学願書を出した時、何番目の志望校でしたか？ (1) 第一志望　(2) 第二志望　(3)
    第三志望　(4) 第四志望　(5) 第五志望又はそれ以下

APPENDIX E
THE WRITING SECTION OF THE EIKEN CAN-DO QUESTION-NAIRE

Level	Contents
2nd Level	Can write texts of some length about topics from everyday life.
	Can describe the details of memorable experiences (e.g., school events, trips).
	Can write a simple description introducing his/her own school or workplace.
	Can write a simple description introducing the areas in which he/she lives.
	Can describe his /her impressions of books he/she has read or films he/ she has seen.
	Can write letters and e-mails of some length (e.g., describing recent news and events to a homestay host family or friends).
Pre-2nd	Can write simple texts about things that he/she is interested in.
	Can write about his/her future dreams and ambitions for his her future (e.g., the countries he/she would like to visit, the career he/she would like to pursue.
	Can write simple texts describing his/her favorite things or familiar items (e.g., a pet or favorite book).
	Can write a short letter and e-mails (e.g., a simple letter to friends or pen pal)
	Can write a simple notice (e.g., the date, time and place, of a party , the program for school festival).
	Can write your simple plan on a calendar or in a personal planner or schedule book (e.g., "Meet Yoko at the station at ten." "Go shopping with Jill.").
3rd Level	Can write simple texts about himself / herself.
	Can write a simple self-introduction (e.g., name, where he/she lives, family).
	Can write about his/her own hobbies and interests.
	Can write what he/ she likes, dislikes and explain why (e.g., food, sports, and music).
	Can write a short diary entry (from one to three sentences).
	Can write a simple card and postcard (e.g., birthday cards, postcard sent while on vacation).
	Can write short messages (e.g., "Ken called at 3 p.m.").
4th Level	Can write simple sentences and messages.
	Can write sentences using English word order, provided that the sentences are short (e.g., "I went to the park yesterday.").
	Can write short messages by putting words and phrases together (e.g., birthday party at 6:00 p.m.).
	Can write sentences joining clauses with conjunctions (e.g., and, but, so, when, because).
	Can write dates and days of the week.

APPENDIX F
THE ORIGIONAL JAPANESE VERSION OF THE CLASSROOM CAN-DO QUESTIONNAIRE
（中西、林、小林、佐久間、2010）

第 12 週目の Can-Do リスト

2 年 a 系統 A・B グレード（担当者：小林和歌子）	
Controversy（賛成と反対のあるトピック）のエッセイ（100 語以上）を書くことができる。	到達度%
1. 指定の箇所の単語テストを行い語彙力を増強させる。	60%
2. Controversy（賛成と反対のあるトピック）のエッセイ（100 語以上）を書くことができる。 例（①日本の学校のシステムの長所と短所、② e-learning の長所と短所、③一人暮らしの長所と短所、④一戸建てではなくてアパートに住むことの長所と短所）	90%

APPENDIX G
CLASSROOM CAN-DO QUESTIONNAIRES AND DEGREE OF ATTAINMENT (ENGLISH VERSION)
(Nakanishi, Hayashi, Kobayashi, & Sakuma, 2010)

Second-year English Communication Class (Reading & Writing)
Instructor: Wakako Kobayashi
Week 12, 2009

	Attainment %
You can write an essay on a controversial topic in more than 100 words	
1. Can learn assigned vocabulary, take a vocabulary quiz, and develop knowledge of vocabulary.	60%
2. Can write an essay on a controversial topic in more than 100 words in 45 minutes.	90%
(e.g., What are the advantages and disadvantages of the Japanese school system?	
What are the advantages and disadvantages of e-learning?	
What are the advantages and disadvantages of living alone?	
What are the merits and demerits of living in an apartment rather than in a house?)	

The original Classroom Can-Do statements are written in Japanese (see Appendix F).

184 APPENDICES

APPENDIX H

CLASSROOM CAN-DO QUESTIONNAIRES AND DEGREE OF AT-TAINMENT: IN THE 2010 AND 2011 ACADEMIC YEAR

English Communication Class: B classes in the Music College, the First Semester 2010

Week	Classroom Can-Do questionnaire item	Attainment %
1	Can understand the framework of paragraphs.	80%
2	Can write a self-introduction in 45 minutes in more than 100 words.	90%
3	Can write the new words on pages 179-180 correctly.	80%
	Can write a self-introduction letter in paragraph style.	90%
	Can edit sentences, such as connecting the sentences with *and* and *but*.	90%
	Can write a short comment in 10 minutes after reading a partner's essay.	90%
4	Can understand the omission of the relative pronoun, and write the sentences using that pattern (from English Quest, Unit 8)	70%
	Can understand the framework of the essay about Special Places.	80%
5	Can write the new words on pages 180-181 correctly.	70%
	Can write the essay about *Special Places* in 45 minutes (> 100 words).	40%
	Can write connected sentences using *and* and *but*.	80%
	Can write prepositional phrases to refer to places, such as *at school, on a bench, in the park*.	90%
6	Can edit the essay on Special Places using the prepositional phrases, *at, on,* and *in*.	60%
	Can write a comment after reading a partner's essay on Special Places.	80%
	Can write English sentences, using relative pronouns such as *which, whose, what,* and *that* (from English Quest, Unit 9).	70%
7	Can write the new words on pages 182-183 correctly.	70%
	Can use words such as *First, Second,* and *Third* to put information in order.	90%
	Can use *because* to give reasons in writing.	90%
	Can write English sentences, using relative adverbs (e.g., *when, where, how*)	60%
8	Can write English sentences using relative adverbs, such as *when, where, how* and *why*.	80%
	Can write an essay about My Ideal Partner in 30 minutes in more than 100 words.	40%
9	Can write the new words on pages 184-185 correctly.	70%
	Can finish writing an essay about My Ideal Partner in 30 minutes.	90%
10	Can write English sentences using comparatives and superlatives (from English Quest, Unit 11)	80%
	Can complete the chart in English as a prewriting activity with regard to My Favorite Photo.	60%
11	Can write the new words on pages 186-187 correctly.	70%
	Can write a summary of each paragraph after reading *The Comic Café*.	70%
	Can write a summary of each paragraph after reading *Green Tea is Booming*.	70%
12	Can write an essay in English titled *My Favorite Photo* in 50 minutes in more than 100 words.	90%
13	Can write new words on pages 188-189 correctly.	60%
	Can write a summary of each paragraph, titled *Should Smoking be Banned in the Public Places* and *Euthanasia*.	70%
14	Can write an essay in more than 100 words, and answer the grammatical questions in English. (The final examination)	70%

Classroom Can-Do Questionnaires and Degree of Attainment

English Communication Class: B classes in the Music College, the Second Semester 2010

Week	Classroom Can-Do questionnaire item	Attainment (%)
1	Can write three English sentences for the question *What did you do during the summer vacation?* in ten minutes.	90%
	Can write the English sentences with auxiliary verbs, such as *can, may should, have to, had better* (from English Quest, Unit 12).	80%
	Can write the personal symbols that represent each student's character and give reasons for that.	60%
2	Can write the essay on My Personal Seal in 45 minutes in more than 100 words.	90%
	Can write the new words on pages 190-191 correctly.	70%
3	Can edit the essay titled My Personal Seal in 5 minutes using *because*.	90%
	Can write comments or questions to the partner's essay.	80%
	Can write a summary of each paragraph in *Sociology and Anthropology*.	60%
4	Can write the new words on the pages 192-193	70%
	Can write the English sentences with conditional clauses and subjunctive (from English Quest Unit 13)	70%
	Can complete the chart in English as a prewriting activity for Party Notice	50%
5	Can write more than three sentences about the topic, *What did you do last weekend* in 10 minutes.	90%
	Can write a summary of each paragraph after reading *Holy Europe* in 20 min.	70%
	Can write the Party Notice in 30 minutes.	60%
6	Can write the new words on pages 194-195 correctly.	70%
	Can write the Party Notice in 45 minutes in more than 100 words.	90%
7	Can write the English sentences with conditional clauses and subjunctives (from English Quest Unit 14)	80%
	Can complete the chart in English as a prewriting activity for Thank you letter.	70%
8	Can write a summary of each paragraph in *How to join in a discussion*.	70%
	Can complete the chart in English as a prewriting activity for Thank you letter.	80%
	Can write the plan of thank you letter in 10 minutes.	60%
	Can write the new words on pages 196-197 correctly.	60%
9	Can write more than 3 sentences about *What do you want to do after graduation?* in 10 minutes.	70%
	Can write Thank you letter in 50 minutes in more than 100 words.	80%
10	Can write the new words on pages 198-199 correctly.	60%
	Can write the English sentences using modification clauses	90%
	Can complete the chart in English as a prewriting activity for Movie Review.	40%
11	Can write more than 3 sentences about *What is your favorite music* or *Who is your favorite musician* in 10 minutes.	90%
	Can write a summary of each paragraph after reading Christmas.	70%
	Can complete the chart in English as a prewriting activity for Movie Review.	50%
12	Can write the new words on pages 200-201 correctly.	70%
	Can complete the chart in English as a prewriting activity for Movie Review.	60%
	Can write an essay about Movie Review in 20 minutes.	30%
	Can complete the Can-do questionnaire in 5 minutes.	100%
13	Can write an essay of Movie Review in 50 minutes in more than 100 words.	80%
14	Can write an essay in more than 100 words and answer the grammatical questions in English. (The final examination)	70%

186   APPENDICES

Classroom Can-Do Questionnaires and Degree of Attainment

English Communication Class: A classes in the Music College, First Semester 2010

Week	Classroom Can-Do questionnaire item	Attainment (%)
1	Can understand the essay framework consisting of reasons and conclusions.	80%
2	Can write an essay in support of the abolishment of capital punishment.	70%
3	Can write the new words on pages 179-180 correctly.	90%
	Can write an essay on one of the following topics in 50 minutes using more than 100 words.	90%
	Should English be taught in primary school?	
	Should mothers stay at home until their children go to school?	
	Should the marriage system be abolished?	
	Should children leave home after they reach the age of twenty?	
	Should university entrance examinations be abolished?	
4	Can understand the omission of the relative pronoun, and write sentences using that pattern (from English Quest, Unit 8)	70%
	Can understand the essay framework of analysis.	80%
5	Can write the new words on pages 180-181 correctly.	80%
	Can write an essay on "Why are coffee shops popular in Japan," referring to the Japanese translation.	70%
6	Can write English sentences, using relative pronouns, such as *which, whose,* and *that*. (From English Quest, Unit 9)	80%
	Can write an original essay on one of the following topics in 40 minutes.	60%
	Hot springs are now popular again.	
	Chinese noodles are booming.	
	Why have personal computers spread so quickly?	
	Why have mobile phones spread so quickly?	
	Why are karaoke boxes so popular?	
7	Can write the new words on pages 182-183 correctly.	70%
	Can edit the original essay in 20 minutes.	80%
	Hot springs are now popular again.	
	Chinese noodles are booming.	
	Why have personal computers spread so quickly?	
	Why have mobile phones spread so quickly?	
	Why are karaoke boxes so popular?	
	Can write a summary of each paragraph in the model essay, Your eyebrows express more than your eyes.	70%
8	Can write a model essay on Pavlov's Dogs, referring to the Japanese translation.	60%
	Can understand the essay framework of theory and proof.	80%
9	Can write new words on pages 184-185 correctly.	70%
	Can write English sentences, using relative adverb, such as *when, where, how,* and *why*. (From English Quest, Unit 10)	90%
	Can write the essay on "Women can do more things at the same time than men" in 30 minutes.	50%
10	Can write and edit the essay on "Women can do more things at the same time than men" in 40 minutes.	90%
	Can write a summary of each paragraph, titled Abortion.	70%

APPENDIX H CLASSROOM CAN-DO QUESTIONNAIRES AND DEGREE OF ATTAINMENT: IN THE 2010 AND 2011 ACADEMIC YEAR   *187*

	Can write a summary of each paragraph, titled What are the merits and demerits of the life time employment system?	80%
11	Can write new words on pages 186-187 correctly.	70%
	Can write a summary of each paragraph, Euthanasia.	80%
12	Can write a model essay, titled The merits and demerits of paper swapping in classroom quiz referring to the Japanese translation.	90%
	Can write sentences using comparatives and superlatives.	80%
13	Can write new words on pages 188-189 correctly.	70%
	Can write an original essay on the following topics in 70 minutes using more than 100 words.	80%
	What are the merits and demerits of the Japanese school system?	
	What are the merits and demerits of e-learning?	
	What are the merits and demerits of living alone?	
	What are the merits and demerits of living in an apartment rather than a house?	
14	Can write an essay using more than 100 words, answer the grammatical questions, write a summary of the long passage. (The final examination)	70%

188   APPENDICES

Classroom Can-Do Questionnaires and Degree of Attainment

English Communication Class: A classes in the Music College, the Second Semester 2010

Week	Classroom Can-Do questionnaire item	Attainment (%)
1	Can write more than three sentences in 10 minutes for the question, What did you do during the summer holidays?	90%
	Can write English sentences with auxiliary verbs, such as *can, may, should, have to, had better* (from English Quest, Unit 12)	80%
	Can write a summary of each paragraph after reading the model essay, Japanese and British university entrance systems.	80%
2	Can write the new words on the pages 190-191 correctly.	70%
	Can write the model essay on Comparing co-educational and single-sex schools referring to the Japanese translation.	70%
	Can write a summary of each paragraph in *Sociology and Anthropology.*	70%
3	Can write more than three sentences in 10 minutes about the topic, What did you do during the last weekend?	90%
	Can write a summary of each paragraph in *Japanese and Western Employment Systems.*	80%
	Can write the essay on the following topics in 40 minutes using > 100 words.	40%
	Compare Japanese and American family life.	
	Compare television news and newspaper news.	
	Compare public school education with private school education.	
	Compare city life and country life.	
	Free essay title.	
4	Can write the new words on pages192-193 correctly.	70%
	Can write the essay in 30 minutes using more than 100 words.	90%
	Can write a summary of each paragraph in *Communism and Capitalism.*	80%
5t	Can write more than 3 sentences in 10 minutes about the topic, Explain about your major in this college.	90%
	Can write the model essays, Divide the countries of the world into three groups: those surrounded by the sea, those partly facing the sea, and those that are landlocked in 30 minutes, referring to the Japanese translation.	60%
6	Can write a summary of each paragraph in *Holy Europe and Religious Worlds.*	70%
	Can write a plan of the essay on the following topics in 5 minutes.	
	Developed, rapidly developing and still underdeveloped countries.	80%
	Countries with hot, temperate, and cold climates.	
	Europe, Asia, Africa and America.	
7	Can write an essay in 60 minutes using more than 100 words.	80%
8	Can write English sentences with conditional clauses and subjunctives.	80%
	Can write the new words on pages196-197 correctly.	60%
9	Can write more than three sentences in 10 minutes about the topic, What do you want to do after graduation?	80%
	Can write the model essay, How to succeed in an interview referring to the Japanese translation.	80%
	Can write a summary of each paragraph in *How to join in a discussion.*	
10	Can write a summary of each paragraph after reading How to prevent a suicide.	80%
	Can write an essay on the following topic in 60 minutes using > 100 words.	70%
	How to save paper / water / electricity. (Choose one topic.)	

How to succeed in an exam.

How to make friends.

How to stay fit. (How to stay healthy.)

11	Can write a summary of each paragraph after reading The Falling Birthrate.	80%
	Can write English sentences, using modification clause (from English Quest, Unit 7).	90%
	Can write an essay, What effects do you think a five-day school week will have on society? referring to the Japanese translation.	70%
12	Can write more than three sentences in 10 minutes about, What is your favorite music? or Who is your favorite musician?	90%
	Can write the new words on pages 200-201 correctly.	80%
	Can write an essay on the following topic in 30 minutes using > 100 words.	50%
	What effects have personal computers had on society?	
	What is the influence of the spread of mobile phones on society?	
	How did the Meiji Restoration affect Japanese history?	
13	Can write an essay on the following topics (continued from the 12th class)	80%
	Can complete the Can-do questionnaire in 5 minutes.	100%
14	Can write an essay using more than 100 words, answer the grammatical questions, and write a summary of the long passage. (The final examination)	70%

190 APPENDICES

Classroom Can-Do Questionnaires and Degree of Attainment

English Communication Class: C classes in the Music College, the First Semester 2011

Week	Classroom Can-Do questionnaire item	Attainment %
1	Can write self-introduction using more than 50 words in 15 minutes.	80%
2	Can introduce people and name some nationalities	60%
	Can write what they are doing.	60%
3	Can write an email letter of self-introduction using > 100 words in 40 minutes.	70%
	Can write about different jobs.	
4	Can write the answers to the question after reading the article.	80%
5	Can write answers to the questions about the article.	80%
	Can write about everyday activities using collocations.	80%
6	Can write about the life events.	70%
7	Can write about a special place and what happened there using more than 100 words in 40 minutes.	60%
8	Can write the answers to the questions about life story.	70%
	Can write answers to the mid-term examination.	80%
9	Can write the vocabularies at the station.	80%
10	Can answer the comprehension questions in *The Gardener.*	70%
11	Can write the past continuous and past simple correctly.	80%
	Can use the articles with geographical names correctly.	60%
12	Can express doubt.	80%
	Can describe a person's appearance.	70%
	Can describe personality, likes and dislikes,	70%
13	Can complete the Can-do Questionnaire in 5 minutes	100%
	Can answer the final examination in 60 minutes.	60%
14	Can write an essay on your favorite photo and why it is important to you using more than 100 words in 50 minutes.	70%

APPENDIX H CLASSROOM CAN-DO QUESTIONNAIRES AND DEGREE OF ATTAINMENT: IN THE 2010 AND 2011 ACADEMIC YEAR   *191*

Classroom Can-Do Questionnaire and Degree of Attainment

English Communication Class: C classes in the Music College, Second Semester 2011

Week	Classroom Can-Do questionnaire item	Attainment
1	Can write what you did during this summer holiday in 10 minutes.	80%
	Can write about TV program.	70%
	Can write the everyday expressions (ex. expressing opinions).	90%
2	Can write about some health problems.	60%
	Can write advice for travelers.	60%
3	Can write an essay on "My seal" in 40 minutes in more than 100 words.	60%
	Can write vocabulary about cooking.	70%
4	Can write the answers to the questions in the text.	70%
	Can write everyday expressions on annoyance.	80%
5	Can write the different kinds of shops.	60%
	Can write about money.	70%
6	Can write the answers to the questions in the text.	60%
	Can write everyday expressions about money problems.	70%
7	Can write a thank you letter in more than 100 words in 40 minutes.	60%
	Can write about activities.	70%
8	Can write the answers to the questions in the mid-term examination.	50%
	Can write the answers to the questions after reading the passage.	70%
9	Can write Wordsworth's poetry correctly.	50%
	Can write the answers to the questions after reading "Dream Holidays".	60%
10	Can write Wordsworth's poetry correctly.	60%
	Can write sentences about everyday office activities.	60%
	Can write answers the questions after reading the story.	60%
11	Can complete the Classroom Can-Do Questionnaire in 5 minutes.	100%
	Can write Wordsworth's poetry correctly.	60%
	Can write the things and jobs in the home.	60%
	Can write the answers to the questions after reading the passage, "I promise to love, honor and wash up."	50%
12	Can write Wordsworth's poetry correctly.	70%
	Can write the vocabularies of materials.	60%
	Can write everyday expressions (Responding to information).	70%
13	Can complete Can-Do Questionnaire in 5 minutes.	100%
	Can write an essay, "Should English be taught in primary school" in more than 100 words in 40 minutes.	70%
14	Can answer the questions in the final examination in 60 minutes.	60%

192   APPENDICES

Classroom Can-Do Questionnaires and Degree of Attainment

English Communication Class: B classes in the Music College, the First Semester 2011

Week	Classroom Can-Do questionnaire item	Attainment %
1	Can ask about and give personal information.	70%
	Can write self- introduction in more than 50 words in 15 minutes.	80%
2	Can give information about myself and complete a form.	80%
	Can write about people's working lives.	80%
3	Can write an email letter of self-introduction using > 100 words in 40 minutes.	80%
	Can write how to make appointments.	60%
4	Can write how to make appointments	70%
	Can write the events in the pasts.	80%
5	Can write the summary of Vijay and Seema's story.	80%
6	Can write the questions about events in the past.	80%
	Can write the respond to the news.	70%
7	Can write about a special/favorite place using > 100 words in 50 minutes.	70%
	Can write sentences using present continuous.	80%
8	Can write answers to the mid-term examination.	80%
	Can write sentences using present continuous.	80%
9	Can write sentences about past activities in progress, and give directions.	80%
10	Can write a summary of the interview about the travel on a yacht.	60%
11	Can write a summary of Rachel and Stefan's journey.	70%
	Can describe things and activities.	70%
	Can describe things in a shop.	70%
12	Can write the present perfect correctly.	70%
	Can change the newspaper headline into full sentences.	30%
13	Can complete the Can-do Questionnaire in 5 minutes.	100%
	Can answer the final examination in 60 minutes.	60%
14	Can write an essay on your favorite photo and why it is important to you in more than 100 words in 50 minutes.	70%

APPENDIX H CLASSROOM CAN-DO QUESTIONNAIRES AND DEGREE OF ATTAINMENT: IN THE 2010 AND 2011 ACADEMIC YEAR   *193*

Classroom Can-Do Questionnaires and Degree of Attainment
English Communication Class: B classes in the Music College, Second Semester 2011.

Week	Classroom Can-Do Questionnaire item	Attainment
1	Can write the newspaper headlines in full sentences.	50%
	Can write about accidents.	80%
2	Can write the sentences using present perfect and past simple.	60%
	Can write the expressions at the doctor's.	70%
	Can write a recipe for Summer Pudding.	70%
3	Can write an essay on My seal in 40 minutes in more than 100 words.	70%
	Can write the quantity expressions, countable nouns and uncountable noun.	70%
4	Can write comparatives and superlatives forms correctly.	80%
	Can write about the different kinds of shopping.	70%
5	Can write expressions about buying clothes.	80%
	Can write about the future using *will*.	80%
6	Can write about future possibility and certainty using *if* and *when*.	70%
	Can write everyday expressions to look a hotel room.	70%
7	Can write a thank you letter in 40 minutes in more than 100 words.	70%
	Can write about obligations (*must* and *have to*)	80%
8	Can write the answers to the questions in the mid-term examination.	80%
	Can write the answers after listening to "My journey".	30%
9	Can write Wordsworth's poetry correctly.	70%
	Can write answers after listening to "My journey".	60%
10	Can write Wordsworth's poetry correctly.	70%
	Can write the sentences using *should* and *shouldn't*.	70%
	Can write everyday expressions which are dealing with faults.	60%
11	Can complete the Classroom-Can-Do Questionnaire in 5 minutes.	100%
	Can write Wordsworth's poetry correctly.	80%
	Can write the sentences using passive.	80%
	Can write answers after listening to each speaker describe a festival.	30%
12	Can write Wordsworth's poetry correctly.	80%
	Can write the sentences using relative clause.	70%
	Can write everyday expressions on asking what the things are called.	80%
13	Can complete the Can-Do Questionnaire in 5 minutes.	100%
	Can write an essay, *Should English be taught in primary school?* in more than 100 words in 40 minutes.	80%
	Can write the sentences using present perfect: for and since.	70%
14	Can write answers to final examination questions in 60 minutes.	70%

194   APPENDICES

Classroom Can-Do Questionnaires and Degree of Attainment

Advanced English Classes in Sakura University, First Semester 2011

Week	Classroom Can-Do questionnaire item	Attainment %
1	Can write a self-introduction using more than 50 words in 15 minutes.	90%
2	Can write the answers to the questions in the text.	70%
	Can complete the Can-do Questionnaire in 5 minutes.	100%
3	Can write an essay using more than 100 words in 40 minutes.	
	Skills for Better Writing: Unit 1 Conclusion / Reasons	80%
	• Should English be taught in primary school?	
	• Should mothers stay at home until their children go to school?	
	• Should the marriage system be abolished?	
	• Should children leave home after they reach the age of twenty?	
	• Should university entrance examination be abolished?	
4	Can write answers to the questions in the text.	80%
5	Can write answers to the questions in the text.	70%
6	Can write answers to the questions in the text.	70%
7	Can write an essay using more than 100 words in 50 minutes.	
	Skills for Better Writing: Unit 2 Analysis	
	• Hot springs (*onsen*) are now popular again.	
	• Chinese noodles (*ramen*) are booming.	
	• Why have personal computers spread so quickly?	
	• Why have mobile phones spread so quickly?	
	Why are karaoke boxes so popular?	
8	Can write answers to the questions in the text.	70%
9	Can write answers to the questions in the text.	70%
10	Can write answers to the questions in the text.	70%
	Can write phrasal verbs in an appropriate blank.	60%
11	Can complete the Can-do Questionnaire in 5 minutes.	100%
	Can write an essay using more than 100 words in 50 minutes.	80%
	Skills for Better Writing: unit 4 Controversy.	
	• What are the merits and demerits of the Japanese school system.	
	• What are the merits and demerits of e-learning?	
	• What are the merits and demerits of living alone?	
	• What are the merits and demerits of living in an apartment (flat) rather than in a house?	
12	Can answer the questions on the final examination.	70%

Classroom Can-Do Questionnaires and Degree of Attainment
Advanced English Classes in Sakura University, Second Semester 2011

Week	Classroom Can-Do questionnaire item	Attainment
1	Can write the answers to the questions in the text.	80%
2	Can write the answers to the questions in the text.	
3	Can write vocabulary about movie making.	80%
	Can write the answers to the questions in the text.	80%
4	Can write an essay in more than 100 words in 40 minutes.	70%
	• Compare Japanese and American family life.	
	• Compare television news and newspaper news.	
	• Compare public school education with private school education.	
	• Compare city life and country life.	
5	Can write the answers to the questions in the text.	80%
6	Can fill in the blanks with an appropriate word.	70%
	Can write the answers to the questions in the text.	80%
7	Can write the answers to the questions in the text.	80%
	Can write vocabulary about Unit 7: Men and Women.	70%
8	Can write the English compositions on How to succeed in an interview.	70%
	Can write an essay in more than 100 words in 40 minutes.	
	• How to save paper / water / electricity.	
	• How to succeed in an exam.	
	• How to stay healthy.	
	• How to make friends.	
9	Can write the reaction in 3 English sentences after reading Obama's Inaugural Address.	80%
	Can write the prepositions to the blanks in the Obama's text.	40%
10	Can complete the Classroom Can-Do Questionnaire in 5 minutes.	100%
	Can write the answers to the questions in the text.	80%
11	Can write the answers to the questions in the text.	80%
12	Can complete the Can-Do Questionnaire in 5 minutes.	100%
	Can write a thank you letter in more than 100 words in 40 minutes.	90%
13	Can write the answers to the questions in the text.	80%
14	Can write the answers to the questions in the final examination in 60 minutes.	80%

APPENDIX I
THE CLASSROOM CAN-DO QUESTIONNAIRE (ENGLISH VERSION)

1 = Cannot do at all   2 = Can do slightly   3 = Can do fairly well   4 = Can do very well

C level class in the music college (Fall semester 2011)

1	I can write an introductory paragraph.
2	I can write a topic sentence for a paragraph.
3	I can write a conclusion paragraph.
4	I can write a paragraph that develops a single idea.
5	I can write supporting details in a paragraph.
6	I can check my spelling.
7	I can write a five-paragraph essay.
8	I can write the answers to the questions in the textbook.
9	I can write an essay (*My seal*, and *Thank you letter*) using more than 100 words in 40 minutes.
10	I can write the answers to the comprehension questions after reading *Dream Holidays* (p. 55).
11	I can write vocabulary for the activities on page 53.
12	I can write the answers to the comprehension questions after reading *What will the future be like?* (p. 51).
13	I can write vocabulary concerning money (p. 49).
14	I can write vocabularies concerning shops (p. 45).
15	I can write the answers to the comprehension questions after reading *Eat as much as you like* (p. 43).
16	I can write vocabulary concerning cooking (p. 41).

THE CLASSROOM CAN-DO QUESTIONNAIRE

1 = Cannot do at all   2 = Can do slightly   3 = Can do fairly well   4 = Can do very well

B level class in the music college (Fall semester 2011)

1   I can write an introductory paragraph.
2   I can write a topic sentence for a paragraph.
3   I can write a conclusion paragraph.
4   I can write a paragraph that develops a single idea.
5   I can write supporting details in a paragraph.
6   I can check my spelling.
7   I can write a five-paragraph essay.
8   I can write the answers to the questions in the textbook.
9   I can write an essay (*My seal,* and *Thank you letter*) using more than 100 words in 40 minutes.
10 I can write everyday expressions concerning faults (p. 64).
11 I can write sentences using *should* or *shouldn't* correctly (p. 62).
12 I can write answers after listening to the speaker talk about *Daily journey* (p. 59).
13 I can write sentences using *must* or *have to* correctly (p. 58).
14 I can write everyday expressions for *booking a hotel room* (p. 56).
15 I can write sentences using *the first conditional* correctly (p. 54).
16 I can write sentences using *will* correctly (p. 41).

THE CLASSROOM CAN-DO QUESTIONNAIRE

1 = Can not do at all   2 = Can do slightly   3 = Can do fairly well   4 = Can do very well

Advanced English class in Sakura University (Fall semester 2011)

1	I can write an introductory paragraph.
2	I can write a topic sentence for a paragraph.
3	I can write a conclusion paragraph.
4	I can write a paragraph that develops a single idea.
5	I can write supporting details in a paragraph.
6	I can check my spelling.
7	I can write a five-paragraph essay.
8	I can write the answers to the questions in the textbook.
9	I can write an essay (*Comparison*, and *Instructions*) using more than 100 words in 40 minutes.
10	I can write the sentences for *How to succeed in an interview.*
11	I can write the sentences for *Comparing co-educational and single-sex schools.*
12	I can write the answers to the comprehension questions after reading *Spotting communication problems* (p. 58).
13	I can write the answers to the comprehension questions after reading *Men, women, and sports* (p. 52)
14	I can write the answers to the comprehension questions after reading *The knight in shining armor* (p. 50).
15	I can write the answers to the comprehension questions after reading *The incredible shrinking family* (p. 46).
16	I can write the answers to the comprehension questions after reading *Father's day* (p. 44).

APPENDIX J
THE CLASSROOM CAN-DO QUESTIONNAIRE (JAPANESE VERSION)

1 = 全くできない   2 = 少しできる   3 = かなりできる   4 = とてもよくできる

C level class in the music college (Fall semester 2011)

1	序論のパラグラフを書くことができる。
2	パラグラフのトピックセンテンスを書くことができる。
3	結論のパラグラフを書くことができる。
4	ひとつの考えを発展させるパラグラフを書くことができる。
5	パラグラフで支えになる詳細を書くことができる。
6	スペリングをチェックすることができる。
7	5パラグラフからなるエッセイを書くことができる。
8	教科書の設問に答えることができる。
9	マイシールや感謝状のエッセイを40分で100語以上使って書くことができる。
10	*Dream Holidays* (p. 55) を読んだ後、内容理解の設問に答えることができる。
11	Activities (p. 53) に関する語彙を書くことができる。
12	*What will the future be like?* (p. 51) を読んだ後、内容理解の設問に答えることができる。
13	money (p. 49) に関する語彙を書くことができる。
14	shops (p. 45) に関する語彙を書くことができる。
15	*Eat as much as you like* (p. 43) を読んだ後、内容理解の設問に答えることができる。
16	cooking (p. 41) に関する語彙を書くことができる。

THE CLASSROOM CAN-DO QUESTIONNAIRE

1 = まったくできない   2 = すこしできる   3 = かなりできる   4 = とてもよくできる

B level class in the music college (Fall semester 2011)

1	序論のパラグラフを書くことができる。
2	パラグラフのトピックセンテンスを書くことができる。
3	結論のパラグラフ書くことができる。
4	ひとつの考えを発展させるパラグラフを書くことができる。
5	パラグラフで支えになる詳細を書くことができる。
6	スペリングをチェックすることができる。
7	5パラグラフからなるエッセイを書くことができる。
8	教科書の設問に答えることができる。
9	マイシールや感謝状のエッセイを40分で100語以上使って書くことができる。
10	faults (p. 64) に関する日常表現を書くことができる。
11	*should* や *shouldn't* (p. 62) を使って正しい英文を書くことができる。
12	*Daily journey* (p. 59) を聞いた後、設問に答えることができる。
13	*must* や *have to* (p. 58) を使って正しい英文を書くことができる。
14	*booking a hotel room* (p. 56) に関する日常表現を書くことができる。
15	*the first conditional* (p. 54) を使って、正しい英文を書くことができる。
16	*will* (p. 50) を使って、正しい英文を書くことができる。

APPENDIX J THE CLASSROOM CAN-DO QUESTIONNAIRE (JAPANESE VERSION)   *201*

THE CLASSROOM CAN-DO QUESTIONNAIRE

1 = まったくできない　　2 = すこしできる　　　3 = かなりできる　　　4 = とてもよくできる

Advanced English class in Sakura University (Fall semester, 2011)

1	序論のパラグラフを書くことができる。
2	パラグラフのトピックセンテンスを書くことができる。
3	結論のパラグラフを書くことができる。
4	ひとつの考えを発展させるパラグラフを書くことができる。
5	パラグラフで支えとなる詳細を書くことができる。
6	スペリングをチェックすることができる。
7	5パラグラフからなるエッセイを書くことができる。
8	テキストの設問に答えることができる。
9	エッセイ（比較と指示）を40分で、100語以上使って書くことができる。
10	面接での成功の仕方について英作文を書くことができる。
11	共学と別学の比較について英作文を書くことができる。
12	*Spotting communication problems* (p. 58) を読んで、設問に答えることができる。
13	*Men, women, and sports* (p. 52) を読んで、設問に答えることができる。
14	*The knight in shining armor* (p. 50) を読んで、設問に答えることができる。
15	*The incredible shrinking family* (p. 46) を読んで、設問に答えることができる。
16	*Father's day* (p. 44) を読んで、設問に答えることができる。

202   APPENDICES

APPENDIX K
SAMPLE QUESTIONS OF THE EIKEN PLACEMENT TEST B
(STEP, 2009)

(The original questions are written in Japanese)

Section 1: 30 items.

1. Fill in the blanks. Choose the most appropriate answer from (1) to (30). Check the mark sheet.

(1) Tom really ( ) himself in South America last year. He wants to go again this year.
1 enjoyed 2 sent 3 passed 4 told

(2) A: Hi, Tim. Did you remember to bring the book I lent you?
 B: Oh, no! I'm sorry. Aya. I ( ) forgot. I'll bring it tomorrow.
 1 previously 2 formerly 3 nearly 4 completely

(3) When I'm short ( ) money, I usually ask my father to lend me some.
 1 of 2 by 3 in 4 with

(4) A: This is a report ( ) I wrote in Japanese yesterday. Could you check it for me, Jiro?
 B: Ok, Laura.
 1 which 2 when 3 who 4 whose

(5) A: I need to get my car ( ). Is there a gas station near here?
 B: Yes. There's one two blocks from here.
 1 wash 2 washing 3 washed 4 to wash

APPENDIX K SAMPLE QUESTIONS OF THE EIKEN PLACEMENT TEST B *203*

2. Arrange the order of the sentences so that the sentences make sense. Choose the second and forth one and check the mark sheet. We use the small letters for the blanks.

Naoko went to Malaysia on vacation. She was looking forward to eating Malaysian food. She had eaten it before in Tokyo and liked it. But when she went to restaurant in Malaysia, (31) than what she had eaten in Tokyo.

(31) 1 ate 2 the food 3 hotter 4 she 5 was much

The Great Wall of China is 2400 kilometer long and 9 meters high, and stretches across most of the country. It was built more than (32). Today millions of people from around the world visit the Great Wall every year, making it China's main tourist attraction.

(32) 1 to 2 China from 3 attack 4 protect 5 2000 years ago

(In all, 5 items)

3. Choose the most appropriate one from (36) to (40). Check the mark sheet.

(36) A: You don't look well. Maybe you should go to the doctor.
B: ( ).
1 Sure, there is. 2 I'll do it well. 3 I'm all right. 4 That looks great.

(37) A: Happy birthday, Nancy! Here's your present.
B: Thank you very much. Can I open it now?
A: Sure. ( )
B: Oh, I do. What a beautiful necklace!
1 You said it was OK. 2 You should do it later 3 I hope you like it 4 I'll buy it for you.
(5 items)

4. Read the English article, and then choose the best answer for each question below. Check the mark sheet.

Alaska's Great Dog Race

Every year in the state of Alaska in the United States, a special kind of race is held. This is the Iditarod Trail Sled Dog Race. Using dog to pull their sleds* across the snow, people race about 1100 miles between the cities of Anchorage and Nome.

The winner of the race in 1999 was Doug Swingley, a 45-year-old lover from the town of Lincoln, Montana. Swingley first began to practice racing with dogs in 1989 because he wanted to win the Iditarod race. He has joined the every year since 1992. When he finally won for the first time in 1995, he had the fastest time in the race's history. He became famous because he was the first person from outside Alaska to win this difficult race.

Swingley certainly had trouble winning the race in 1999. Even before he reached the halfway point, he had broken two sleds. The first time, he fixed the sled with a piece of wood from a tree until he could reach the next stop. There he changed to a new sled, but then that broke, too. So the judges decided that Swingley could use the first sled again. He and his 11 dogs finally reached Nome at 1:31 a.m. It had taken 9 days, 14 hours, 31 minutes and 7 seconds to win the race. The person who came second finished nine hours later.

As the winner, Swingley was given $60,000 and a new truck. Swingley, the father of two grown-up children, looked very happy when he was asked about his plan. The tired champion smiled and said, "I'm going to take a long rest."

*sled: そり

(41) Doug Swingley

1 is a 45-year-old dog lover from Anchorage.

2 first entered the Iditarod race in 1989.

3 set a new record for the race in 1995.

4 is a native Alaskan from Nome.

APPENDIX K   SAMPLE QUESTIONS OF THE EIKEN PLACEMENT TEST B   *205*

(42) What does Swingley plan to do next?

1 He will take a long rest.

2 He will buy a new sled.

3 He will take a trip abroad.

4 He will buy some new dogs.

(43) Which of the following statements is true?

1 Swingley began racing with dogs just for money.

2 People have to race, 1100 miles in the Iditarod Race.

3 No one from outside Alaska has won the Iditarod Race.

4 Swingley gave up in 1999 when his sleds were broken.

(10 items total)

Listening Test

Part 1: Listen to the conversation, and choose the answer for the questions (15 items).

Transcript

No. 1

M: Excuse me, waitress.

F: Yes, sir. How can I help you?

M: I'd like another glass of water, please.

F: Certainly, sir. I'll bring one over right away.

Question: Why did the man call the waitress?

1 He dropped his water.

2 He wanted some water.

206   APPENDICES

3 He brought some water.

4 He forgot to bring water.

Transcript

No. 2 M: Excuse me. I think you're sitting in my seat

F: Really? Here's my ticket. See? Seat number 16 C.

M: Your ticket is for the train to Jacksonville. This is the train to Miami.

F: Oh, I'm sorry. I guess I'd better find my train before it leaves without me.

Question: What must the woman do right away?

1 Change to another train.

2 Get a ticket for this train.

3 Get off at Miami.

4 Look for her ticket.

Part 2: Listen to the English sentences, and answer the questions (15 items).

Transcript No. 16

John wants to be professional tennis player someday. He practices tennis at school for more than three hours every day. Twice a week John has a lesson at a tennis club near his house.

Question: How often does John have tennis lessons at tennis club?

1 Every day.

2 Once a week.

3 Twice a week.

4 Three times a week.

Transcript No. 17

Kruger National Park in South Africa is one of the most famous wildlife parks in the world. It is also one of the biggest and oldest. Many tourists come to visit the park every

APPENDIX K   SAMPLE QUESTIONS OF THE EIKEN PLACEMENT TEST B   *207*

year to see the lions, elephants, and cheetahs. People say that animals living in their natural environment look very different from those they see in zoos.

Question: What can tourists do at Kruger National Park?

1 Visit famous zoos.

2 Watch wild animals.

3 Catch different animals.

4 Live in a natural environment.

208   APPENDICES

APPENDIX L
THE PROMPTS FOR EACH WRITING ASSIGNMENT AND WRIT-
ING SAMPLES

Directions: Write the essay using more than 100 words in 45 minutes.

Suzuko (Grade= A)

Should English be taught in primary school?

Some people say that pupils should learn Japanese rather than English in primary school. That may be true, but my opinion is different. I think pupils should learn English for two reasons.

Firstly, English is said to be the universal language. In fact, English is spoken in a lot of countries. So I think that learning English can acquire the international communications ability.

Secondly, we had better study English as soon as possible. Because the younger we are, the easier it is to lean a lot of English words. Therefore, it is important to study English in the elementary school

These are the reasons why I think that English should be taught in primary school.

Maki (Grade = B)

Should English be taught in primary school?

Many people say that English should be taught in primary school because English is the world's most common language. That may be true, but I don't think so. I think English shouldn't be taught in primary school for two reason.

Firstly, I think we should put native language before English. It often find that young people use wrong Japanese. If English be taught in primary school, I think such young people will be more than ever.

Secondly, I think we put stress on other subjects. For example, there are school that teacher do not experiment in science.

APPENDIX L THE PROMPTS FOR EACH WRITING ASSIGNMENT AND WRITING SAMPLES *209*

Consequently, many young people are not interesting in science. So we should put stress on science for developing of science. If English is taught in primary school, young people will use more wrong Japanese and lose interest in other language. Therefore, English shouldn't be taught in primary school.

Megumi (Grade = A)

Why have personal computers spread so quickly?

Now personal computers have become indispensable for most of us in our everyday lives. What factors have spread them so quickly? Different people use them for different reasons.

Firstly, businessmen would not dream of working without personal computers. They use their personal computers in order to form data, to gather information, to make a presentation, and so on.

Secondly, students are taught how to use personal computers in their schools. Young people may understand quickly. So they often get to use them.

Thirdly, some people create a Website. They renew their Website frequently. Other people watch someone's Website. Information spread among people and people who use personal computers increase.

These are the reason why have personal computer spread so quickly.

Kanon (Grade = B)

Why have personal computer spread so quickly?

Today, almost household have personal computers 1 and above. Why have personal computers spread?

Personal computers is necessary for work to businessmen. If they can't use computer, they can't work. Young people are different directions for businessmen. They watch interesting animation when they use personal computers and they contribute animation of them own composition to website. They are personal computer schools for aged people recently. Perhaps the day will soon come when every aged people can use personal computer.

These people are supporting personal computers' popularity.

210 APPENDICES

Haruna (Grade = A)

Women can do more things at the same time than men.

Women always do a lot of housework all at once. While, men are poor at doing many thinks at one time. An experiment was performed to find whether women can do more things at the same time than men.

In this experiment, 30 women and 30 men who are twenties read the newspaper, talking over on the phone. And then, their perception of its content was observed. The results showed that women can remembered much more than men.

It was found from the results that women can do more things at the same time than men.

Madoka (Grade = B)

Women can do more things at the same time than men

Is this supposition really true? As experiment was performed to find whether women can do more things at the same time than men.

An experiment is as follows. Subject are 30 men and women in their 20's. They talk by phone and read a newspaper at once time. A researcher examined they comprehension how much newspaper's contents.

The results showed that women remember contents better than men. These results lead us to the conclusion that women can do more things at the same than men.

Misaki (Grade = A)

What are the merits and demerits of e-learning?

Opinions are divided on e-learning. Some people say that e-learning is a good way to study English. On the other hand, some people say it isn't a good way.

The merits of e-learning are as follows: First, we can study English at home when we want to. So we can study at our own pace. Second, e-learning is cheaper than enter the English conversation school.

The demerits of e-learning are as follows: First, we can't speak English if we didn't study steadily. So we have to be strict on ourself. Second, se can't speak English in public for the

APPENDIX L THE PROMPTS FOR EACH WRITING ASSIGNMENT AND WRITING SAMPLES *211*

tenseness. We have to be accustomed to speak English in from of real people. However, e-learning is an individual based.

Thus, there are merits and demerits with e-learning. We should consider these merits and demerits before deciding which stance to choose.

Uran (Grade = B)

What are the merits and demerits of e-learning?

Today, e-learning is popular among various people. But, there are proponents and opponents with regard to this issue.

Proponents of e-learning are busy people at work and housework. They think that it is convenient, because they learn free time. Proponents say that it is an efficient way for learn at their own pace.

On the other hand, opponents think that learn by teacher directly is better than e-learning. They say that it can ask teacher a question when they have incomprehensible problem.

Thus, there are proponents and opponents with regard to this issue. We should consider these merits and demerits before deciding which stance to choose.

Yuka (Grade = A)

Self Introduction

Dear classmates,

My name is Yuka Tanaka. I am 19 years old. I am from Kyoto, so I am staying dormitory. My major is piano. My favorite composer is Maurice Ravel. So I like French music very much.

I have a father, a mother, and a younger brother. Younger brother plays the trumpet at the club. I don't have an animal. I want to have a hamster.

I have not decided my future plans yet. I want to work that concern music Being with everyone who play music companion here is comforting.

I want to spend a happy time in this English class. I hope to see you more of everyone.

Best wishes,

Yuka

Shiori (Grade = B)

Self Introduction

Dear everyone!!

My name is Shiori Kobayashi. I'm 19 years old. I live in Uenohara city in Yamanashi. I go to college by train an hour every day. I haven't brother, sister, and pet. My hobby is reading book, just reading 1Q84. This book is very interesting!! I like Pooh! Pooh is very cute. I have many Pooh goods–a towel, a stuffed, cup, dishes, a spoon, a fork, chopsticks etc. I have a dream. It is teach of piano many people. So, I just study music in this College of Music.

Best wishes,

Shiori

Yukina (Grade = A-)

Special Place

Near my home, there was a park. One day when I was junior high school students, I took my dogs out for a walk to the park. My dogs was playing with a branch. Then, one dog ran away in the park. Her name is Momo. I chased Momo but her figure disappeared into the distance. When Momo ran away, always she came back at once. But she didn't came back home 2 hours in the day.

So I was looking for Momo with my family. Then Momo and a stray dog broke out woods. We were very surprised.

After a few days, Momo's pregnancy came to light. Everyone in my family was very surprised.

Daiki (Grade = A)

Special Place

Hello everyone. I'll talk about my special place. My special place is my room (composition room).

My house stands near the railway track in Yokohama. It's very small apartment. So I share a room with my brother. My desk is in a mess. There are many printed music score

APPENDIX L THE PROMPTS FOR EACH WRITING ASSIGNMENT AND WRITING SAMPLES   *213*

and a lot of books on my desk. So I clear up the mess when I start composition. Composition is very hard work. I often spend a lot of hours to write to write one note. I fell stress and tiredness. Last week, I finished to compose new music. I was Happy. So I like composition very much.

I will make a lot of music in this room from now on.

Takuto (Grade = A)

My Ideal Partner

What kind of partner do I want?

First, I would like a partner who likes chatting because I like to be talkative.

Second. I would like a partner who is active. Because I am very vigorous I like to be cheerful, bright, outgoing and mischievous. And I like sports very much. I fell so delighted that who likes spots, too.

Third, I would like a partner who likes music. Particularly if she knows contemporary music, instrumental, rock music, healing music and ensemble, I'm very pleased. And I want to talk about music.

Ayana (Grade = B-)

My Ideal Partner

What kind of partner do I want?

First, I would like a partner who can respectable. Because I think that great respect each other.

Second, I want a partner who likes music. Because I love music. I want to listening music and play the instrument together. And I want to talk about music a lot.

Third, I would like a partner who is calm. Because I want to derived from the mere fact of his existence a sense of inward security. I don't like quarrel and I want to friendly every day.

Sachiko (Grade = A)

My Favorite Photo

My favorite photo is of my pet. Her name is Hoshi. Her kind is beagle. Body color is black, brown, and white. She is very cute. We first met when I was ten. Because I had wanted a dog, my parents gave her. I was very happy.

Usually we keep Hoshi outside, but my mother and I put her into house when my father go out. We enjoy playing with her. I like this photo because it reminds then. I want to meet her soon.

Thank you.

Kahori (Grade = B)

My Favorite Photo

My favorite photo is of my friends and me on the day we went to Harajuku. It was taken about two months ago. My friends name is Ai and Mayuko. They major vocal music in college of music. Mayuko is the same college.

We watched a moview. The title of movie is "Lier Game." A man sit the seat from the front who was angry because we spoken a little in the middle of the movie. We said, "I am very sorry". Then, I staid Ai's house. We talked until the middle of the night.

Note. Mistakes in the essays have been retained.

APPENDIX M
RATING CRITERIA FOR STUDENT ESSAYS
(Adapted from Jacobs et al., EFL Composition Profile 1981)

1 = Poor   2 = Fair   3 = Average   4 = Very Good   5 = Excellent

Criteria	Specific Criteria	Score
Contents	Does the writer respond to the writing topic appropriately? Is all necessary information (who, what, where, how) included?	
Organization	Does the writer have a topic sentence? Does the writer develop the idea(s) stated in the topic sentence? Are logical connecters used appropriately? Is the order of the information appropriate?	
Vocabulary	Are the choices of words appropriate? Are a variety of words and expression used?	
Grammar	Is grammar (subject-verb agreement, tense, numeral article, preposition, pronoun, and reflexive pronoun) accurate?	
Mechanics	Are punctuation, spelling, and capitalization accurate?	
Total		

APPENDIX N
AFFECTIVE ORIENTATION QUESTIONNAIRE (ENGLISH VERSION)
(Adapted from Beglar, 2009; Gardner 1985b)

1	Strongly disagree	全くそう思わない
2	Disagree	そう思わない
3	Slightly disagree	あまりそう思わない
4	Slightly agree	少しそう思う
5	Agree	そう思う
6	Strongly agree	すごくそう思う

Desire To Write English (DWE)

1　I plan to write as much as possible during the class.

2　I want to write English outside English communication class if I have a chance to do so.

3　I would like to take this English communication class, even if it were an elective.

4　I would like to be able to write English to people in English-speaking countries, such as the US or UK.

5　I would like to be able to write English to people on the Internet.

6　I would like to be able to write English well.

Attitude Toward Learning To Write English (ALWE)

1　Writing English is really enjoyable.

2　I look forward to my English writing class (English communication class).

3　I like writing English more than reading English.

4　I have enjoyed previous English writing class.

5　I feel a sense of accomplishment when I learn to write new things in English.

6　Learning to write English is a challenge I enjoy.

APPENDIX N   AFFECTIVE ORIENTATION QUESTIONNAIRE (ENGLISH VERSION)   *217*

Motivational Intensity (MI)

1 I plan to study hard in writing class.

2 I want to write English better than many of my classmates.

3 I plan to do homework for this English writing class very carefully.

4 I will try to understand the mistakes that I make when writing English so that I can improve in the future.

5 I want to write English more than many of my classmates.

6 I plan to improve my writing ability as much as possible while at this College.

Instrumental Orientation (IO)

1 Improving my English writing ability is important because it will help me get higher test scores (e.g., on the Eiken).

2 Improving my English writing ability is important because it will help me get a better job.

3 Improving my English writing ability is important because it will help me earn more money in the future.

4 Improving my English writing ability is important because it will help me get a higher position in Japanese society.

5 Improving my English writing ability is important because it will make me a better-educated person.

6 Improving my English writing ability is important because it will help me communicate successfully when I am abroad.

L2 Writing Anxiety (ANX)

1 I feel nervous when I write English.

2 I feel nervous when I think my English writing skills.

3 I feel nervous when I think my English grammar ability.

4 I feel nervous that other students will feel that my English writing ability is bad.

5 I feel nervous that the teacher will think that I do not write English well.

6 I feel nervous when participating in class writing activities.

L2 Writing Self-Confidence (SC)

1 Compared to other students, I think I can write English well.

2 I can write about common topics (e.g., hobbies and vacation) in English.

3 I can write about academic topics (e.g., social issues and environment) in English.

4 I can write a 1-page paper in English.

5 I can write a 5-page paper in English.

6 I can write my opinion about common topics (e.g., Japanese TV programs and movies) in English.

7 I can write a 1-page blog every week about my daily activities in English.

8 I can write email message in English to a native speaker of English.

APPENDIX O
AFFECTIVE ORIENTATION QUESTIONNAIRE (JAPANESE VERSION)
(Adapted from Beglar, 2009; Gardner 1985b)

Desire To Write English (DWE)

1 授業中、出来るだけ英語を書こうと思う。

2 もしも機会があれば英語コミュニケーションのクラス以外でも英語を書きたいと思う。

3 この英語コミュニケーションのクラスが選択科目だったとしても履修するだろう。

4 アメリカ合衆国やイギリスのような英語を話す国の人々に対して英語を書けるようになりたい。

5 インターネットで人々に英語を書けるようになりたい。

6 英語で上手に書けるようになりたい。

Attitude Toward Learning To Write English (ALWE)

1 英語を書くことはとても楽しい。

2 英語のライティングのクラス（英語コミュニケーション a 系統）が楽しみだ。

3 英語のリーディングよりもライティングの方が好きだ。

4 私は去年の英語のライティングのクラスを楽しんだ。

5 英語で新しい書く表現を覚えると、達成感を覚える。

6 英語で書くことを学ぶことは、楽しい課題である。

Motivational intensity (MI)

1 ライティングのクラスで一生懸命勉強するつもりだ。

2 クラスメートよりももっと上手に英語を書きたい。

3 このクラス（ライティング）の宿題は真剣に取り組むつもりだ。

4 自分のライティングの間違いは上達する為に出来るだけ理解するつもりだ。

5 クラスメートよりももっとたくさんの量の英語を書きたい。

6 大学に在学中、英語ライティングの力を出来るだけ伸ばすつもりだ。

Instrumental Orientation (IO)

1 英語のライティング力を伸ばすことは、テスト（英検など）の点数を上げるために重要だ。

2 英語のライティング力を伸ばすことは、より良い仕事を得るために重要だ。

3 英語のライティング力を伸ばすことは、将来より高い給料を得るために重要だ。

4 英語のライティング力を伸ばすことは、日本社会でより高い地位を得るために重要だ。

5 英語のライティング力を伸ばすことは、より教養を身につけるために重要だ。

6 英語のライティング力を伸ばすことは、海外で上手くコミュニケーションを取るために重要だ。

L2 Writing Anxiety (ANX)

1 英語を書く時緊張する。

2 自分の英語のライティング力を考えると緊張する。

3 自分の英語の文法力を考えると緊張する。

4 他の学生に自分の英語のライティング力が低いと思われるのではないかと緊張する。

5 先生に、自分の英語のライティング力が低いと思われるのでないかと緊張する。

6 授業中ライティング活動に参加する時緊張する。

L2 Writing Self-Confidence (SC)

1 他の学生に比べて、自分は英語が上手く書けると思う。

2 英語で趣味や旅行の話など一般的な話題について書ける。

3 英語で社会問題や環境問題など学問的な話題について書ける。

APPENDIX O   AFFECTIVE ORIENTATION QUESTIONNAIRE (JAPANESE VERSION)   *221*

4　英語で1ページ書くことができる。

5　英語で5ページ書くことができる。

6　テレビ番組や映画など、日常的な話題について英語で自分の意見が書ける。

7　英語で日常生活について毎週1ページのブログを書くことができる。

8　英語の母語話者に対して英語でEメイルを書くことができる。

APPENDIX P
WILLINGNESS TO COMMUNICATE (WTC) IN WRITING (ENGLISH VERSION)
(Adapted from Weaver, 2010)

1	2	3	4	5	6
Very unwilling	Unwilling	Slightly unwilling	Slightly willing	Willing	Very willing

1   I would be willing to write about a recent vacation on a postcard in English.

2   I would be willing to write a self-introduction in English.

3   I would be willing to write about my daily life in English in more than 100 words.

4   I would be willing to write an explanation of why I chose this college in English.

5   I would be willing to write about my future plans in English.

6   I would be willing to write an essay that recommends my favorite musician's CD.

7   I would be willing to write about Japanese culture in one paragraph (e.g., new year and summer festival)

8   I would be willing to write a short report that explains my hometown.

APPENDIX Q
WILLINGNESS TO COMMUNICATE (WTC) IN WRITING
(JAPANESE VERSION)
(Adapted from Weaver, 2010)

1	2	3	4	5	6
全くあり得ない	あり得ない	あまりありそうにない	ややあり得る	あり得る	かなりあり得る

1　最近の休暇について英語で絵葉書を書くことを進んでやる。

2　英語で自己紹介を書くことを進んでやる。

3　英語で100語以上で自分の日常生活について書くことを進んでやる。

4　何故この大学を選んだのか英語で説明を書くことを進んでやる。

5　将来の計画について英語で書くことを進んでやる。

6　自分の大好きな音楽家のCDを買うように勧めるエッセイを英語で書くことを進んでやる。

7　日本の文化について（例えば新年や夏祭りなど）1パラグラフで英語で書くことを進んでやる。

8　自分の出身地についての短いレポートを英語で書くことを進んでやる。

224   APPENDICES

APPENDIX R
SELF-ESTEEM (ENGLISH VERSION)
(Adapted from Rosenberg, 1965)

Indicate your level of agreement with each of the following statements by choosing one
number on the rating scale that best describe the way you feel about yourself. Use the following scale as your guide.

1	2	3	4	5	6
Strongly Disagree	Disagree	Slightly Disagree	Slightly Agree	Agree	Strongly Agree

1.   I believe that I have a number of good qualities.

2.   I am able to do things as well as most other people.

3.   I feel useful most of the time.

4.   I feel that I am a person of worth.

5.   I respect myself.

6.   I feel that I am a success.

7.   I have a positive view of myself.

8.   I am able to do things better than other people.

9.   I feel that I am at least on an equal plane with others.

10.   I have more good points than weak points.

APPENDIX S
SELF-ESTEEM (JAPANESE VERSION)
(Adapted from Rosenberg, 1965)

次の項目について、あなた自身にどの程度当てはまるか、尺度上の該当する項目を選びなさい。

1	2	3	4	5	6
全くそう思わない	そう思わない	あまりそう思わない	ややそう思う	そう思う	強くそう思う

1. 私にはたくさんいい所があると思う。
2. 私はたいていの人ができる程度には物事ができる。
3. 自分はたいていの場合において役に立つ人間だと思う。
4. 私は自分は価値ある人間だと思う。
5. 私は自分のことを尊敬できる。
6. 私は自分が成功者だと思う。
7. 私は自分に対してポジティブな見方をしている。
8. 私は人よりも物事を上手に出来ると思う。
9. 私は他人と少なくとも同レベルの人間だと思う。
10. 私は短所よりも長所の方が多いと思う。

226 APPENDICES

APPENDIX T
COGNITIVE COMPETENCE (ENGLISH VERSION)
(Adapted from Harter, 1982)

Indicate your level of agreement with each of the following statements by choosing one number on the rating scale that best describe the way you feel about yourself. Use the following scale as your guide.

1	2	3	4	5	6
Strongly Disagree	Disagree	Slightly Disagree	Slightly Agree	Agree	Strongly Agree

1. I am good at schoolwork.
2. I like school and am doing well.
3. I am just as smart as others.
4. I can figure out answers.
5. I can finish my schoolwork quickly.
6. I can remember things easily.
7. I can understand what I have read.

APPENDIX U
COGNITIVE COMPETENCE (JAPANESE VERSION)
(Adapted from Harter, 1982)

次の項目についてあなた自身にどの程度当てはまるか、尺度上の該当する項目を選びなさい。

1	2	3	4	5	6
全くそう思わない	そう思わない	あまりう思わない	ややそう思う	そう思う	強くそう思う

1. 私は学業が良くできる。
2. 私は大学（学校）が好きで、良くやっている。
3. 私は他の人と同じくらい頭が良い。
4. 私は解答を探し当てることが出来る。
5. 私は大学（学校）の勉強（宿題）をはやく終わらせることが出来る。
6. 私は簡単に暗記が出来る。
7. 私は読んだものを理解できる。

228   APPENDICES

APPENDIX V
GENERAL SELF-WORTH (ENGLISH VERSION)
(Adapted from Harter, 1982)

Indicate your level of agreement with each of the following statements by choosing one number on the rating scale that best describe the way you feel about yourself. Use the following scale as your guide.

1	2	3	4	5	6
Strongly Disagree	Disagree	Slightly Disagree	Slightly Agree	Agree	Strongly Agree

1. I am sure of myself.
2. I am happy the way I am.
3. I feel good the way I am acting.
4. I am sure that I am doing the right thing.
5. I am a good person.
6. I like my personality as it is now.
7. I am doing things fine.

APPENDIX W
GENERAL SELF-WORTH (JAPANESE VERSION)
(Adapted from Harter, 1982)

次の項目についてあなた自身にどの程度当てはまるか、尺度上の該当する項目を選びなさい。

1	2	3	4	5	6
全くそう思わない	そう思わない	あまりそう思わない	ややそう思う	そう思う	強くそう思う

1. 私は自信がある。
2. 私は今幸せだ。
3. 私は自分のやっていることに満足している。
4. 私は正しいことをしていると確信している
5. 私は良い人間だ。
6. 私は自分の今のパーソナリティが好きだ。
7. 私はうまくやっている。

230   APPENDICES

APPENDIX X
CONFIGURATION OF THE VARIABLES AFTER PARCELING

Instrumental Orientation items 1-6 were parceled into three groups: item IO 1+ item IO 3 were PIO 1, item IO 2 + item IO 4 were PIO 2, and item IO 5 + item IO 6 were PIO 3.

Intrinsic Motivation, Motivation, Self-Esteem items 1-10 were parceled into five groups: item IM 1+ item IM 3 were PIM 1, item IM 2 + item IM 4 were PIM 2, item IM 5 + item IM 7 were PIM 3, item IM 6 + item IM 8 were PIM 4, and item IM 9 + item IM 10 were PIM 5.

General Self-Worth items 1-7 were parceled into three groups: item GSW 1 + item GSW 2 + item GSW 3 were PGSW 1, item GSW 4 + item GSW 5 were PGSW 2, and item GSW 6 + item GSW 7 were PGSW 3.

Self-Image, Cognitive Competence items 1-7 were parceled into three groups: item CC 1+ item CC 2 + item CC 3 were PCC 1, item CC 4 + item CC 5 were PCC 2, and item CC 6 + item CC 7 were PCC 3.

L2 Writing Self-Confidence items 1-8 were parceled to four groups: item SC 1 + item SC 3 were PSC 1, item SC 2 + item SC 4 were PSC 2, item SC 5 + item SC 7 were PSC 3, and item SC 6 + item SC 8 were PSC4.

L2 Writing Anxiety items 1-6 were parceled into three groups: item ANX 1 + item ANX 3 were PANX 1, item ANX 2 + item ANX 4 were PANX 2, and item ANX 5 + item ANX 6 were PANX 3.

Willingness to Communicate in L2 Writing items 1-8 were parceled into four groups:

APPENDIX X CONFIGURATION OF THE VARIABLES AFTER PARCELING   *231*

item WTC 1 + item WTC 3 were PWTC 1, item WTC 2 + item WTC 4 were PWTC 2, item WTC 5 + item WTC 7 were PWTC 3, and item WTC 6 + item WTC 8 were PWTC 4.

The Eiken Can-do Questionnaire items 1-24 were parceled into six groups: item CD 1+ item CD 2 + item CD 3 + item CD 4 were PCD 1, item CD 5 + item CD 6 + item CD 7 + item CD 8 were PCD 2, item CD 9 + item CD 10 + item CD 11 + item CD12 were PCD 3, item CD 13 + item CD 14 + item CD 15 + item CD 16 were PCD 4, item CD 17 + item CD 18 + item CD 19 + item CD 20 were PCD 5, and item CD 21 + item CD 22 + item CD 23 + item CD 24 were PCD 6, in Measurement Model C'.

About the Author

Wakako Kobayashi received her Ed.D. in curriculum, instruction and technology in education from Temple University, the USA. Her research interests include listening strategies, extensive reading, Vygotsky's sociocultural theory, and application of Can-Do statements by CEFR. She received a B.A. in language and culture from Tokyo Woman's Christian University in Japan and a M.Ed. in TESOL from Temple University, the USA. Currently, she is Associate Professor in College of Humanities and Sciences, Nihon University, in Tokyo, Japan where she teaches courses: English reading, Sightseeing English, and TESOL, etc.. She was a visiting colleague in University of Hawaii at Manoa from February to March, 2019. She published articles: "Bringing Extensive Reading into Practice: A Case Study in a Japanese University" *Bulletin of Nihon University, No. 97*, (2019), "Theory and Practice for Effective Listening Activities −An Action Research Study−", *FD Research of Nihon University No. 5*, (2017), and "What is an Acquisition-rich Classroom from SLA Perspective? −A Theoretical Investigation−" *The LCA Journal, No. 30* (2016)

Structural Equation Modeling of
Writing Proficiency Using Can-Do Questionnaires

2019 年 9 月 30 日　第 1 版第 1 刷発行　　　　　　　　検印省略

著　者　小　林　和　歌　子

発行者　前　　野　　　隆

発行所　株式会社　文　眞　堂
東京都新宿区早稲田鶴巻町 533
電　話　03（3202）8480
FAX　03（3203）2638
http://www.bunshin-do.co.jp/
〒162-0041 振替00120-2-96437

印刷・モリモト印刷／製本・高地製本所
©2019
定価はカバー裏に表示してあります
ISBN978-4-8309-5056-8　C3037